Running Home

Running Home

A Memoir

Katie Arnold

RANDOM HOUSE

NEW YORK

Running Home is a work of nonfiction. Some names and
identifying details have been changed.

Copyright © 2019 by Paper Sky LLC

Published in the United States by Random House, an imprint and
division of Penguin Random House LLC, New York.

Random House and the House colophon are registered trademarks
of Penguin Random House LLC.

LIBRARY OF CONGRESS CATALOGING-IN-PUBLICATION DATA
Names: Arnold, Katie, author.
Title: Running home : a memoir / by Katie Arnold.
Description: First Edition. | New York : Random House, [2019]
Identifiers: LCCN 2017060112 | ISBN 9780425284650 (Hardback : acid-free paper) |
ISBN 9780425284667 (Ebook)
Subjects: LCSH: Arnold, Katie. | Women runners—United States—Biography. |
Marathon running—Biography. | Fathers and daughters. | Grief. | Extreme sports.
Classification: LCC GV1061.15.A75 A3 2019 | DDC 796.42092 [B]—dc23 LC record
available at https://lccn.loc.gov/2017060112

Printed in the United States of America on acid-free paper

randomhousebooks.com

2 4 6 8 9 7 5 3 1

First Edition

Book design by Caroline Cunningham

For Steve

and Pippa and Maisy—

I'm always running home to you.

Be who you really are and go the whole way.

—LAO TZU

Miles from Nowhere

2012

Valles Caldera, New Mexico

'm floating alone through a million-year-old volcano. Less than a week from now, a wildfire will torch the edges of this high, scooped-out basin, but the only thing burning here today is me. I'm just a body in motion, arms and legs firing in unison, swallowing the dirt beneath my feet, spraying a fine mist of silt in my wake.

The caldera extends for miles in each direction, tawny grassland fringed by fir trees, which from this distance look as tiny as toothpicks. At ten thousand feet above sea level, the air is thin and the sun ferocious, beating down on me from a cloudless sky. In the stark light, everything stands out in sharp relief: chunks of glossy black obsidian strewn across the rocky track, bleached white elk ribs, a lumpy cow skull. A knee-high dust devil swirls across the trail ahead of me, a miniature cyclone throwing its arms in the air.

It's late May 2012 in the mountains of northern New Mexico, and I'm twenty-one miles into a fifty-mile ultramarathon. After nearly four hours on the trail, my brain has gone quiet at last, lulled by the repetitive motion of limbs, lungs, beating heart. It has ceased its tireless, stubborn spinning. Without words for pain and fear, without the conscious thought of them, the discomforts of the day have lifted, like skin sloughed off by the wind.

I'm a speck on this enormous land, suspended between earth and sky, more sky than earth. More flying than running. For the first time in months, I'm no longer afraid. I wonder, briefly, if I've lost my mind. The answer is yes. Finally.

Everyone follows a different path. The path starts with a persistent voice inside, nudging you to try the unexpected, the improbable. This is the voice to listen to, not the voice saying *No*. Not the one saying *Are you crazy?* Don't worry if you don't understand it yet. You can't possibly see where the path will take you, twisting and kinking out of sight. Follow it anyway. Sometimes the path will be faint and you will think you've lost the way and you will be afraid. This is normal. The path will lead you on, out of your known world and into a new one, and deeper into yourself than you've ever been before.

Running is my path.

I've run through winter, on steep, snow-packed peaks with metal spikes strapped to my shoes so I won't slip. I've risen early to sneak out at first light in late spring, the air sweet with lilacs. I've run high above the tree line at twelve thousand feet in late August, climbing through wildflowers and into the clouds until the world below feels like a dream. I've run across river canyons, hurdled rattlesnakes, startled bears, and outsprinted mosquitoes in damp, boggy woods. I've run to win and to be loved and I've run not to be noticed but to disappear, into the forests and my own heart. Some days I can no longer tell if running is madness or the clearest kind of sanity.

When I began, I did not have a map of where I was going or how I would get there or where *there* even was. In the span of three months in 2010, my younger daughter was born and my father died. I'd lost him once before, but this time was for good. My world flipped upside down, and the ground dropped out from beneath my feet. Consumed by grief and terrified that I was dying, too, I fumbled forward into the wilderness alone. I lived in terror of my body breaking down, but I pushed it to its limits almost every day. I had two young daughters at home who needed me, whom I needed even more. But I went anyway. I had so many questions and so few answers. All I could do was see where running would lead me.

A caldera is a large, shallow crater formed when a volcano explodes and collapses in on itself. The crater at Valles Caldera National Preserve, in the Jemez Mountains, is not one crater but seven, strung out like pearls on a necklace, nearly thirteen miles across, a staggeringly huge sea of grass that dwarfs everything within it.

A week before the Jemez Mountain 50 Mile Trail Run, a friend of a friend named Jacob, who'd run the race before, sent me a message on Facebook. "You need to keep it together in the caldera," he warned, "because the climb out of it is brutal. You're going to be pulling yourself up by tree branches. It's like a sick joke."

On the morning of the race, my alarm went off at 3 a.m. I dressed in the darkened bedroom so as not to wake my husband, put the kettle on for instant oatmeal, drank a glass of vitamin C–spiked water, and was out the door by 3:30. It was still cool, the black sky gleamed with stars, and the highway north was empty and lonesome. When I pulled into the starting line at 4:30, the night hadn't brightened one bit. My heart whomped against my ribs and goosebumps pricked my bare arms and legs; how I longed to be home, snug with my family in our sleeping house. Then the race director shouted *Go!* and my legs began to churn and there was no turning back.

I picked my way through rocky arroyos under my headlamp's dim beam. Except for the narrow cone of light illuminating the ground beneath my feet, I could see nothing. It is difficult to gauge speed when you run in the dark. You have to go more slowly to avoid falling, but without visible landmarks, just colorless, indistinct shapes lunging up at you—trees, boulders, sharp turns—you feel as if you're careening along at a reckless velocity. Sensory deprivation creates the illusion of speed.

As the sky gradually lightened to dull gray, the objects around me became recognizable. I was on the side of a rugged, dun-colored canyon, steep and treeless in places, forested in others. The sky appeared cloudy, but there were no clouds, just the absence yet of sun, the eastern horizon whitening on its way to blue. When the sun rose, an hour later, I whooped with joy; daylight was a shot of optimism straight to my heart. Far below, the canyons puckered and wrinkled, slouching downstream to the Rio Grande.

Halfway to the summit of 10,440-foot Pajarito Mountain, I hooked my foot on a rock and slammed into the ground. I knelt in the dirt and licked my gritty palm and used my spit to wipe my bloody shin, remembering horror stories of runners who'd nicked their knees on a root and kept running, only to look down hours later and find that the scrape had bled down to the bone.

Barreling down the other side of the mountain, I watched the runner in front of me trip and rag-doll through the air, landing in a heap, and then stagger to his feet and keep running. My fingers turned into fat sausages and I peed urine the color of Dijon mustard and I force-fed myself two energy gels and a few swallows of electrolyte water to bring myself back from the brink of dehydration.

I'd been running for three and a half hours, and I hadn't even gotten to the caldera yet.

Running is linear, almost tiresomely so. You're moving forward through space and time, sometimes for a very long time, over a very long, sometimes idiotically long, distance. Even when you're running in a loop, your progress is forward—arms and legs aligned, you take one step ahead and then another until you reach the end. Your mind, though, takes a more circuitous route: jumping from the past to the future and back again, like a movie reel or a time machine. Sometimes it projects a whirring jumble of memories and impressions, zooming in on minute details. Other times it pans out and makes cinematic leaps. At the beginning of a long run, you may be excited and impatient to see what will happen. Did I train enough? Will I make it? What's going to happen? So many questions. You're running to find out.

The middle miles are the hardest. The early thrill has worn off, and you still have so far to go. You just have to put your head down and do the work. There's no glory in the middle, but it's beautiful in its own way, because at last your looping mind has nowhere to go but right where you are: your shoes striking the ground, dust puffing up around your ankles. Can you smell the pine trees? Like magic, they've been there all along. It's every runner's dream—maybe *everyone's* dream—to make this feeling last.

Eventually you cross the threshold where you're closer to the end than the beginning. You can't see it, but you can feel it. With each step the finish is calling you forward, reeling you in. It's a force bigger than you, invigorating and impossible to resist. You're running home.

There's no way to enter a crater without going down. The trail into the Valle Grande, the largest of the seven calderas, pitches down through thick forest, loose rocks, and bare roots at a nearly thirty-five-degree angle. I leaned back on my heels in a semicontrolled slide, grabbing for branches and tree stumps, anything to keep myself from somersaulting all the way to the bottom. My shoes and socks filled with pebbles and dirt, and sand sloshed between my toes, but I was too impatient to stop.

It was then that my brain detached from my body, a kite cut loose from its string. It was no longer calling the shots, as it had been all morning—*slow down, speed up, don't trip, don't fall, eat more, drink more, keep going, don't die.* Instead it said to my body, *You take it from here.* Suddenly I was all legs, no thoughts. It was much easier this way, and faster.

The trail across the caldera is a wide, rolling dirt track, so for the first time all day I don't have to watch my feet. Instead, I lift my eyes and look around. It's nothing but grass, waving in the wind. I can see twelve miles across to the scallop of trees on the far side, tugging me forward like an invisible cord. I'm running faster and with less effort than I have all morning.

This must be what it feels like to hallucinate, a lightness in my body, my senses absorbing every detail: the skeleton bones and swirling earth. Far in front of me, a shimmery pond glints like a dime-size mirage. As I get closer, I see that it's real and I'm overcome by the urge to jump into the water. Toy trucks waver like vehicles in a model town. It's a faraway aid station.

The caldera was once a scene of cataclysmic change, but time has turned it into a place of stillness and silence. Half a mile ahead of me, a black spot lopes along the contours of the rough road. Another runner. He's slowly, almost imperceptibly, getting bigger. I'm gaining on him, if only by inches. Beneath this massive sky, I'm outrageously lonely, but as the runner grows closer I realize that I don't want to talk to him, or anyone. Solitude is my fuel.

People think long-distance running is about speed, about getting from point A to B as fast as possible, but really it's about slowing down. In the quiet of prolonged effort, time stretches, elongates. I look around at the hot blue sky, summer settling down on northern New Mexico, and feel my legs moving automatically and do what comes naturally. I run.

Twelve miles disappear beneath my feet. The back side of Pajarito Mountain rears up, the off-kilter doubletrack road disappearing into tall grass. I stop at the aid station and the race volunteers press watermelon slices into my palms and send me on my way. Past the pond, the course goes up, up, up the slope, trees stacked upon trees stacked upon trees: ponderosa pines, Douglas firs, blue spruce, aspens greening with the first heat of spring. This is the climb Jacob warned me about. It's so steep I can't see the top.

I've run all day to get out of the caldera, but now that I'm almost there, I have the strangest sensation that I will miss it. I will miss the scale and solitude, the simplicity of the task before me. Running reduces life to its bare essentials: sky, ground, skin, breath, flesh, bones, muscle.

Then, as if on cue, the orange flags marking the course vanish. There's no trail, just knee-high bunchgrass atop tussocky earth. The footing is uneven, and the course could be anywhere on the side of the mountain. I slow to a walk, scouring the meadow for the neon stick flags. Nothing.

In every long run, there comes a moment when you ask yourself, *What the* hell *were you thinking?* This is it. I stare at the ground, the steep slope rising above me, and think about my father and my daughters, and how I ended up alone and lost on a mountain in New Mexico. A million steps along a crooked path have led me here. And only I can find my way out.

PART ONE

Leavings

I would like to beg you . . . to have patience with everything unresolved in your heart and to try to love the questions themselves as though they were locked rooms or books written in a very foreign language. Don't search for the answers, which could not be given to you now, because you would not be able to live them. And the point is, to live everything. Live the questions now. Perhaps then, someday far in the future, you will gradually, without even noticing it, live your way into the answer.

—Rainer Maria Rilke

1

Home Stretch

Fodderstack 10K, Flint Hill, Virginia, 1984

The journey has taken all day. We got up before dawn and we're still not there. The road before us winds and swerves, up hills and down. It is very narrow, and you can't see around the curves, so you have to stay to the edge and hope that no one's coming in fast from the other direction. My older sister, Meg, is driving, like she always did. My three-month-old daughter, Maisy, is in the back, asleep in her car seat.

There are fences and walls on either side of the road and, beyond them, green fields and horse pastures unfurling to dense woods. I'd forgotten that trees get so tall, taller than the second story of a house. I'd forgotten that there *are* second stories of houses. I'd forgotten about grass. I've been away so long.

We pass a small sign for Huntly. There's nothing here but a low white house where the rural post office used to be. It shut down years ago, and now Huntly is just a name on the map. A mile later, we turn left onto a smaller road. Meg slows down as the asphalt gives way to gravel, as Dad taught us to do out of respect for the neighbors. The lane tightens as it passes a row of mailboxes and a neglected stucco chapel that was once a slave church. To our right is a house abandoned when we were children, its rusting swing set still lurching in the weeds. On the left is the overgrown apple orchard where a horse named Mack used to graze, so skinny we could count his ribs.

My heart skips the way it used to when I was a girl and we'd come back after a long absence. What was waiting for us? What had changed while we were away? We were gone far more than we were here. Always I had so many questions.

Now, at last, I see it: the wooden sign, HUNTLY STAGE, hand-carved in large black letters, hanging from its post. We ease in and creep between two long rock walls overhung by persimmon trees, giving way to grass on both sides. The field to our right slopes up a long hill that hides the house, until it doesn't, and there it is, rising right out of the grass, all the lights on, calling us back.

I've been coming to Huntly Stage since 1978, after my parents divorced and my father bought the property with his girlfriend, Lesley. I was six that year. Through much of our childhood living in New Jersey with our mother and stepfather, Meg and I visited the farm four times a year; this dwindled to once or twice a year after we went to college, and considerably less when we got jobs and,

PHOTO: DAVID L. ARNOLD

Dad, Meg, and me, summer 1978

later still, had children of our own. A quick computation yields a disappointing sum—fifty-two weeks, a year of my life at most.

Because of the infrequency of our visits, Huntly Stage has never felt entirely like home, yet it's as familiar to me as any place I've ever known. I can close my eyes and summon it in my mind: a two-story wooden house overlooking twenty-seven acres of fields and streams and forest. After a summer rain, no greener place exists than this corner of Rappahannock County, in northern Virginia, at the foot of the Blue Ridge Mountains. Dad likes to joke that he can watch the grass grow, but I've seen the way he studies his fields and tends to them like children, and I know he's not kidding.

As with so many things we come to know well over a long period of time, at some point I began to take Huntly's constancy for granted, or perhaps I always had. I thought it would never *really* change, just as I thought my father would never change.

I was wrong.

Three weeks ago, Dad was diagnosed with stage IV kidney cancer. Shortly after getting the news, I flew east with Maisy from

Santa Fe, where I've lived for fifteen years. My husband, Steve, stayed home with our two-year-old daughter, Pippa. Meg caught a flight from her home in California, and together we rented a car and drove an hour and a half from Dulles airport to the farm for a long weekend to help however we can. On the plane, I worried that Dad would have cancer written all over his body, but when we pull up the driveway, he's ambling down the walk to greet us.

"Hello!" he bellows. He looks okay, a little wan but still sturdy, himself.

"Dad," I say, hugging him hard and handing him the baby. He puts his arms around her, and I put my arm around him and together we walk slowly inside. Through his sweatshirt I can feel his shoulder blades moving up and down with his breath.

The house is comfortably cluttered and largely unchanged from my childhood. Books line the shelves in the living room, paintings and photographs hang on the walls. In the kitchen, the refrigerator is plastered with cartoons; a plastic Queen Elizabeth figurine sits on the windowsill, gracing the room with her regal, solar-powered wave when the sun shines. Lesley, who married my father in 1981, is from England and still goes back every other year.

What's different is the way the house *feels*. The air inside is heavier and quieter, sleepier, but there's too much to do to just droop around the house. Meg and I run errands in our rental car, hauling in supplies from Kmart, ten miles away in Front Royal: a case of chocolate Ensure, because Dad's losing his appetite, and a new pair of plaid pajamas, because his old ones are threadbare. Both seem like terrible portents of what's to come.

In the late afternoons, when our chores are finished and Maisy and Dad are resting, I slip out the back door, sit on the stoop, and put on my running shoes. It's early October and the sun is hot on my skin. I'm tired and I don't feel like going, but I need fresh air. I need to move.

I jog down the long arc of the driveway, between two pastures bounded by a curving split-rail fence, past Lesley's barn, where she runs a small horse-breeding business, one foal a year, for show. The grass is so immaculately trimmed, it looks painted on. At the bottom of the hill, I swing left along the creek and past the Huntly Stage sign. Dad and Lesley gave the farm this name, after the faint, grassy track that cuts across one corner of the property, which they liked to imagine was once a stagecoach road traveled by George Washington.

My legs are heavy and slow, but I don't care. I'm not running for speed or fitness. I'm running to get out of the house and escape the dread of what's to come. I'm running to feel the humid air swoosh through my lungs, to feel normal again, and just a little bit alive. I'm running to forget, and to remember.

I became a runner by accident. It was April 1979, and I was seven. Meg and I were visiting Dad, as we always did over Easter break. Spring was the best time of year in Virginia: the cherry blossoms were in bloom, and the grass and leaves were greener than they were in New Jersey. Easter was Dad's holiday with us, just like Thanksgiving and New Year's and the last few weeks of August. Often when we were with him, I had the uneasy feeling that this was not enough time and also too much. Dad was always trying to think up clever things to do with us.

Now he had an idea.

"What do you think about running a race?" he announced at breakfast. "Six miles, from Flint Hill to Little Washington?"

"*How* far?" I asked, between bites of peanut butter toast.

"Six miles," he repeated. "On the Fodderstack Road."

I knew the road he was talking about. It was famous in our family for its short, steep hills—tummy-funnies, we called them whenever Dad intentionally revved his rust-colored diesel Rabbit over the small rises, sending our stomachs into our throats, as if we were hurtling down a roller coaster.

Six miles. The distance was so audacious that it meant absolutely nothing to me. I had never run a race, never a single mile, let alone six, all in a row. Dad might as well have been suggesting we run home to New Jersey.

Meg, sitting next to me, bent over her bowl of Corn Flakes and shrugged noncommittally. At ten-going-on-eleven, she was the cool, discerning big sister, capable of withholding judgment until she deemed an endeavor worthy of her time and interest. A slight sneer of her upper lip indicated it was not. I, meanwhile, was the overeager puppy, ready to leap at anything. We played to our birth order perfectly.

Dad smiled, his mouth curling into a sly, crinkled grin. It was, like so many of his ideas, a lark. He was half daring us to say yes but not really believing we would.

"Running?" I said again. Never in my life had I seen my father run or heard him talk about running. He liked hiking and camping and riding his bicycle along country roads, exploring. This was often what we did when we were together, rambling around with no apparent destination, up and down trails in the woods, in our red Keds, bashing at brambles with our bare arms, dying of boredom and fatigue but not wanting to quit, because this was the only time we got with Dad and we didn't want to waste it.

Dad nodded. He'd thought it all out. "You two can run the race, and I'll be waiting in Little Washington, taking pictures."

I nodded. This made complete sense to me. Dad was a *National Geographic* photographer. Just the thought of this gave me a little shiver of pride. The kids I knew in New Jersey had banker dads or lawyer dads or dads who ran Chinese restaurants, but my dad walked around with cameras dangling from his neck and wore a mesh khaki vest and got his pictures on the cover of the most famous magazine in the world. In my eyes, this was a grand and noble pursuit that bestowed upon him, and, by extension, me, the faint glow of celebrity. Picture-making was important work, and it trumped everything, even the craziest of things, like running six miles without any training or parental supervision.

Dad assured us that other kids would be running the race, too, and lots of grown-ups, some of whom were his friends, so even though he wouldn't be with us, we wouldn't be alone. If we got tired, we could always walk, and, he chuckled, he'd be there to capture our triumphant finish on film. Those were his actual words: *triumphant finish.*

I was a stringy second grader with a Dorothy Hamill haircut and perpetually skinned knees. For the past three months, the bathroom scale hadn't budged from forty-nine pounds. Mom joked that maybe I would always be forty-nine pounds, and part of me worried that she was right. Meg had Princess Di cheekbones and skinny supermodel legs and was on her way to becoming six feet tall. She might actually have a legitimate chance of finishing the race, but I was the long shot, the underdog, the scrappy kid sister desperate for Dad's attention.

"Sure," I said, tugging my mouth into a grin to match my father's. "Okay."

Meg and I made an unlikely, woebegone pair on the starting line of the second annual Fodderstack 10K Classic. We wore holey Tretorn tennis shoes that, much to our mother's chagrin, were fashion-forward in 1979; ankle socks with purple pom-poms; and terry-towel gym shorts destined to become soggy with sweat, like clammy kitchen sponges, at the slightest exertion. The collar on my raspberry-pink Izod shirt was turned up, and I'd stuck a ribbon barrette in my hair to kept my bangs out of my eyes.

The instant the gun went off, we lit out hopefully for Little Washington, sneakers slapping, limbs flailing. Two-tenths of a mile in, where the course turned right onto the Fodderstack Road, we were decisively dropped off the back of the pack. We inched forward in a bumbling, ill-advised combination of running, jogging, walking, limping, and staggering. The effort engulfed us—Meg and I locked in our own private circle of hell, yet too dwarfed by the distance to stray far from each other. It seemed desperately unlikely that we would ever make it, and yet how could we quit? We had no choice but to push on. Few words passed our lips, just the occasional pained grunting.

The course was pretty, passing hundred-year-old brick farmhouses with high hedges and stone walls. Dogwoods bloomed pink in the meadows. The road rolled up and over short climbs and down the other side. Every couple of miles, farmers in denim overalls stood at the roadside holding out Styrofoam cups of water from wobbly card tables. Meg and I stopped at all of them, drinking as though we'd been lost in the desert for all of eternity. At about the three-mile mark, the course ascended a long hill. Dad had actually referred to it in jest as a "mountain," and from the bottom, staring up at the long squiggle of blacktop disappearing beneath a canopy of oak and maple trees, it looked as menacing as any I'd ever seen. I leaned into the slope, trying to will my legs to move, trying not to cry. Beside me on the road, Meg attacked the climb. Her gangly legs were so long that for every step she took, I had to take two just to keep up. I had to keep up. Somewhere in the distance, Dad was waiting to capture the moment on film for posterity.

Dad wore his camera everywhere he went, like an extra appendage, as familiar to me as his thick horn-rimmed glasses and his wavy black hair that crept back slightly from his high forehead. Slung around his neck, the Nikon was part of his dress code, just like the thick gray ragg wool socks we teased him mercilessly for wearing, day in and day out, winter and summer. Just as we made fun of him for taking too many pictures. He never took just one—*never*. "One more shot," he'd murmur as the shutter went *click, click* and Meg and I held our positions, eyeballs rolling back in our heads with exasperation, faint smirks twitching at the corners of our mouths. "Okay, just one more, one more." Our expressions changed as we got older, tinged with the aloof superiority of teenagers who'd learned to tolerate his relentless, occasionally mortifying documentation, but only barely. He was so intent on making the picture that he lost track of his words, and of time. "Good, one more, good.

Good! Last one. Good!" Behind the lens, Dad seemed to disappear and become the camera itself.

In film, there are two sides to every picture. Negatives render dark subjects light and light subjects dark: reality inverted. But the positive image is not infallible, either. To tell the truth of something, you need both light and dark, sun and shadow, transparency and secrecy, things exposed and others withheld. If you are patient and pay attention, these details might begin to arrange themselves into a recognizable shape, a pattern that starts to make sense. Dad believed that the most important element of a photograph is what you leave out, so as to frame only what is most significant. But for himself, he seemed to want the opposite—to amass the world, gather it all up in his sights, to capture everything possible of this life. It wasn't always comfortable, this deep, persistent hunger. But I recognized it in myself. For as long as I can remember, I've felt this way, too.

When the redbrick houses of Little Washington appeared over the final hill of the Fodderstack 10K Classic, I was so stunned and ecstatic, I began to sprint. My legs were on autopilot, the world funneling to a single point. All I wanted—all I had ever wanted in my whole life—was to cross the finish line and collapse in a jubilant heap at my father's feet. I'd grown miraculous new legs, and they were powerful and fast, wheeling me along to him.

I could pick Dad out from half a block away: five feet eleven inches, navy-blue crewneck sweatshirt, khaki work pants, L.L. Bean leather work shoes. Meg was gone, ahead of or behind me; it no longer mattered. With two hundred feet to go down the homestretch, it was every girl for herself. I barreled across the finish line and straight into Dad, nearly knocking him over. My lungs were scorched, and my legs were spasming so hard from fatigue that I couldn't have slowed down if I wanted to. I'd been running for nearly two hours, and now I couldn't stop.

The Fodderstack finish, 1981

"I'll be damned!" Dad bellowed, fumbling for his camera. But it was too late. Maybe it was my spastic, unexpected dash or the miraculous fact that I wasn't lying crumpled in the fetal position on the side of the road, but he was too distracted and befuddled to get the shot.

"Whoa! There you go, old girl!" he cried, grasping my shoulders to steady me. "Well done!"

Somehow I managed to lower myself onto the curb, where I slouched, panting and red-faced, until my heaving breath begin to settle. Dad handed me a Mountain Dew and patted me a few times on my back. This was his signature gesture, a firm, reassuring thumping that conveyed both comfort and approval, if not exactly gentle affection.

I might have sat there all afternoon, stuffing my face with brownies from the finish-line picnic, but I could tell by the mischievous glint in Dad's eye that we weren't done yet.

"Okay, girls," he told Meg and me. "Now go back and pretend to crawl across the finish line!"

Dad was serious about his photographs, but he had a silly side, too. Often he'd arrange us into joke poses and fake scenarios, the exact opposite of his documentary pictures for *National Geographic*. "Stand up on that rock and look tough," he'd say, positioning us on a rocky precipice atop Mount Washington or Old Rag, chortling from behind the camera as we flexed and grimaced like the Incredible Hulk. "Okay, back up. Just one more step, and one more. *Ha ha ha.*" That we always obliged him with mock exasperation but never fell for the gag was a time-honored part of the game.

Meg and I rose stiffly to our feet, groaning a little for effect. We limped a few feet onto the course and got down on our hands and knees, looking furtively around at the other runners; we were just barely old enough to feel embarrassed. Dad pointed his camera. "Look like you're really in pain!" he commanded, laughing, as we dragged ourselves over the fraying strip of duct tape laid across the road. Did he not realize we really *were* in pain? Obligingly we rearranged our faces into masks of pretend agony that only moments before had been real. *Click, click, click* went the shutter. "Okay, one more, just one more!" *Click, click.*

Meg and I must have come in dead last that day, but it didn't occur to me to care. In the picture Dad took of me, I'm grinning madly, all my freckles popping, my expression one of delirium and relief. I know that look. It's runner's high. It's the look that says *I ran 6.2 miles and survived the improbable, and nothing will ever feel hard or annoying again!* Not even posing like a fool on my hands and knees in front of complete strangers.

We drove back to the farm the same way we'd run, covering the same demented distance in not much more than fifteen minutes. Meg and I rode in the bed of Dad's pickup, the wind slapping my hair, my legs stiff as logs, elated. Flooded with endorphins and a crazed surge of optimism, I had a flash of understanding: Suffering and perseverance were their own rewards. They could make me stronger. They could make all the tricky bits of life seem easier.

2

Dares

Huntly Stage, summer 1980

Dad's MRI shows a tumor the size of a fist. "It's a rather massive ugly thing," he writes in an email a couple of weeks after his diagnosis, a sinister image that lodges in my mind. There are spots on his lungs. "Suspicious," he calls them. "The assumption is that the cancer has spread."

When I was little and felt sad or out of sorts, Mom always gave me the same advice: "Just get busy and do something." Had I botched a multiplication quiz? Just get busy and do something.

Was I mad at Meg for locking me out of her room? Just get busy and do something. When my sixth-grade friend's father killed himself in the guest bedroom where only the week before she and I had made electrical circuits for our science project? Just get busy and do something. *Anything.* Being busy kept us out of trouble, but it also saved us from having to feel, think, or talk about what might lie beneath our restless moping.

After Dad's diagnosis, our phone conversations and emails become a volley of medical updates revolving around a single urgent question: What do we *do*?

I remember what my doctor told me right after Pippa was born: "Whatever you do, don't look anything up on the Internet. It will drive you crazy." But going crazy seems preferable to sitting passively as Dad navigates the worst health crisis of his life, so at night, after the girls are asleep, I flip open my laptop and Google kidney cancer. I find pages of specialists, discussion boards about new drugs, and case studies. Maybe if I look hard enough, if I scour the digital universe for cancer treatments all night until my eyeballs fall out, if I go OCD on Dad's cancer, I will save him.

I deluge Dad with links. "MD Anderson is where everyone goes," I declare confidently late one night, long after Steve has gone to sleep and begged me to do the same. I don't care that it's in Texas and Dad's in Virginia and he's told me he wants to be treated locally, at the county hospital. I'm going to find him the best of the best—someone tells me Columbia is first-rate!—and he will go there and be treated and he will live.

"I'm tired," Dad writes. "I like my oncologist."

I spend hours researching experimental treatments: hypnosis, macrobiotics, laughter therapy! I buy him an iPod and upload soothing hypnosis sessions set to droning New Age music. Meg and I split the cost of a monstrous juicer, so that Lesley can pulp vegetables into pea-green juice, supposedly a miracle cancer cure.

Then, serendipity! I come across a study asserting that breast milk may combat cancer cells. I'm still nursing Maisy six times a day and pumping milk once or twice in case she gets hungry while I'm out working or running. Now I attach myself to my breast pump three times a day to increase my supply. The tiny motor, disguised in its black nylon working-lady tote, sounds like someone whispering *Oh shit, Oh shit,* over and over. By the end of three days, I've filled three big bottles with breast milk. I pack them in a small cooler with dry ice and drive to the FedEx store, feeling valiant. "The contents are perishable," I tell the man behind the counter, a hint of pride creeping into my voice.

I call Dad to tell him the milk is on its way. "Just blend it up with some bananas in a smoothie!" I say, hoping my enthusiasm will disguise the fact that this is the grossest idea in the history of the world.

A couple of days later, I get an email from Meg. "There's a fine line between having a fighting spirit and being in denial," she writes. She's been talking to Dad. *I'm not in fucking denial!* I want to yell back at her, but part of me knows she's right.

On our second day at Huntly, Meg and I move Dad's computer and hard drive upstairs to his bedroom. It tires him out to go down two flights of stairs to his basement office, but he has work to do. He's trying to finish archiving the many thousands of photographs he's taken over the years, for *National Geographic* and for himself. He refers to this simply as the Project, and it's all-consuming. He's been working on it since he retired, in the mid-nineties—long days burrowed in his basement, digitizing, captioning, editing, backing up, and filing every image. Dad's turned retirement into a test of endurance.

Lesley has bought him a new desk at Office Depot, which, we're disheartened to discover, comes packed flat, in dozens of pieces. Meg and I sit on the carpet with flimsy, unmarked parts scattered all around us, trying to decipher the half-baked illustrated instructions and fumbling to screw tiny screws into the particleboard. In any other circumstance, this would irritate me beyond words, but we seize on the project with grateful, almost manic enthusiasm. Dad's tumor may be beyond our control, but not this damn desk. Here is something useful we can do.

When it's finally assembled, Meg goes downstairs to make lunch, and I turn on his computer. Dad's stretched out on his bed, talking to me with his eyes closed.

"I've got all the digital photos cross-referenced on the hard drive," he says, "and there are duplicate copies in the white folders in the basement. A complete copy of everything is on a zip drive in my safety-deposit box at the bank, all my pictures." For as long as I can remember, he's always enunciated this word slowly and deliberately, as though he's savoring it: *pick-chures*.

I open the hard drive. Dad worked at *National Geographic* for nearly thirty years. There are hundreds of folders, labeled by year or subject matter or story, each folder containing hundreds of images.

"The *Geographic* pictures are marked with file names and dates," Dad goes on. I know I should be paying attention, but I'm so transfixed by the mountain of digital memories that I'm only half listening.

I scroll down to a folder marked KIDS. A long column of tiny thumbnail photographs pops up on the screen, in which are contained even tinier bodies, Meg and me in miniature. Dad documented nearly everything we ever did together. I start clicking on pictures at random. Some I've seen before, in my grandparents' photo albums or in frames on Dad's desk at work, but there are so many others I've forgotten, so many days we spent with him, yet also so few.

I look up from the screen and glance over my shoulder at Dad. He has dozed off and is snoring lightly. Beside me on the floor, Maisy rustles in her car seat, batting absently at a quilted giraffe dangling from a plastic hook. She catches my eye and smiles, a soft, sleepy grin that makes her bright eyes crinkle. She's always been this way: agreeable and undemanding. She slid into the world, be-calmed, without a sound. Her hair was strawberry, her skin as wrinkled as a walnut. At home she slept off childbirth like a bad hangover, napping in her car seat on the kitchen counter or propped up on our knees on the couch. She can sleep anywhere, in the midst of any commotion, for hours.

I rock her car seat gently with my bare foot and open the folder labeled CAMPING. Here are dozens of variations on the same picture: Meg and me huddled in Dad's mustard-yellow Sears tent, standing in front of the tent, sitting in the open tent flap, roasting marshmallows over a charcoal fire. The canvas tent was of ancient vintage, tall enough for Dad to stand up in without stooping, with high peaks and billowy valleys, where water pooled when it rained. The long awning above the door was a hopeful thing, as though made for a grand party, though poorly executed. It sagged in the middle, collecting dew. In the morning you had to be careful not to knock into the poles that held it up or water would drip down your neck. In my memory the tent was ornate, even festive, like a circus big top, but inside it smelled like musty basements, and our plaid flannel bedrolls were placed directly on the ground, a fact that eventually gave rise to Meg's intractable loathing of camping. Seeing it now, I'm struck by how run-down it was, even then, as though wilted by poor weather and unfulfilled expectations.

These were the foggy first years after my parents split up but before we moved with Mom to New Jersey, when Dad took us on weekend camping trips to state parks in Maryland and West Virginia. We cooked watery scrambled eggs or baked beans in a blackened frying pan and wore leather sandals with knee socks and wool cardigans, outfits my mother had packed for us. In a disproportionate number of these pictures, Meg and I are shoving hot dogs into our mouths, nearly whole, and staring with dazed wonder at the sodas in our hands. Mom would never have fed us hot dogs for dinner at home; she would never let us guzzle Cokes straight from the can as if they were water. Meg's expressions throughout range from uncertain to sullen. Even when I'm smiling, I look slightly bewildered.

Meg and I were tomboys. She was mildly cross-eyed and needed braces, and I knocked out both my front teeth before I was three, falling off the plastic trapeze we called Hanging Bar, hung by a fraying rope over the basement's black-and-brown-checked linoleum floor. I was always getting hurt, like the time I ran headlong into a tree at a park. I was so busy looking over my shoulder and grinning at my mother that I hit the trunk and bounced off, got up, laughing, and kept running. Mom clipped our brown hair in short bowl cuts and trimmed our raggedy bangs with the kitchen shears. Little girls don't wear their hair long, she told us.

Meg (left) and me, Lincolnville, Maine, 1976

Below that are folders marked MAINE. In the summer of 1975, we stayed with Dad in a yellow one-room cabin on Penobscot Bay. My parents had separated, and it was our first long trip away from home with just him, the first of many we would take to Maine. We drove north in his green VW microbus, Meg and me flinging around the two white vinyl bench seats in back, pretending the bus was a plane. Dad was the captain, and whoever rode in front was the co-pilot, responsible for pushing the AM radio's fat, useless buttons (the radio never worked) while our father steered the craft north on I-95, the day growing cooler, the air smelling like the sea and damp old forests.

I am three and a half. The trip wobbles in the mind. We kick a red rubber ball in a meadow of Queen Anne's lace and skip down dirt lanes bordered by blackberry bushes, arms streaked purple from reaching through the prickers for handfuls of berries. We glop bare-foot across the mudflats at low tide, foraging for mussels, hazy ocean waves curling in the distance. On the summit of Mount Battie, Meg bites into a pear and leaves her front tooth behind. It lies bloodied like a shark's tooth in the white flesh, prompting great hilarity and immortalized forever, like so much of our childhood, on film.

Dad's in all of these pictures, even when he's not. He's the unseen presence in every frame, the photographer behind the lens. Look into our eyes and it's his eyes we are trying to catch, his smile we seek, his face we most want to see. Our expressions tell only half the story; the photos tell it all. We're not looking at the camera but at *him*.

There's one photo I want to find but can't, from a day that stands out in my memory more than almost any other. Ironically, it's one of only a few days together that Dad didn't document.

It must have been November 1979, the fall after the Fodderstack, the second winter he and Lesley lived on the farm. It was a crackly, bitter afternoon after Thanksgiving, and we went traipsing through the woods, Dad and Meg and I. The pale sunlight slanted through spindly trees in its dizzying, fatiguing way. This was the hated sea-son of shortening days, night shouldering in too soon, and morn-ings with a glaze of frost on the grass. I wore a belted navy-blue down parka and red rubber boots with thin cotton socks. My knees were chilled through my corduroy pants. I was cold and wanted to go home, but I would never admit it.

In this part of Virginia, there is water everywhere, splicing through pastures, along the rock walls Dad laboriously restacked by hand, over the far hills and between this field and that. On sticky August days, we braved the itchy pasture and cut across two fields, hopped the stone stile Dad built, and crossed over into the neighbors' property. We skirted their house and followed a faint path that switchbacked down to a swimming hole on the Rappahannock River.

That day in November, though, there was a papery skin of ice at the river's edge, dead leaves swirling in an eddy created by a small boulder. It was likely not as frigid as I remember, because if it was, Dad probably wouldn't have done what he did next. "I'll give you five bucks if you go in," he said, with a sly grin. The river was low, little more than a trickling creek, and the swimming hole looked deep enough for me to dunk up to my waist, but barely.

Dad always liked to make bets. "Let's bet who will get home first," he'd say. "Us or Lesley?" Money, rarely offered and almost never rewarded, was never the point. Trying to guess and be gutsy, to outsmart the other, was. He was a walking Trivial Pursuit game, quizzing us constantly about geology, engineering, nature: *Where do we get iron? What makes gunpowder? How do glacial moraines form?* Beneath his tests and gags—some fun and others, frankly, annoying—lay his long-held conviction that if we pushed ourselves, we were capable of big things.

The river glimmered uninvitingly, but it didn't scare me. I'd learned to swim when I was three, flinging myself off of docks into chilly lakes. I loved the shivery rush of soaring through the air, the moment of anticipation just before you hit the water.

I thought about the five dollars. The cash meant nothing to me. I knew that if I did it, it wouldn't be for the money. I'd do it to prove I could.

"Okay," I said, with a conviction that surprised me. "Watch me."

I stripped off my coat and turtleneck and tugged down my corduroy pants and knee socks. I stood there, shivering for a moment in my white cotton underwear and undershirt, watching the wind rustle the branches, trying to anticipate the cold, for which I had no precedent. I took a deep breath and plunged in up to my waist. Over the rush of blood in my ears, I could hear Dad gasp; his bushy eyebrows shot up and down frantically. Meg looked disdainful but also sort of impressed.

It might as well have been Antarctica. The water sliced me open, karate-chopping my shins, my stomach. I counted to ten, forcing myself to stay in long enough to make it count.

"Good grief, old girl!" Dad cried, waving me out. When I crawled onto the bank, the air seemed colder, prickling my splotchy red skin as I patted myself dry with my clothes. Dad clapped me on the back and reached into his wallet, stretching it wide open and pulling from it, with a flourish, a wrinkled five-dollar bill. I was wet as an oily muskrat and shaking uncontrollably, laughing through chattering teeth, half-deranged from the chill.

Now, remembering the day, I stare out of the sliding glass door that opens onto the balcony, overlooking the fields and the cleft in the hills where the river flows. Wallowing in the water had been an awful idea, pure torture. But it was the stuff of family legend— even as I stood shivering in my underwear on the bank, I sensed it would be—a bold feat I could pocket for future use, as insurance against indecision and doubt, as proof of courage I didn't always feel but wished I did, that would bond me to Dad forever. If he loved nature, so would I! And beneath this was my secret hope: If I could be brave and daring and fully committed in the tiny wedge of a world we shared—outside, in the fields, on the rivers and trails—maybe Dad would forgive me for leaving him. Maybe, somehow, I would get him back.

On the floor beside me, Maisy has fallen asleep. She's suckling her pacifier through wobbly lips—in and out, in and out—her plump cheeks expanding and contracting slightly with each breath. Her mouth makes a tiny sound, like a kitten lapping milk with its sandpaper tongue. Dad's still asleep, too, flat in his bed, so still I have to look twice. They make a mournful pair: one just born, the other slowly dying.

The heaviness in my chest is old and familiar. It's not quite grief, not yet, though I can feel that coming, but a hitch in my heart, a tick of apprehension—something is missing, but I don't know what. I feel as young as the girl in Dad's pictures. I'm homesick. That discomfiting in-between feeling—not quite there, not quite here—that I've felt my whole life with my father. Our relationship has been a constant cycle of coming together and moving apart, hellos and goodbyes. The excitement of arriving and the guilt of going all twisted up like a tangled skein of wool. Happy! And sad. Now that we're heading toward our last goodbye, the word has a terrible new meaning: home-*sick*.

That first summer we went to Maine, Dad made up a game that he called Morsel. He would lie on his back on the ground, pretending to be some sort of big monster. Meg and I would run around him, squealing, daring each other to make ever tightening circles, while he stretched his arms out and tried to grab us with his lurching monster limbs. When he did, he would roar and pull us in, tickling us and holding us tight while we laughed and laughed, pretending to be devoured, tender little morsels of prey. After a while we would grow tired, all of us, and Meg and I would sag down on either side of him, his arms wrapped around us, giggling and tired, our stomachs and faces sore from laughing. We would lie that way for a while, until it seemed like maybe Dad had fallen asleep, and maybe we would, too. I felt as though if we lay still, we could stay that way forever.

I look down at Maisy and picture Pippa, at home in Santa Fe. They're almost the same ages Meg and I were when my parents' marriage began dissolving, not long before they separated. I think of the lengths I went to impress Dad and to bridge the distance between us—the stamina this required and the person I became be-cause of it. And suddenly I wonder if I'm still trying to prove myself, to myself and to my father—if maybe my whole life up to this point hasn't been one long dare.

And who will I be when he's gone?

3

Edge of Memory

Meg and me, Washington, D.C., 1974

No one tells you anything when you're little. You have to gather clues. The story of your life is made from these clues, random shards stuck together at haphazard angles that don't always make sense. They will not necessarily match the recollections of those around you; everyone collects their own evidence.

It's nearly impossible to untangle my earliest memories from Dad's photographs. In his first picture of me, I am one second old. I have just cleared the birth canal. The masked doctor holds me, squalling, furry with mucus, splattered with blood, eyes squeezed shut, mouth in an uproar. The fingers of my right hand are flung open and blurry, in motion already.

I foraged for clues the same way Dad made pictures: voraciously. "Your memory is like a steel trap!" Mom liked to tell me. I could tell by the fullness of her voice that this was a very good trait, and that she had it, too. Memory was proof that you were clever, that you were observant, and *this* was a quality that my father, as a photographer, deeply admired.

Remembering, then, became a way to please both of my parents at the same time. This was not always easy to do, as they were nearly as opposite as two people could be: my mother the buoyant go-getter, my father the thoughtful, introverted artist. I loved them both with great and equal, though entirely separate, devotion, so I kept my eyes and ears open, harvesting scenes and details and smells, imprinting them into the nubby weave of memory. There they lodged, crisscrossed and notched one upon another like the miniature pioneer cabins I built out of Lincoln Logs, imagining wayward wolves prowling the perimeter and plucky sisters in calico bonnets, safe inside, standing guard.

Entire years and passages of time were blank, while other moments stirred out of the shadows and stuck. The barrel of roasted peanuts at the wine store, the hollow, dusty crackle the shells made as I squished them open between my fingers; sitting with Meg on the carpeted landing of the stairs in our house, neither up nor down but halfway in between. There was a hexagonal window at ankle height on the landing that was too low for grown-ups to see out but was for us a secret child-size porthole.

One memory is recurring: standing in my crib in my upstairs bedroom, staring into the mirror on the wall. I can't be more than two. On the bottom right pane, someone—me?—has stuck a small, round yellow smiley-face sticker. The idea it stirs in me is: *happy*. The rectangular glass is divided into six panes and hangs horizontally, like a window. I grip the rail, puzzling at the reflection staring back, looking out at the same time I am looking in.

We lived in an off-white clapboard-and-stone colonial on Legation Street, in a residential neighborhood of northwest Washington, D.C. My parents stretched and bought the house for $29,500 in 1967, two years before Meg was born, the year my father, David L. Arnold, landed his dream job as a picture editor and photographer at *National Geographic*.

Dad had always loved pictures. As a seven-year-old growing up in Claymont, Delaware, he would sit on the front steps every Friday afternoon, waiting for the mailman to deliver *Life* magazine. He studied the first grainy images of the Normandy invasion, the Americans taking Rome. He examined the textures and faces, the expressions of joy and pain, of the places and people he didn't know but thought he could, if only he observed them carefully enough.

His father, Harold, a chemist at DuPont, built a darkroom in the basement of their house, using tin cans with their bottoms snipped out, a paper safe made out of plywood. For the timer, he gutted an old electric clock—two dark-red bulbs, filaments like glowing worms. Dad was eight when he was invited in for the first time. My grandfather closed the door, turned on the enlarger, and slid the paper into the liquid. Wordlessly, my father watched the faint gray ghosts appear on paper, slowly thicken, and gradually take on substance, rising from the celluloid negative into recognizable black-and-white forms.

Through the ceiling Dad could hear the radio in the kitchen, his mother, Mary, making pot roast and his younger brother, Philip, pushing a toy car along the floor. Philip had been brain-damaged at birth when the doctor yanked him out too forcibly with forceps. Mary was small and birdlike, with a propensity for worry. Her own mother had died of cancer when she was eleven, and she'd been raised by her older sister and her father. After Philip was born, Mary became ever more fragile, rattling with nerves, expecting the worst, because it had already happened.

Though he was still young himself, Dad believed that Philip was his responsibility now. Privately, he tried to teach him to read, pulling slips of paper from a hat, helping him decipher the letters. Philip managed only a few words at first, then sentences, eventually a whole book, *Fun with Dick and Jane*. Dad was sure there were depths to his brother that no one, not even he, could see. Dad carried this duty the rest of his life. Several times a year, he visited Phil at the communities where he lived in upstate New York and, later, Wisconsin, took him on road trips, sent him funny cards and pictures, and brought him to Huntly Stage for holidays. Below Dad's loyalty lay the guilt. The healthy son would have to be the one to shine, to live out his life not only for himself but for his parents and his brother, too.

As a boy in the cozy basement cave, though, Dad was free of all entanglements. How could there be such a beneficent, quiet place to hide in his own house? It reminded him of his favorite book, *Robinson Crusoe*. His bed was the sailing ship that wrecked in the great storm, and the darkroom his hut, all of the castaway's necessities cached and close at hand, fashioned out of imagination and simple, utilitarian things—salvation in the wreckage.

Years later, Dad inherited his father's darkroom equipment for his first job, as photographer for *The New Era*, a weekly newspaper in Essex, Connecticut. It fit perfectly into a crude little closet in the apartment he rented. After he met my mother, Betsy McDonald, in 1961, and she dropped out of Smith to get married, he lugged the darkroom with him as they moved around the Northeast, lighting out from one photography job to another.

PHOTO: DAVID L. ARNOLD

Dad aboard the *Talitiga*, South Pacific, 1973

October 29, 1973: an ordinary slow Monday at the National Geographic Society. A cable arrives from the governor of American Samoa, inviting the magazine to send a representative on a voyage aboard a vessel called the *Talitiga,* leaving in two days' time. The expedition will visit tiny, uninhabited atolls in the South Pacific to survey seabirds and nesting green turtles and assess the need for conservation in the region. Dad gets the nod. By noon, expenses have been advanced, film drawn from the locker, six cases of photographic equipment organized, wife consulted, plane reservations requested. He packs hastily, and the next day, my second birthday, Dad's on a flight to Los Angeles.

A few days after he left, our furnace broke. It was damp and cold in Washington that fall, and Meg and I both got sick. Mom had to go down to the Geographic to ask for an advance on his salary so she could afford a new one. Dad's only communication was a cable he sent to the magazine while steaming toward their last port of call.

The *Talitiga* was a roller, grossly unfit for high seas. She pitched back and forth with an abandon that my father initially found exhilarating but that soon turned nauseating in twenty-foot swells. Dishes ricocheted off the galley shelves, the engine caught on fire and was swiftly doused, and all on board were felled by a horrific, churning seasickness. Dad lay sweating and hallucinating in his overheated berth, emerging two days later to calm seas and high opera playing on the deck. At one stop, they exhumed the body of a Samoan man whose bones they would return to his proper home, and at another they performed emergency surgery on a wizened old hermit with skin cancer. Dad shot dozens of rolls of film. On the flights back to Washington, he transcribed his notes, wrote haiku, drank one too many gin and tonics.

Even when Dad was home, though, he seemed to hover just out of view, the suggestion of someone rather than the person himself—appearing at bath time, and after, stretching out on Meg's bed beside us, the picture book *One Morning in Maine* propped open on his lap—a transient figure slipping back into darkness. Often in my memory he is a blurred silhouette climbing the stairs to the third floor, a cramped room under the eaves with shag carpet the color of flames. I see only his back, disappearing from view. The attic was his private place, where he played his bass violin and recorder, where we ventured only when we'd been invited.

Music had been his first love, even before photography. It was his family's language. In the evenings, his parents sat together at the piano, his father singing in his booming bass-baritone while his mother's fingers raced across the piano, trying to keep pace. When he was seven, Dad began taking recorder and violin lessons; by high school he was playing second chair in the All-Eastern Orchestra. At Wittenberg University, in Ohio, he learned to play the bass violin, joined a jazz trio, the Collegiates, and made a record.

PHOTO: DAVID L. ARNOLD

Dad and his father, Delaware, 1945

His bass violin was six feet tall—taller than him by an inch. Made from a glossy maple, it loomed in its corner of the attic, fragile and intimidating. I feared it a little, in the same way I must have feared my father, abstractly, the passing shadow of authority whom I so badly wanted to please.

The blur in my mind is Dad, whirling after me, or maybe it is me, toddling away in the seconds after I accidentally bumped into the bass and knocked it to the ground, breaking its delicate neck in two. In that moment, the music is gone from the house, replaced by a bellowing rage, brief, and then buried. What I remember is not his anger as much as my shame. *I* had done this. I had broken his beautiful instrument, which he loved almost as much as us, and some days maybe even more.

On May 24, 1974, two days shy of their twelfth wedding anniversary, my parents split up. Dad was thirty-seven, Mom just thirty-three, Meg barely five. I was two and a half. For many years, no one talked about the day Dad moved out or what came later. It was the strangest kind of demarcation: utterly forgettable but absolutely defining.

Dad took his bass violin, its neck repaired with wood glue, his jazz records, the darkroom equipment, a few books, his tent and camping gear, and a rough slab of driftwood shaped like a fish, a black knot for an eye. Everything else he left behind. Later, according to the terms of the divorce, Mom would get the white Peugeot sedan with red vinyl interior and an unreliable starter, 60 percent equity in the house on Legation Street, and, as was typical of the time, full custody of Meg and me.

With Dad gone, the music in our house changed. Mom listened to sappy seventies love songs on the radio as she whirred the vacuum across the carpet, leaving straight lines in the pile like stripes in fresh-cut grass. *You'd think that people would have had enough of silly love songs.* Sometimes while she made dinner, Meg and I crawled under the side tables on either end of the sofa, pressed our ears to the stereo speakers, and sang along to plaintive lyrics we didn't understand: *Walkin' in the rain and the snow when there's nowhere to go and you're feelin' like a part of you is dying . . .*

One evening before bed, Mom lay facedown on the living room floor and wept. Alarmed, I lay next to her and reached for her hand. What had I done wrong? It must have been that night, in my tiny, hammering heart, that I vowed not to do anything that might make her cry again, that I began my silent, stalwart campaign to keep myself together, always, no matter what, so that she would, too.

In the 1970s, there wasn't a road map for how to get divorced. My parents' separation dragged on for nearly three years as they muddled along, in and out of each other's lives. Dad occasionally came over to tinker in his workshop. Sometimes he minded us—"babysitting,"

Mom, Meg, and me at the C & O Canal, Washington, D.C., 1976

it was called back then when fathers watched the children—while Mom finished night school to become an accountant.

Some weekends, we stayed with Dad at his apartment on Newark Street. Dinner was fried chicken at Roy Rogers, spinning on the shiny red plastic stools while a jolly, larger-than-life Roy in his red neckerchief beamed down on us from above the counter. His winking smile lit a flame of pure joy in my heart. How could you possibly be sad, basking in the glow of a grin like that? Afterwards, Dad would tuck us into sleeping bags on canvas cots he'd set up under his desk. On one wall he'd painted an enormous mural of the sun setting behind a thatch-roofed cabana, inspired by his trip to the South Pacific. We fell asleep to Miles Davis on the stereo, turned down low.

The year I started kindergarten, Mom got a full-time job as a CPA at Price Waterhouse. Meg and I walked ourselves six blocks home every day after school, crossing Nebraska Avenue, the front door key dangling like a cliché from a red-and-white bakery string around Meg's neck. Sometimes we stopped at the corner store to buy long sticks of grape-flavored Big Buddy bubble gum, which we gnawed on, smacking bubbles all the way home.

We had a string of live-in babysitters, *TrishSharonTrishLaura,* who snuck cigarettes in Dad's attic, which Mom had converted into a guest room. They wore their long brown hair parted in the middle and pulled back in pigtails and smelled of smoke and wool sweaters. Their chief duties seemed to consist of being in the house with us in case their cigarettes caught fire and reheating the tuna fish casserole that Mom fixed for dinner when she worked late.

On weekends, Mom took us ice skating or pedaled us around on the plastic seat on the back of her ten-speed bike. We walked through the woods in Rock Creek Park and went out to Arlington to watch the planes roar over the bike path on their descent into National Airport. Sometimes in the evenings, when it was still light, we'd ride our tricycles down the alley that sloped past our one-car garage to the street.

In our neighborhood of northwest Washington, alleys functioned as shared driveways. Ours ran up from Legation Street, along the side of our house to Military Road; halfway up it T'ed into the back alley that came in from 32nd Street. A tall wooden fence enclosed our backyard on two sides, with a gate leading from the alley to our kitchen door. When the neighbor boy came over to play, he slithered under the fence rather than opening the latch. His name was William, but we called him Lowly Worm, after the character in the Richard Scarry books Dad read to us at bedtime.

The alley is long and steep, a thrilling sliver of fast-flying asphalt. Mom positions herself in the street at the bottom while we push our tricycles to the top. Mine is a plastic Big Wheel, Meg's an orange, metal trike with white handlebar streamers. They are too small for us, and we have to pull our knees up to our chins so our feet don't drag on the ground, hunch over the handlebars, and wait at the top until Mom gives us the go-ahead that the coast is clear.

Side by side, we haul off down the hill, gathering speed, lean on the foot brakes, and clatter to a stop in front of Mom. She is clapping and beaming the way she did with her whole face—her green cat eyes and straight white teeth and deep dimples. The plastic wheels jar and bump along the uneven asphalt. We do this again and again, until it's too dark to see. It seems entirely probable we'll whiz right past Mom, clear across the street, and into the neighbor's front shrubs, like an avalanche thundering down its slide path and up the other side.

At the time, I thought this was what all mothers did: work full-time and fix leaky toilets and wash our wool tights by hand and run the car pool and call us down the hill until it's almost dark, and then get up and do it all again, by herself. Only now that I'm a mother do I see how radical this was, how tired and lonely she must have been.

Not that she ever let on. In my memory, she is waving madly, her smile throwing sparks at the bottom of the alley, yelling "All clear!"

On Wednesday afternoons, Dad took us out for mint-chocolate-chip ice cream cones at Baskin-Robbins. Maybe it was on one of those Wednesdays that he taught me how to ride my blue two-wheeled Raleigh. There I am, high astride the bicycle seat, head turned back to look at Dad and make sure he's still holding on, and he is, pushing and grinning at the same time. I look ahead, pump the pedals uncertainly, look back again. Dad five steps behind me, mouth stretched wide in a silent cheer, arms flung open in a last big send-off, palms to the sky as though in supplication. I am riding, flying. I'm off.

This is where I stop. This is where my memories of Washington cluster together, pressing inward like fortress walls, summoning a defense, as though they might possibly prevent what happens next.

I don't want the girl to leave.

The girl leaves.

My mother has met a man named Ron, and they've decided to get married. Ron is a divorced naval officer and self-made Wall Street investment banker, with a son and daughter almost exactly our ages. He lives in New Jersey. We're moving there. That's all I am told.

I tell no one we're moving. Not my teachers, not Lowly Worm, not my friends. In mid-April, I walk out of Lafayette Elementary School for the last time. I've left my first-grade cubby cluttered with books, pens, and papers—all of my school supplies shoved into the back of my desk in a miserable pile. I imagine my teacher's shock when she finds them the next day, after I don't return. The mess shames me, but not nearly as much as leaving does.

There is one thing I take: a library book called *All-of-a-Kind Family*. The cover depicts five sisters in old-fashioned blue-and-white pinafores on the steps of their brick New York City apartment at the turn of the century—the safe, sure confines of home. The due date is stamped on the slip in the back: 6 APR 1978. It is already overdue. I take it deliberately, for keeps, knowing I will never bring it back.

My memory of the day we leave Washington is fuzzy and unreliable. Is it true or a conflation of all our subsequent partings, merged into one burned-on-the-brain goodbye? Dad stands on the sidewalk, squinting into the bright April sun. Or maybe it is raining. He has come to see us off. The dogwood in the front yard is bursting with pale-pink blossoms, and the magenta azalea unleashes its fragrance as it has every spring, indifferent to our departure. Meg and I are on the front steps, watching men load cardboard boxes into the green-and-white moving van; the dining room table is shrouded in cotton batting. Unaware of how our lives are about to change, we hang upside down by our knees on the curlicue black metal railing, spinning round and round until we're so dizzy we have to stop. Then the truck is pulling away, with all our belongings in it. Dad shields his eyes with his hand, watching it go, knowing that in a moment we will, too. His face begins to buckle, a single fat tear squeezing out of the corner of one eye.

This goodbye is much harder than the day he moved out, because I remember it. Because it changes everything for real, forever. We are leaving and Dad is crying and leaving him seems an unforgivable abandonment, the most wretched kind of betrayal. Guilt lodges itself in my gut like an indigestible pit that won't go away.

4

Signals

Me, Summit, New Jersey, 1980

'm six and a half years old, and I am running.

Smocked dress, navy-blue party shoes with a buckle and leather soles. Bare legs pumping down the sidewalk in Summit, New Jersey. Behind me, my mother in her pale-pink belted dress and pantyhose, screaming *Stop!* I reach the corner, hesitate for half a second, look left, look right, and then hurl myself across the street alone. My Mary Janes make a scuffing sound on the concrete.

I'm in my body and outside of it. I know I'm being naughty, frightening my mother. But I can't stop myself.

Ahead, the church, its sharp granite steeple stabbing the sky. It's my mother's wedding day.

I have no idea where I'm running or why. The urge to flee overwhelms reason, outweighs my deep-seated desire to be good no matter what. All I know now is the sensation of flight, a brief, flickering freedom, the sudden realization that my legs can carry me away, where no one can catch me.

We rolled into Summit a few days before the wedding. My about-to-be new stepsister, Amy, seven years old, with an enviable blond bob, and I played Othello in Ron's apartment on the morning of the ceremony, my fingers clutching the smooth black-and-white game pieces, stroking the board's soft green felt for comfort. My wedding hair parted down the middle and pulled back with white plastic butterfly barrettes. I remember: clutching a small bouquet of roses; the hot, panting terror I felt while running to the church; nothing of the ceremony.

We lived on top of the highest hill on the highest ridge due west of New York City, in the Watchung Mountains. At 450 feet above sea level, "mountain" was an exaggeration. It was more of an escarpment, spindled with trees and rising modestly like the face of a small breaking wave. Mom told us that this was the crest where George Washington once stood, lighting beacons for his troops stationed on the island that is now Manhattan, to warn them of the coming redcoats. I liked this image of danger and heroism buried beneath the sidewalks where, two hundred years later, I rode my bicycle and played hopscotch.

Our new house on Fernwood Road was a drafty hundred-year-old Victorian, marigold yellow, with glossy black shutters, one house down from the true summit of Summit. "Don't split hairs," Mom used to say when we bickered over whose turn it was to sit in the front seat (always Meg's). This was, when you think about it, an odd sentiment for an accountant, whose job it *was* to split hairs. But that was Mom: cheerfully determined to smooth over the sharp edges, always willing to round up.

In September, I started second grade at Lincoln School. On Fridays in Mrs. Volz's classroom, we played spelling bingo; when you won, you got your pick of miniature chocolate bars from a bowl on her desk: Mr. Goodbars, Krackle, and my favorites, the chalky, bitter Special Darks. My class launched helium balloons from the playground, our hopeful messages tied on with ribbons. *This balloon belongs to Katie A., 2nd grade, Lincoln School, Summit, New Jersey*—a tenuous time capsule adrift in the clouds.

I am seven. My nickname is Minniscule, a play on my middle name, Minnis, a family name. I am the littlest in my new family, the youngest in my grade. "May I please have a Minnis pancake," my new brother, Ronnie, asks; *Minnis* is code for "small." Ronnie is ten and swings his wooden baseball bat at all hours of the day; he and Amy live with their mom in the next town over. I am dwarfed by the scale and complexity of my new life. Bigger house, twice the siblings. But half the scaffolding is gone, the sure hands pushing me forward, the protective tent under which we sheltered now flapping in the wind, letting the great world blast in. Unspoken is the gaping distance that separates me from Dad. My balloon sailing into the infinite sky, the uncertainty of its journey feels just like loneliness. Who will find my balloon? Who will know me now?

I'm learning the rules of our new house. Chores are assigned. "Many hands make light work!" Mom trills, by way of pep talk. My job is to empty the wastepaper baskets. They are wicker, made with a crisscrossed basket weave that traps tiny debris. I'm making my rounds, room to room, emptying baskets into a large garbage bag, when I hear Ron calling me. He beckons with one finger, and points to an empty wastebasket. I look closer. There at the bottom, plastered to the wicker, is half a cinnamon gum wrapper, glistening and sticky. He peels it off with two fingers and holds it up for me to inspect.

"There's a right way and a wrong way," Ron admonishes me. His authority baffles me. How can he be so sure? And who gets to decide which is which?

"Do it right the first time," he says, dropping the tiny fleck of torn wrapper into the garbage bag. "Touch it once."

This is his motto, but it's not mine. I already know that life can't possibly be this neat. Not when you love two families, back and forth, here and there, as best you can but never perfectly. You mess up again and again and keep going. Life is about touching it all as many times as possible.

A week later, my balloon makes landfall in the yard of another human being in another town. That person licks a finger, flips through the phone book, dials Lincoln School. My scrawled card arrives by mail a few days later, and I hold it in my hands, dazed by the distance it has traveled back to me. It has survived its improbable flight. I've won the balloon launch. Things lost can be found again.

It was understood that we didn't talk about Washington or our old life, just the three of us, Mom and Meg and me. We pretended that we had always lived this way, a family of six, coming and going, going and coming, in an elaborate charade of unity that might eventually come true if only we acted like it would. To gauge the mood in our house, you had to go on raised eyebrows, the purse of Mom's lips, the emphatic clink of Ron's spoon against his teacup. Our job as children was to adapt and not make trouble. We were expected to do well in school, and be happy and keep busy, as Mom had, growing up in Toronto in the forties and fifties.

My mother, Betsy, was the fair-haired, deeply adored daughter sandwiched between two sons. When she was two, her mother put her in her playpen in the front yard, and tied her wrists loosely to the wooden slats with cotton sewing scraps so she wouldn't climb out. A few moments later, the polished black telephone began to ring. It was the neighbor across the street. "Peggy," she said, "I think you'd better look out the window." My mother had flipped out of her playpen and was dragging it behind her down the middle of the road.

PHOTO: DAVID L. ARNOLD

Mom, Stony Lake, 1961

When she was nine, my grandparents bought a cottage on an island north of Toronto, without running water or electricity. Mom had her own cedar strip canoe, with *Betsy* painted in red cursive on the bow, and a sixteen-foot sailing sloop she named *Scurry*. She was the only girl on Stony Lake who sailed, and she took pleasure in beating the boys in the races. "You can do anything you set your mind to," her father told her over and over. Her mother said, "You're the luckiest girl in the world!"

This was the same thing Mom told us whenever she caught us pouting or feeling sorry for ourselves. "We are the luckiest girls in the world!" The way she practically sang it, so melodiously, I knew she believed it down to her very soul, and I wanted to, too. All signs pointed to yes: We lived in a big house on a hill and belonged to the Y. Dad called Meg and me every Thursday like clockwork and when they spoke, my parents were always cordial. I never once heard them say a bad word about the other. I had my own bicycle and a pair of metal circus stilts and a mother who loved me and drew silly faces on my hard-boiled eggs for lunch.

Mom worked part-time in an accounting firm downtown, but she was always home to greet us after school, the cookie jar full of oatmeal-and-walnut hermits just out of the oven. She'd sit with us at the kitchen table while we did our homework, a Pink Pearl eraser tied to a twine around her neck and a yellow accounting pad by her side, clacking away at her adding machine with mesmerizing sureness and speed. The paper roll spewed out mysterious sums in a long, unstoppable curl, a language that gave her a deep satisfaction and that only she understood. She could do all this and talk to us about our day without once looking at the keys.

Within a month of moving in, Meg and I knew every kid on Fernwood Road. Like most children in the seventies, we had a supremely unsupervised childhood. We were responsible for our own entertainment. "If you're bored, it's your own fault" was Mom's refrain. We rode our bikes to school, drew a four square court in the street with soap, and made up elaborate charades. In one, Meg was the horse and Amy and I the pioneers and we would hook Meg up to the garden cart with invisible reins and sticks for crops. As Meg trotted us up and down the driveway, we fed her handfuls of instant oats we'd pilfered from the pantry. We insisted that she actually eat the oats, not just pretend. Everything else about the game—the exaggerated whinnying, the fake nasal snorting—she could tolerate, but the oats Meg found deeply, rightfully insulting. The game would grind to a halt, and she would stomp up to her room and slam the door.

Meg had been given a typewriter for her tenth birthday and was writing a trilogy about the colonization of Saturn by a band of children. Many afternoons, she didn't come out of her bedroom. I could hear her clacking away on the keys, the metallic *thwap-thwap* taunting me. "Please come out and play!" I'd beg her through the closed door, and her wordless answer would echo through the woodwork—*thwap, thwap, thwap*. I knew from peeking that a stack of double-spaced typed manuscript pages sat faceup on her desk, the mark of a true professional.

I'd lie on the floor outside her room for a while, feeling empty and alone, but her concentration was unshakable, and eventually I'd lose hope and drift off to play by myself. The aimlessness of those suburban afternoons could suck the life right out of you, but you couldn't expect your family to save you from the cloying inertia. You had to create your own energy. It came from within, like an engine or a flywheel. The important thing was to keep it spinning.

I spent as much time as possible outside, free from the complicated rules and allegiances of my new family. In the fresh air, my restless longings became less acute. Time seemed to stretch and settle, and my energy settled, too. I liked to pretend I was Harriet the Spy, fictional heroine of the children's book by the same name. Harriet was eleven. She had freckles like me and wanted to become a writer, so she devoted herself to spying on people to get material. She mapped a sleuthing route around her neighborhood, taking detailed notes for the books she hoped someday to write.

I wanted to be a writer, too, but Meg had beaten me to it. She had the typewriter, after all, and when she broke the keys from pounding too hard, Mom and Ron bought her an electric Brother. She was working on a *trilogy,* for God's sake! Human beings have been telling stories since the dawn of time, but in my dubious reasoning, this gave her ownership over the entire enterprise.

I wrote secretly, where no one could see or hear. Before dinner, I played basketball alone in the driveway. I'd position myself in front of the hoop and throw the ball against the backboard, over and over. I was small for my age and had no talent for the sport, nor did I love it. What I loved were the elaborate stories I invented, entire sagas that came to me while I did my layups. I never wrote them down; they lived in my head, and when they disappeared, new ones would come. I felt a rush of almost indescribable joy in these moments, a secret thing flapping inside me: my imagination.

The one story I did write down was about a girl whose parents had divorced and who was scheming ways to get them back together. I wrote the title in bubble letters ("What a Choice!," *exclamation point*) and tied the pages with cheerful orange and yellow yarn that I hoped would disguise the trepidation I'd felt while writing it. Couldn't I have made the story about something fantastical or perilous, like Meg's novel? No. I had to go and base it on a girl my age, like me but *not me*. My writing in comparison seemed shabby, lacking in both imagination and ambition. My teacher pulled me aside and told me she was going to submit it to a children's literary journal. I was mortified. The thought of my parents reading it and talking to my teacher made me cringe. They would think I was writing about *me*! That I was unhappy and wanted my parents to reunite. Did I? *Was* I? I didn't think so, but I'd made up so many stories in my head that it was hard to keep track anymore.

I stuffed the story with its babyish yarn and drawings into a shoebox in my closet. Writing was best kept as a private happiness, like bike riding and making up spy stories in my head. It was much better to not be so serious. Look where it got you.

Instead, I made my own spy route. I rode my bike around the block, scouring the sidewalk along Summit Avenue for torn bits of handwritten notes and receipts dropped from pockets, evidence in a mystery of my own invention. I would fold them into my pockets and pedal home. Our garage was a carriage house dating to the 1890s, with three stables and rusted feed bins that still smelled like hay. Upstairs in the coachmen's quarters was a wooden ladder up to the cupola. The cupola had four low rectangular window openings, covered in thick fencing wire that allowed a view of neighbors' backyards while obscuring the watcher from view. You could see rooftops and trees, sheds and garages, people emptying their trash, coming home from work. It was the ultimate stakeout.

The cupola didn't have a floor, just a narrow beam spanning the middle. To get to the beam, you had to lunge out from the top rung of the ladder and hook one leg around the beam, then scoot out on it until you were straddling it, perched ten feet above spools of pink insulation. Ron had cautioned us that the pillowy rolls were made of flecks of glass and might cut us if we slipped off. The possibility of falling frightened and fascinated me equally. I imagined plunging through suffocating clouds of cotton fluff, sailing through darkness and beyond, landing in another world.

Alone on the beam, I examined my haul and scanned the territory below for signs of subterfuge. I could sit for an hour, noting my observations and speculations in my second-grade composition book labeled SPY WORK, PRIVATE! and by the time I was done, I would believe my own stories totally:

> *The Case of the Plant Divice [sic]. Who we think is the person causing this? Mrs. S. is. What makes us think she is the person? Because she ran up her driveway suspishishly. . . . She bent down into the hole. Rocks were messed with and her panse were dirty. How did she get the divice down in hard ground? All she had to do was place it down and when it rained it froze. It was packed down . . . More explanations later.*

The world contained many inscrutable things, of this I was certain. I could not grasp how I had arrived here or where I was going, but I liked a mystery almost as much as I liked solving it.

My old life became subsumed by my new life, what I thought of as *real* life. Washington was buried so far below the surface that most of the time I wasn't even aware of what we'd lost, except when I was getting scolded, and then it was tempting to think wistfully of Dad. But the truth is, I had no point of comparison. I didn't remember living with him. In the calculus of old life versus new life, there were too many variables to compute, no clear winner or loser, just all the moments blending together into a kind of cockeyed whole.

On a regular day in that highly irregular year—the year everything changed—I wandered aimlessly into my bedroom and sat cross-legged on the floor. Mom had covered my walls in pale-blue wallpaper patterned with perky sprigs of daisies and baby's breath. Around me the house was quiet. A full-length mirror hung on my door and I inched closer, studying the person looking back: a skinny girl with a brown pixie cut, freckles across my upturned nose, striped T-shirt, boxy front teeth too big for my small mouth, sparrow limbs, bruised shins, fingernails bitten down to the skin. I had the uncanny impression that I was seeing myself for the first time, not as a reflection in the mirror but as I actually existed: real and of this world, a flesh-and-blood entity.

I regarded myself in a plain, detached manner. I saw myself not as perfect or flawed, not with gray-blue eyes or lavender OshKosh overalls. Instead I saw, beneath that, a body. And beneath that a self. Maybe even all the way down to a soul, though I wouldn't have used that word or even known what it meant. The essence of myself. I understood for the first time that there was a correlation between the world and me. I was part of it, but separate. I was separate from my sister in the next room, from my green rain slicker hanging on the doorknob, from our pet hermit crab that Meg and I would one day tire of and throw, mercilessly, out the second-floor window. Separate even—as unthinkable as it was—from my mother in the kitchen. I sat there feeling my atoms crawl and move in my body in a way that they crawled and moved in no one else's body, and I felt distinct for the first time in my life—fuller and bigger than I had only moments before.

The realization was so obvious, it was startling. I was not a story I'd made up: I was real, embodied. I occupied space within a place and time. Time was finite, here one moment and then gone. I was a girl now, but one day I would not be. The inescapability of it astounded me. Who was I, and what was I going to do with my-self?

5

Matters of Importance

Atalaya Mountain and the Santa Fe foothills

Years from now, when I'm ninety and have just run my last day, I will remember a section of trail high on Atalaya Mountain. At 9,200 feet, it's the tallest of Santa Fe's foothills, pushed up against the Sangre de Cristo Mountains on the east side of town, three miles from the downtown Plaza. I love the whole mountain, but my favorite part is short, less than a quarter mile long. It comes after a three-mile, two-thousand-vertical-foot climb to the summit, followed by a steep descent off the north side. In winter, the north shoulder of Atalaya is snowy; in the summer, it's shaded and cool. Most people climb and descend the peak from the west side, so I'm usually alone among the trees.

My trail hops small boulders and rocks, twists around a corner, then becomes smooth and forgiving, dirt over springy pine needles. Visible to the west through a fringe of ponderosas is Santa Fe, spreading south and west. If I stop to look, I can make out the silvery outline of our adobe house, its pitched tin roof glinting in the sun, notched into a low hill a few blocks east of the state capitol. But I don't stop. I keep running along the ridgeline to Picacho Peak, just north of Atalaya and seven hundred feet lower. In an hour I'll be home, but for now I'm high on my mountains, the world below reassuringly close and just distant enough.

I lean my torso into the turn, my legs soaring with sure-footed relief. It lasts only a few seconds, the sensation of flight, but it's enough. I've put it in my body so it will stay in my heart.

When Georgia O'Keeffe moved to New Mexico in 1940, she rented a small adobe casita in the craggy high desert fifty miles north of Santa Fe. From her studio window at Ghost Ranch, she could look south to Pedernal, a forested peak with a blocky, nearly perfectly flat top. She believed that if she painted the Pedernal often enough, it would become her mountain. For twenty years, I have run and hiked Atalaya so often, in so many moods and in all kinds of weather, that it has become mine. Even now, when I'm scared or happy, when I don't know what to do with myself, I run to the top and sit on the knobby summit and remember how it felt to be young and scared but full of life and certainty, with everything stretching before me.

Every few weeks, I fly to Virginia with Maisy. Traveling between Santa Fe and Huntly Stage as an adult is as disorienting as visiting the farm was as a young girl. I can't figure out where I belong: at home with Steve and Pippa—who, at two, is still a baby herself, and whom I miss terribly, viscerally—or here with Meg, helping Dad and Lesley.

Sadness burrows in my bones. It crawls into my joints, the space between my shoulder blades, the muscles at the base of my neck that contract when I nurse Maisy. My eyes are itchy, my skin pale, my neck stiff. Even my wrists ache. I shed long strands of my hair on couches, pillows, my own wool sweaters.

Every night at Huntly, I take long, scalding showers, trying to wash Dad's sickness off my skin. I actually think that if I scrub hard enough, it will come off. When I get home to Santa Fe, I drive to the fancy Japanese spa on the mountain and pay a woman to rub coarse salt all over my naked body. The treatment is pure, overpriced agony, and when she wipes me down with a warm towel, the sticky, granular sadness is still there and I feel worse. Each trip back to Virginia adds a new layer of despair, so uncomfortable it feels like its own disease.

Except for a prostate scare a decade ago, Dad, who is seventy-three, has always been healthy. He never smoked, he doesn't drink much, and his lungs are strong. He's the one we *didn't* worry about. Sometimes I would lie awake at night, filled with foreboding that Mom, who has the energy of an eighteen-year-old, was going to die one day. And when she did, who would help me with the babies and answer the phone in her delighted, singsongy voice that immediately made me smile? Who would exude such wacky, childlike optimism and look out at a cold, rainy night and chirp, without a trace of irony, "Aren't we lucky we're not squirrels!" Mom was mandatory, the clear skies to Dad's partly cloudiness, the sunny MVP of everyday life.

Over the years, Dad's thrown himself into various enthusiastic fitness binges: jogging, stationary cycling, a ninety-day diet-and-training plan. Most of his athletic pursuits started normally enough but soon morphed into mild infatuation, which eventually morphed into full obsession, followed swiftly by burnout. Eventually he'd quit and start something new. His latest fixation was

the Bowflex home gym he'd sent away for and set up in the basement.

"Whee!" he joked in an email six months before he learned he
had cancer. "It'll be just weeks before I achieve 'a strong, sexy
core,' but there goes your inheritance!" A month passed with little
contact, an eternity in Dad-land; then, an email: "Sorry for the
radio silence! Don't get me started on the wonders of the Bowflex!"

As much as Meg and I like to tease Dad about his monomaniacal
fixations, this is what you want for your retired parents: for them
not to act retired. He has more hobbies than anyone I know his age.
Four years ago, he took up the saxophone; until recently, he drove
to the county high school, in Little Washington, once a week to
take lessons from his nineteen-year-old teacher. "There are some
good days, some awful," Dad wrote genially not long after he started
playing. "Watch for my album soon!"

Still, he could sometimes wear himself out with his own enthusiasm. "I'm seemingly powerless to poke a stick in its spokes and
stop the whole mess," Dad confided to me by email about his photography project last spring before he got sick. He sounded weary,
maybe wearier than I'd ever heard him—the first faint alarm bells
ringing out from Huntly—but I was pregnant and too preoccupied
to pay much attention. I brushed it off, as I always did, as just one
of his compulsions, faintly annoyed that he was still pushing himself so hard. Why did he labor so over his pictures when he could
be visiting his grandchildren or planning new adventures? Couldn't
he just hang out? But I knew that he couldn't, wouldn't. His creativity was what moved him, even when it exhausted him.

Virginia is in the middle of the worst stinkbug infestation in decades, and the whole house is crawling with them. They drag their
miniature pewter shields on their backs, as though to war, oblong
bodies clacking, tiny pincer feet scraping against the wide-plank
pine floors. We flick them from beds and bookshelves. They cling

to the plaster walls and skitter across the kitchen counter, emitting a terrible stale odor of sickness. But no matter how many we squish or flush down the toilet, the army of stinkbugs is winning. They remind me of Dad's cancer: stalwart and insidious and determined to outlast us all.

It's amazing how tiring it is to care for an infant and a sick parent, both of whom sleep a lot and eat often, but in Dad's case never enough. As his illness has advanced, his appetite has diminished. He can't stand the pressure of having to eat, so we scurry around the kitchen preparing calories in little batches, bestowing upon him trays with modest portions. Nor are we allowed to call meals by their proper names—breakfast, lunch, and dinner—as this is too discouraging for Dad. We've learned to retreat hastily from his room, leaving him alone so he can properly concentrate on eating. When I linger too long, he swats the air impatiently and I go downstairs, feeling lonely for both of us—Dad, eating by himself in his bed, and myself, missing him already.

Later we carry the same dishes back to the kitchen, their contents more or less intact, minus a couple of bites of omelet or a few stewed prunes and a quarter-glass of milky Ensure. Sometimes Dad is awake, propped up on pillows, smiling with the corners of his eyes. "How long has it been since I kicked you out?" he asks apologetically. But other times he just lies there, slack-jawed, glasses off, his gray-green eyes open but eerily blank, and I can't help but wonder where he's gone and what he's seeing.

Not long after we left Washington, Dad did, too. He'd met Lesley on a scuba diving trip to Jamaica, in 1976, and eventually they moved in together, renting a split-level in Bethesda. In 1978, they bought Huntly Stage. Though it had only just been built, the house had already slipped into disrepair, as though the previous owners had run out of money or interest before they could finish. With rough-sawn vertical planks and a wooden deck upstairs and down, it sat like a tall, lonely ship on the prow of the hill, surrounded by drought-singed grass trampled to a stubble and not a single tree. They drove three hours round-trip to their jobs in D.C. each day. Back then, no one had heard of a three-hour commute—it was the energy crisis, after all—but their love for Huntly trumped the tedium of the drive, and their diesel Rabbit got forty miles to the gallon, which Dad verified every time he filled up the tank, dutifully scribbling the mileage in a log book he kept in the glove box. On weekends and evenings they fixed up the house, repairing the chicken coop, seeding the lawn, planting trees and a vegetable garden.

The divorce granted Dad "reasonable" visitation rights. In my parents' arrangement, this amounted to one week with him three or four times a year, give or take. Transportation was the tricky part. It was five hours by car from Summit to Huntly Stage, too far for either parent to drive us back and forth, so Mom took us to Newark and put us on the train to Washington by ourselves.

Even by the laissez-faire parenting standards of the seventies, this was borderline nuts. Newark had the highest violent crime rate in New Jersey; the Amtrak station was surrounded by abandoned buildings and smelled of urine. We wore laminated UNACCOMPA-NIED placards looped around our necks, which meant the conductor was supposed to make sure we weren't abducted, though Mom, trying to hide her despair, didn't say this outright.

She gave us each a few dollars of spending money, and once we settled in our seats and the conductor collected our tickets, we'd wander to the Café Car and ponder the candy selections. We always bought the same thing—two boxes of Cracker Jacks and two cans of yellow Country Time lemonade—and we sat on the counter stools, pawing through the caramel popcorn to find our plastic treasures at the bottom.

The Metroliner sped from Newark to Washington in two hours and fifty-nine minutes, and Meg and I remained on high alert for the duration. We did not fear strangers or foul play: What terrified us was the prospect of missing our stop—the train pulling in and out before we could exit, flinging us along to places where no one we knew was waiting. We memorized the stations, north to south, and the time between each one, imitating the nasally way the conductor bellowed them over the loudspeaker: *Met-RO-park!* *Thirtieth Street Station Philadelphia! WILLLLmington, Delaware,*

Meg on the Metroliner, 1983

Wilmington! Balmore, Balmore. Now arriving Warshington's Union Station. Warshington! At least ten minutes before we were due to roll into the platform, Meg would slam shut her copy of *Little House on the Prairie* and yelp, "Time to go!" and we would leap to our feet, pull our monogrammed suitcases from the overhead rack, and lurch down the aisle to one end of the car. There we'd stand, waiting in the wobbly vestibule, clutching each other and our bags as the train jiggled back and forth and the track sped beneath us through the crack in the metal floor.

Looking back, it seems that the fundamental terms of our sisterhood, maybe even our characters, were established on those train rides. The seeds of self-reliance had been planted, and the conditions of our survival made clear: Despite what might go on in either of our homes, the vagaries of our parents and stepparents that remained beyond our control and understanding, we two constituted our own independent, inviolable unit—separate yet united, Meg buried in her book, me pressing my nose to the train window, watching the gritty cities flash by, the narrow houses with yards that backed right up to the tracks. It was a wordless agreement. *We must stick together at all costs.*

When the train finally came to a stop, we'd rush down the stairs, scanning the platform for Dad's familiar form: wavy black hair, owlishly round glasses, straight from the office in his tweedy blazer and pressed khaki slacks. He liked to pretend to hide from us, in plain sight—*now you see me, now you don't.* Sometimes we saw only his hunched back, cowering obviously behind a concrete pillar, shaking up and down in silent laughter. Other times he'd be slouching against a bench, pretending to have fallen asleep, whistle-snoring a little for effect. We'd make a big show of finding him and nudging him awake, his face cracking wide open at the sight of us.

"Hello, girls!"

The sweet relief of arrival.

If Summit was a bucolic suburban wilderness—sidewalks, grass, trees, freedom—then Huntly was the sticks. We couldn't ride our bikes downtown to buy candy bars with our allowance or corral the neighbor kids. There *were* no neighbor kids, and the closest shop was at Settle's Grocery and Garage, in Flint Hill, five miles away, where they sold Spam and potato salad in plastic containers and knew Dad and Lesley by name.

Lesley was tall and reedy and very British, with short brown hair layered in waves, always a little mussed, as if she'd just come in from mucking the stables. She was thirty-four, seven years younger than my father, an administrative officer at the World Bank. She'd

Dad, Lesley, Meg and me, Huntly Stage, 1978

never married and had no children of her own. She loved all creatures madly, maternally, and she strode about the farm in her faded
Lee jeans and dark-green Wellies, trilling at her menagerie: horses,
chickens, donkeys, and a rotating cast of cats and kittens she
brought home from the dump in cardboard boxes. The way Lesley
warbled in high soprano for her shaggy, good-natured mutts was
straight out of the Westminster dog show. Yet her brisk English accent and aloofness scared me a little. It was possible that she was
fond of us, but it seemed, to a seven-year-old's wary eyes, as though
her four-legged creatures were simpler and easier to love.

The peacock was Dad's. It showed up in the early nineties, after
it ran away from a nearby farm and started roosting in the trees
behind the house. Dad and Lesley heard its high-pitched, tortured
shrieking before they saw it. Dad phoned around to the neighbors
until he located its owner. "Your peacock seems to have wandered
over to our place," he told him. "You can keep him!" the neighbor
replied. Dad set out a bowl of puppy chow on the lawn each morning, crouching in the grass, calling, in his growly-affectionate way,
"Here, Peacock, Peacock!" Peacock would tiptoe across the lawn
and peck at the kibble. Peacock's head was hardly bigger than a

thimble, his plumage outsized and iridescent. Dad bought him a full-length mirror at Kmart and propped it up against the barn, along with a pair of shiny truck hubcaps, so Peacock could preen to his reflection.

The remoteness of Huntly Stage was unsettling at first. Without school, we had long, yawning days to fill with Dad. We flew kites and built model towns and shot plastic airplanes with rubber bands. We drifted in hot black inner tubes down the Shenandoah River. We took seemingly endless walks on seemingly interminable one-lane country roads that dead-ended in the woods, and then turned around and walked all the way back the same way.

To shuttle between parents at such a young age is to vacillate among every major emotion, sometimes in the very same moment. Did I miss Mom? (Always.) Was I glad to see Dad? (Of course.) Did I believe that the divorce was somehow my fault? Did I occasionally resent Mom for moving us away and Dad for letting us leave? (Yes, yes, and yes.) I existed in a state of near-constant confusion. But when I was outside, I forgot about feeling guilty, torn between families, vaguely unsettled in both homes. I could run bare-legged through the grass, chasing clues in a treasure hunt Dad made for us. I could climb trees and catch tadpoles in the creek. I could be seven and pretend this was normal.

Later in the afternoon, after Meg and I get back from town, we find Dad on the back patio. This is where he likes to relax with a glass of orange juice after a long, sweaty day mowing his fields. Across the meadows, the trees on the lumpy ridge of Rattlesnake Mountain are blazing orange and red, and the chestnut he and Lesley planted shortly after they bought the house casts enormous, droopy shadows over the lawn.

He's sitting at the table facing the sun, working his way through a little black notebook. On the cover he's written OBLIGATIONS in all capitals. It's crammed with envelopes, presumably bills. He flips through the pages, slowly and purposefully, ticking off items with his pen. Every few moments he pulls out his checkbook and writes a check. He's settling his affairs.

Meg and I quietly pull up chairs. Dad appears so focused and unperturbed, I don't want to disturb him. It's kind of awesome and horrifying at the same time, his diligent concentration, his reverence for the tedious minutiae. Dad has always been a vigilant record keeper. He's tabulated every centimeter of rain that's fallen on the farm since they moved in. When Meg and I were teenagers and he was saving up for college, he recorded his daily expenses in a spiral notebook that he kept in his back pocket: thirty cents for a Tab at M Street Deli next to the Geographic, $22.99 for pancakes and pork scrapple for four at the Best Western (or "Worst Eastern," as Dad nicknamed it), in Front Royal. If he forgot his pad, he'd write his expenditures in black ink on the back of his hand. This troubled me. It made him seem poor, though of course he wasn't, as though he was about to spend his last dime. I didn't want him going broke on account of us.

After a minute or two, Dad puts his notebook aside and looks at us expectantly. It would be so much easier to talk about the still-blooming Indian summer, his photography archives, the grass that won't quit growing, but that's not why we're here. We're here to have the Conversation—not *What are we going to do?* but *What do you want?* And the uncomfortable question none of us want to ask: *How much time?*

Dad tells us he's scheduled an embolization surgery in a few weeks that will shunt blood away from his tumor to slow its growth. "It's not a cure," he says quickly, lest we get our hopes up. "There is no cure."

He pauses and takes a long sip of water. Orange juice is out now—sugar feeds the cancer. Wipes his brow, hesitates half a second, working up to the hard stuff. "When it comes time," Dad says, "I'd like to be scattered." It takes me a second to understand what he means—cremated. I can't help but smile at the expression, as though in his next life he will sprout from seed as a maple sapling or, better yet, his beloved grass. A line of verse stirs out of the dimmest crevices of my brain. I wrote my college thesis on Walt Whitman. What was it he'd called it—*the beautiful uncut hair of graves*?

Meg bends over one of Dad's small spiral steno pads, taking notes. "Definitely no funeral," he continues. "Just have some people in for snacks." Now I feel like crying. A whole life he's lived and he wants us to commemorate it with *pretzels*? His face is expressionless, as though he's talking about some distant date in the unknown future, about someone other than himself. But I know that, unlike me, he's not in denial. He can see what's coming and is ready to meet it.

"Play some nice music," he continues. He's already picked out the song: "The Jig," composed by Bach and performed by the organist E. Power Biggs. The CD is on the shelf in the closet, with the rest of his collection. "Play it loud, like *really* loud. So loud it fills the room. So loud you can't talk over it."

In my own notebook, I scribble in a shaky hand: *Biggs. Play @ full volume.*

"I've met with my lawyer and taken care of almost everything here." Dad gestures to his notebook pages, stuffed fat with the provisions of being alive. "But all the flopsy-dopsy . . ." He trails off, sounding dispirited. "All my unfinished stuff—my pictures and research. Someone is going to have to put it away. After I've gone, it won't make a difference to me what happens. You girls should take what you want." He pauses, thinking it over. "*If* you want anything."

Before I can respond, Maisy starts chirping through the baby monitor, waking from her nap. When I bring her out to the patio, Dad reaches for her without hesitation, wrapping one arm around her neck and the other on her belly, propping her up on his lap so she can look out at the lawn. She nuzzles his cheek and tucks her head beneath his chin.

PHOTO: KATIE ARNOLD

Dad and Maisy, Huntly Stage, October 2010

I lean back in my chair, trying to imprint the moment in my mind. If only I hadn't waited until my mid-thirties to get married and have babies. If only Steve and I lived closer to Huntly, so Pippa and Maisy could spend more time with Dad, so we all could. I want to tell him this, but after all this time I don't know how. To fill the silence, I blurt, "I think I'm going to start writing about being a mother." My words come as a surprise to me. I haven't actually thought about this before, but now that they're out, I think they must be true.

Dad stops rocking Maisy and turns to look me in the eye. He's always had a certain way of talking when he wants you to pay attention—emphatic, as if he's speaking in capital letters. Occasionally his tone can be condescending, as if he knows what's Good and Right and he's just waiting for you to catch up. Other times he's quietly assuring, certain that if you pay attention and try hard, you'll eventually figure it out.

Quite possibly many words come out of Dad's mouth—supportive and encouraging. But the ones I hear are: "If you're going to write, be sure it's about something important." My cheeks grow hot with embarrassment. I know his serious tone. He means *Important*. He means: *Don't mess around. Write what matters. Live this way, too.*

6

The Faraway

Abiquiu, New Mexico

I n the picture Mom snapped of me the day I moved to Santa Fe, I'm
standing in front of their house, wearing a faded purple shirt
with a freckled fish screen-printed on the front, my shoulder-
length hair parted low to one side. One hand is cocked on my hip,
my elbow jutting out at a jaunty angle. I'm staring straight at the
camera, a wry grin on my face, not quite defiant but almost. I know
this day belongs to me. All I have to do is smile and open my arms
and pull in the fresh air and drive away, and the future will happen, without even trying. I am twenty-three.

It was the first of July 1995. I was leaving my job at a publishing house in New York City for an internship at *Outside* magazine. I was not cut out for city life. For two years, I walked to and from work every day through Central Park to Rockefeller Center, wearing my white Reeboks and carrying my navy-blue pumps in the sensible saddle-brown briefcase that Mom had given me, just like Melanie Griffith in *Working Girl*. In the evenings after I walked home, I put on my Rollerblades and skated back to the park, circling the paved loop all the way to Harlem and home again. From the Sheep Meadow, when the setting sun lit the buildings along Central Park South orange, I could almost pretend they were mountains.

I'd tried to ask Dad for a referral to *National Geographic*, but he was reluctant. "Oh, I don't know, Katie," he said, sounding uneasy, as if he *did* know but was afraid to say it. "I'm not sure it's the best place for women. I think it's easy to get marginalized in the assistant track." I was trying and almost succeeding at not feeling hurt when he added, "And, well, nepotism makes me uncomfortable. I wouldn't want anyone to think I'd gotten you the job and that you couldn't have gotten it yourself." I felt like I'd been punched. Okay, I thought, I'll have to do it on my own.

It was Ron who encouraged me to apply to *Outside*. I'd subscribed to the magazine in high school, and he'd read in *The Wall Street Journal* that it was relocating its headquarters from Chicago to Santa Fe and was hiring. Six months after I applied, I got the call. After the pinch-me shock passed and the elation set in, after I danced a crazy jig around my studio apartment and eyeballed the calendar and tried to imagine Santa Fe and conjured not one single thing but blue skies, the doubt set in. What had I done? Quitting a real job with health insurance and a 401(k) for a short-term internship that paid $5 an hour without benefits, in a city and state in which I knew no one and had never set foot.

Watch me.

The trip to New Mexico took three days. Arkansas appears flat, but it is actually one very long, gradual hill. My Jetta was so loaded down with my clothing, camping gear, mountain bike, and Roller-blades that I had to turn off the air-conditioning just to keep the speedometer from sagging below fifty. In Oklahoma, I watched an RV drive into a gas station overhang, shearing off its roof like the lid on a can of cat food. I laughed carelessly until the man behind the counter gave me a stern warning. "You're in Tornado Alley now," he said. "If you hear the sirens, you'd better get your ass in a ditch." I'd been so blasé about leaving, but suddenly I felt unsure. I thought about Dad, who, just the day before, had driven half an hour from Huntly to a Howard Johnson's on the interstate in Winchester to see me off. We sat in a booth and ordered BLTs and iced teas and looked at the map spread out on the table, tracing the highway west to New Mexico, two thousand miles away. My internship was supposed to last three months, but I hoped that if I worked hard I could stretch it to six. Beyond that, I had no idea what would happen.

In the parking lot, Dad checked my tire pressure and pulled me in for one last, long hug. "I'm proud of you, old girl," he whispered. I drove away slowly, watching Dad grow smaller, a solitary blue dot beneath HoJo's blue crown, his hand in the air. I was leaving him again.

Santa Fe sits at seven thousand feet at the tail end of the Rocky Mountains, where they peter out into desert. The city was like no place I'd ever seen. Even though it's the state capital and home to 65,000 people, many of the roads near downtown were dirt, and they twisted narrowly, never in a straight line. The buildings were uniformly brown: one-story adobes made from mud bricks or wood frame and then stuccoed the color of paper lunch sacks, with tall brown stucco walls. They looked as if they were simultaneously sprouting from the earth and crumbling back into it. The roofs were flat, the walls sloped, and the windows small, trimmed in turquoise and bright blue that matched the sky. I had never seen sky so big and bright, so saturated with color, with an almost brutal clarity—I had to blink to make sure it was real. You could do whatever you wanted and be whoever you wanted to be under that sky.

Georgia O'Keeffe called New Mexico "the Faraway." As a young artist visiting from New York City for the first time in 1929, she was transfixed by the sprawling desert, its radiant light, the mesas and rooster-comb ridges. "The distance has always been calling me," she wrote. The latitude she felt as she ranged far and wide through canyons and buttes lit her paintings from the inside. "I decided that the only thing I could do that was nobody else's business was to paint. I could do as I chose because no one would care." The faraway was as much a state of mind as a specific place, a way of being wild and sure, a way of seeing and living and making art on her own terms.

On the surface, Santa Fe had a ragged, hard-edged beauty. There was the crumbly dirt and rocks, no grass to speak of, and the shrubby juniper and piñon trees fanned out on the foothills, stunted by lack of rain. The scratchy adobe walls and the sharp glare of the sun, the arroyos chewing away at the ground, the dry air that cracked your skin, and the prickly cacti underfoot—all had a toughness to which I was unaccustomed. The necessities I'd taken for granted in the East were rarities here: oxygen, moisture, greenery, family. And yet there was a softness about Santa Fe, too. I could feel it right away. The earth-tone adobes, with their rounded edges, and the gently rounded mountaintops, so old that all the jagged points had been worn down. Even the openness—the scale of the landscape, its great emptiness—seemed conciliatory. You could see what it was dealing you; you could see the weather coming from half a day away. You knew where you stood.

Nothing about Santa Fe should have made any kind of sense to me. Except for my new friends at *Outside,* there weren't many people my age; the city's traditional Native American and Spanish American populations had been inundated by New Age healers and artists and retirees living out their golden years buying art and going to healers. It was easily misunderstood. People from other places assumed, as I once had, that Santa Fe was just like Phoenix: hot lowland desert. Or they'd mistake it for part of Mexico. "No, *New* Mexico—it's a state, not the country," you'd have to say when someone got confused. (Although sometimes it *did* feel like a foreign country.) Even the license plate was compelled to clarify: "New Mexico USA." While forecasting tornadoes in Texas and heat waves in Arizona on national TV, the weatherman stood in front of New Mexico, blocking the whole state with his body.

It was the blank space in between. Somehow, by chance, I'd landed right where I was meant to be.

PHOTO: DAVID L. ARNOLD

Me with Lesley and Meg, Pennsylvania, early '90s

My job at *Outside* was both an understatement and an overstatement. There were three of us interns at any given time, and our job was to fact-check every word in every story in the magazine. This was in the very last, dying days of typesetting, and at the dawn of the Internet, so we marked up paper copies with pencils— checkmarks when the fact checked out, long marginalia when it didn't—and called all our sources on the telephone, using phone books that lined one long shelf.

The *Outside* staff was predominantly male, in number and attitude. If you weren't a guy, you could still make it at the magazine, but it helped if you acted like one, rode your bike or ran fast like one, and thought like one. And, above all, wrote like one.

When I wasn't calling Burmese refugee camps or virus hunters at the CDC or being patched through via satellite phone to Everest Base Camp, I climbed my own mountains. The first month I lived in town, I rode my bicycle to the trailhead and climbed Atalaya every evening after work. The trail was dusty and loose and stitched together by roots and small rocks that behaved like ball bearings in the dry summer heat. It switchbacked and wound uphill for more than two miles, cresting a false summit, through tenuous sections where it was easy to lose your footing and slide off the edge. The route was marked erratically by blue blazes on trees, and the first time I climbed it, I wondered more than once if I was on the right path and what I was doing out there alone. It was cooler on top, the heat draining off the mountain in waves, and I sat wheezing on a granite ledge, the altitude burning my lungs and all of the little brown bumps of Santa Fe spread out below me. I thought, the way I have on every subsequent Atalaya summit, *I've done it.* Not just the climb, but the whole thing—my new life, all on my own.

Sometimes when we were kids and Meg and I took the train to Washington, Dad would pick us up and we'd ride the Metro to *National Geographic,* at 17th and M Streets, until he finished work. He worked in a narrow shaft of an office on the eighth floor, with a long light table on one wall where we'd mash our eyes against the light boxes, looking at negatives. He organized them precisely in tall stacks, rubber-banded twice around, a dozen or more stacks per story. When we got bored, we'd take the elevator down to Explorers Hall, the museum in the lobby, which consisted, thrillingly,

of a talking parrot named Henry and numerous interactive diora-
mas. The clear glass boxes contained intricate, three-dimensional
scenes, miniaturized renderings of dusty, inhospitable places like
sub-Saharan Africa, with rumpled brown knolls that looked as if
they'd been molded out of clay. You could pull the conical earpiece
from the wall by its curlicue cord and listen to Louis Leakey's ancient voice crackling on about the discovery of the first *Homo sapi-
ens,* lulling you into another land.

Looking down on Santa Fe from high on Atalaya was like peering
into a diorama. Especially at sunset or sunrise, when the light
slanted in, the color of honey, at such a low angle that you could
see all the details in sharp relief. It made the immense desert seem
almost quaint.

Climbing a mountain at nine thousand feet when you are used to
Rollerblading through Central Park feels like blasting a blowtorch
into your open mouth, repeatedly. My breathing was so jagged and
labored, I sounded like I was about to go into cardiac arrest. I'd
heard that it could take six months to adjust to the oxygen-depleted
air. Each week, my panting became a little less pronounced, my leg
muscles more springy, the trail more familiar.

One evening on the way down Atalaya, I skidded on the rocks
and tumbled down the trail, coming to a stop against a piñon tree.
When I pulled myself up, blood was spurting from a gash in my left
kneecap. Except for the key to my bike lock, which I'd shoved in
the front of my sports bra, I carried nothing. No water, no phone,
no first aid. I had nearly two miles and a thousand vertical feet to
descend. I yanked off my T-shirt, looped it around the wound like
a saggy tourniquet, and hobbled gingerly down the mountain.

When I got back to the trailhead, my knee was so stiff I could
barely bend it, and I felt lightheaded. Riding my bike was out of
the question. A woman was getting into her car, and she stared
when she saw me.

"Uh, do you think you could drive me to the hospital?" I asked
nervously, gesturing with raw, blood-streaked palms to my bicy-

cle, locked to the post. "I'm new in town and don't have anyone to call."

"Get in," she said.

At the ER, the doctor gave me the choice of stitches or not, and I foolishly chose not. The scar it left, lumpy and red-fading-to-white—the first of many in Santa Fe—was a reminder of why I'd come: to live on the brink of comfort and risk, between the familiar and the faraway.

New Mexico's official nickname is the Land of Enchantment, but it's often jokingly referred to as the Land of Entrapment. People have a way of washing up here and staying far longer than they'd intended. This is not a recent phenomenon. In 1898, the artists Ernest Blumenschein and Bert Phillips were traveling from Denver to Mexico on a painting expedition when one of the wheels on their covered wagon fell off, stranding them in Taos. Seduced by its vivid light and landscape, they settled permanently there, the first of what become known as the Taos Society of Artists, a loose-knit colony that would later draw legions of painters, photographers, and writers to the sagebrush mesa at the foot of the mountains. Of the winter he spent at a ranch north of Taos shortly before his death in 1925, D. H. Lawrence wrote, "I think New Mexico was the greatest experience from the outside world that I have ever had. . . . In the magnificent, fierce morning of New Mexico, one sprang awake, a new part of the soul woke up suddenly, and the old world gave way to a new."

Six months after I arrived, *Outside* offered me a full-time job, and six months after that, Mom boxed up my Manhattan apartment and sent my furniture west on a moving truck. Eventually she stopped asking when I was coming home. I *was* home.

I'd lived in Santa Fe for three years when I ran up Atalaya for the first time. It was a total whim. No one I knew ran up mountains, but I was lonely and heartsick. My boyfriend of a year had decided to move to New York for business school. I was so crushed I taped a Post-it note to the ceiling above my bed, the first thing I saw when I woke up each morning: *Everything takes you to a new place.*

It was a summer evening, after work. I drove to the trailhead and started slowly, jogging the first half mile. Then I decelerated to a hike. For the next mile and a half, I alternated between a jog and a fast walk. I went only as far as the false summit, less than halfway, then turned around and jogged back down, careful not to trip over my own feet. I did this for a few weeks, maybe a month, going a little bit higher, running a little bit more each time. I was breaking the mountain down into smaller pieces, the way rock climbers practice different sequences of a route for months before trying the climb in its entirety.

Each time I staggered up Atalaya, it felt like a physical catharsis. Sweat poured out of me and evaporated instantly in the dry air, leaving a skim of salt on my skin. I would strip down to my sports bra and shove my T-shirt into the waistband of my shorts and feel the sun on my back and the breath surging in my lungs and chase my shadow all the way to the top.

I couldn't think at all when I ran. It took every ounce of effort and willpower just to get myself up the mountain. I couldn't think about the boy in New York, about losing him through my own stubborn independence. I couldn't think about missing my parents or what would become of me. I could think only about my feet crunching on dirt, the tightness in my hamstrings, and how I was going to make it through the steepest, nastiest section, which I knew lay around the next bend.

I took a perverse pleasure in punishing myself on Atalaya. I was starting to feel things in a new way, and it didn't matter that they hurt. I liked the scratches on my legs, the dirt on my shins. I liked coming home pulverized from the effort, with visible proof that I had persevered. Thrashing myself on a long climb was better than brooding at home, staring up at a Post-it note taped to the ceiling.

Running up the mountain in the last light of day felt like an act of audacious nonconformity. Most of my friends from New York were dating investment bankers and had a closetful of dry-clean-only clothes they wore to their marketing jobs. I had a casita a mile from the trails and scabs on my elbows and a low-paying job I loved. Money wasn't freedom. Running in the beauty of the far-away was.

By the end of the summer, I'd broken down the whole mountain. I could run to the top of Atalaya and down again in just under an hour and a half. Years later, a friend gave me a copy of the book *Running with the Mind of Meditation.* In it, the Tibetan lama and marathon runner Sakyong Mipham explains the four progressive phases of meditation and running. Tiger is the neophyte stage, when you are learning to develop focus and strength. On Atalaya, I was becoming a tiger.

I ran all that year and into the next. I'd started writing for *Outside,* and running was one way I wrote. On the trails, my thoughts unspooled in the silence, one to the next as though in a waking daydream, ideas spilling forth of their own accord, the same way I'd written my stories while shooting the basketball years earlier. It was like the feeling you get when you're talking to someone as you drift off to sleep. You can hear the words coming out of your mouth, but you're not sure who's talking. Whole sentences moved through me, up from the earth and into the soles of my feet. My only job was not to forget them as I ran beneath sun-hot ponderosas, along dry creek beds, to the top of my world and back down again.

7

Progression

Mom, Pennsylvania, 1965

The secret to running isn't speed or stamina. It's progression. Whether you're starting out or training for a new distance, the important matrix isn't time or pace, but improvement. Even if you're just goofing off and having fun, running for no one but yourself, even if you don't care about results, if you pay attention, if you stay devoted, you'll see improvements. Your legs will become stronger, your lungs not quite so winded. Hills that used to seem steep won't feel so formidable. You will progress, a little bit farther, higher, faster. This is what gets you out of bed in the morning, on gloomy days when the sky matches your mood and your calves balk with every step.

I don't consciously think *My father has cancer, I have a new baby, I can't go running*. I don't have time to think this. Almost all my waking hours are spent nursing the baby or rocking the baby or hiking with the baby so she will take a nap or telling the other, bigger baby to please keep her hands off the baby. And swabbing projectile spit-up off every surface in the house. And worrying endlessly that the babies won't grow up to know their grandfather.

This is how regression sneaks in. When you're not paying attention.

Someone once told me that when you have a newborn, you should set one goal for yourself every day. It should be modest and attainable—like brushing your hair or taking a nap or making the bed—something that will give you a small bump of accomplishment without causing you to feel more exhausted than you already are. Now when I consider this advice, I want to cry. I can't choose just one thing. There's so much I miss, so much that needs to be done. I want to run up my mountain and write in my notebook and tickle Maisy's soft toes and lie outside with Pippa and pick out shapes in the clouds. I want to do anything but think about losing Dad.

Breastfeeding has sucked almost all the extra pregnancy weight off of me, but my body is still a stranger to me. Everything is looser, my muscles and tendons jigglier, just a tad off-kilter, like I've been haphazardly slung back together after the physical trauma of childbirth. My gait is different, too. I'm not moving forward as much as diagonally, limbs askew, in a hasty awkward jaywalking. Instead of my normally flat, girlish chest, I have breasts now: smaller than average, but actual cleavage. Even jammed into my sports bra, they bounce and leak when I run.

I'm not ready to suffer on Atalaya, so I stick with a rolling, four-mile loop around the base of the mountain. The key to progression is starting small. Even after a few miles at a torpid pace, the endorphin rush is phenomenal, even better than before the girls were born, when I could run whenever I pleased for as long as I pleased, when my body and time were all my own.

I don't wear a watch and never time myself, but I don't need to gauge whether I'm getting faster. It's a novelty to be out on my own again, remembering what it's like to be unencumbered, a body in motion, to feel my lungs expand and my blood hammer in my ears and all the memories come flooding back.

After our Fodderstack debut, Meg and I went back to Virginia each April to run the 10K. We didn't train, but still we got better and faster, walking less and running more, shaving minutes off our time. Soon we were winning prizes for our age groups: hand-thrown clay pots, one for nearly every year of our adolescence. In the summer of 1980, I became obsessed with Terry Fox, the Canadian amputee who was running five thousand miles across Canada on a prosthetic leg to raise money for cancer. The whole world was rooting for Terry. He ran more than three thousand miles before his cancer spread to his lungs. I remember thinking *How could he go that far?* And then: *How could he* stop? He died in 1981, at age twenty-two. That was the year *Chariots of Fire* came out, and for weeks after Mom and Ron took us downtown to the Strand Theater to see it, I hummed the theme song under my breath as I ran.

Female role models were harder to find. Our next-door neighbor ran marathons, but he was a father, so he didn't count. All the mothers in our neighborhood stayed home, decorating their houses or volunteering for the Junior League; or they worked part-time, like my mom, and went to exercise class at the Y and did *Jane Fonda's Workout* in the den after dinner. I didn't see any of them doing exercise for fun or because they loved it and were good at it, or because they couldn't *not*. It was way at the bottom of the list, below the beef stroganoff and the kelly-green curtains and packing the Hostess Ding Dongs for our lunches.

Only years later did I discover I'd been wrong. I was visiting my mother, fixing Pippa and Maisy their breakfast so I could go for a run, when Mom said, "You know, I just ran out the door while you and Meg were sleeping." The way she mentioned it, almost dismissively, I assumed she meant running an errand. Once. But she meant *running*. Regularly. Sneaking out before dawn almost every day.

"You were little, and I'd go out around 5 a.m., down the street and around the block a ways, out that road in Summit . . . oh, what was it called?" She paused, trying to remember. I felt the color drain from my face. My mother, a *runner*? How had I not known this?

Mom shrugged, smiling demurely at the memory, and her ability to surprise me after all these years. "Well, it was only a couple of miles."

Mom and me, Summit, 1984

Mom had always drilled into us the importance of being indomitable. Weakness or doubt were not to be indulged, much less discussed. This was not delusion or wishful thinking on her part, but a sort of homespun positive psychology, years before its time. "*We* do not get allergies," she told us, a suggestion of superiority in her voice. We did not get sick. We did not get stressed or worried. Our strong constitutions were a direct reflection of her sturdy Canadian stock and our own mental resolve. On the rare occasion we caught a cold, Mom made us Jell-O and safety-pinned a wool sock around our necks and let us watch game shows on television before sending us to bed with a hot water bottle. "You'll be better in the morning," she told us, and, whether by our iron willpower or our immune systems, we usually were.

Laid up on the couch, I binged on *The Price Is Right* and *Family Feud*. The contestants' naked desire to win something tangible yet utilitarian—a new toaster or dinette set—depressed and excited me. It seemed to reveal something important about the force of human optimism: a wild, hands-in-the-air hope that something fabulous awaited behind door number two, coupled with the sanguine acceptance that maybe it was only a washing machine.

When someone you love has cancer, it feels a little like playing *The Price Is Right*. You're faced with a series of doors. *C'mon down!* To the left is life as normal. *Bang*—that door closes. To the right is life with cancer. That one opens. Mild, treatable cancer? Closed. Aggressive, terminal tumor: Open for business! Two years to live? Maybe that just closed. Six months? God, let's hope it's still open. Every doorway, each step, forces you to recalibrate your expectations and make concessions. This in itself is a progression. How much uncertainty can you handle? Every day, a little more than you think.

Dad is on his own progression, only it's a negative progression. Regression. He's dying a little bit every day. I've heard people say that about living—aren't we all dying slowly all the time?—but now that Dad's sick, I realize this is completely bogus. As long as you're healthy, you can still improve, fumble forward, make leaps, slip back, inch up, claw your way out again. Your progress may be measurable, as it is with running, or indistinct, but there's always the possibility of improvement and reinvention. You are evolving.

As it had been for Mom, running was my own thing. The only time all year that I ran competitively was at the Fodderstack. In my mind, racing required a combination of elements that existed only at Huntly Stage: the rolling country roads, the anonymity of being an outsider from someplace else, the thrill of seeing Dad at the finish line. At home in New Jersey, I could run when I felt like it, and how I felt like it, and no one would care. I never joined my school's track or cross-country teams. Meg did those things. She wore the maroon-and-gold-striped satiny thigh-grazers and went to state in hurdles. I ran out the back door in my gray New Balance 990s, clutching my bulky yellow Sony Sports Walkman, and blasting Bananarama and INXS through my headphones, with barely a glance from my mother.

My motives were not always pure. In high school, I ran to catch a glimpse of the boy I liked driving by in his wood-paneled Wagoneer. In college in Vermont I occasionally ran up a forested hill called Snake Mountain. My boyfriend lived in a farmhouse at the base, so I could roll out of his bed and run up and down the mountain, burning off the late-night beer and pizza, and still make it to history lecture by eleven. The trail climbed a thousand feet through the trees, and on the broad clearing on top, I could stick my head out of the forest and look down on the lake and hills, and breathe.

It wasn't until I moved to Santa Fe, though, that I began to love running as much as I needed it. It was all that open space, so much of it still so wild and empty. You could see for thirty or forty miles in any direction on a clear day, often more. Everything was laid out in plain sight, but the distances were deceiving. Even the farthest mountains seemed approachable. Like if you set off and just kept going, you'd eventually get there.

My distances began creeping up. It wasn't a conscious decision, but something that happened naturally. My body was stronger, so I could go longer, and I had a new boyfriend who liked running, too. Steve was twenty-six, six feet tall, a gardener with thick calico hair and a sprinter's lanky frame. His calves were perfectly shaped ovals beneath his summer-brown skin. He had a dimple just to the right of his mouth, and when he smiled, his green eyes did that exaggerated twinkly thing I'd only ever seen in the movies, like a leprechaun winking. He made me laugh all the time, but he didn't need to be the center of attention. He could just be himself: the calmest and most direct person I'd ever met, as steady as I was topsy-turvy.

Steve, Stony Lake, 2005

Steve was from New Jersey, like me. The youngest of four, he rode his bike for miles to the ponds and swamps in his town. His older brothers broke their legs running along railroad trestles and cracked their skulls jumping into stone quarries, and his mother had been worn down by worry. As long as he came home alive, he could do as he pleased. In Santa Fe, he explored the backcountry on skis, raft, bike, and foot. Our runs together were never fast, because he was more interested in covering new ground than competing. We were always bushwhacking, ducking beneath piñon trees, hopping boulders, scouting new routes. I envied his spontaneity, but sometimes I just wanted to make steady progress without being thwacked in the face by a branch.

It was his idea to run our first trail race, a twelve-mile mountain run up and down Aspen Vista, a doubletrack forest road above Santa Fe that climbs from 10,000 feet to 12,000 feet. He hadn't trained, and on the morning of the race we showed up at the trailhead with five minutes to spare, couldn't find a parking spot, and had to sprint to the start just as the gun was going off. Steve finished seventh. I was eleventh, the second woman.

It would be another year before we entered our next race, the Albuquerque Half Marathon. Steve and I ran elbow-to-elbow for 13 miles on a flat, narrow bike path along the banks of the Rio Grande; we were two bodies amid a sea of nylon-clad bodies, pounding along in an asphalt daze. In the final mile, though, a commotion on the curb caught my eye. A spectator was waving and yelling at someone. She was yelling at *me*. "SHE'S *HURTING*— TAKE HER *DOWN*!" The woman was pointing ahead, to someone I couldn't see. "The second-place woman is just ahead!" she screamed frantically, gesturing for me to run faster. "You can catch her. CRUSH HER!" She didn't know either of us, but she wanted a dogfight; she wanted a race to the finish. I glanced over at Steve and he dipped his chin, just barely a nod. *Let's go.* Something in me snapped, and I took off.

I'd be lying if I said it wasn't intoxicating, that final pseudo sprint that carried me past my flagging competitor, with two blocks to go, and into second place; if I didn't think I was sort of the shit as I stood on the podium while the race director looped a silver medal around my neck and the spectators clapped and Steve hollered my name. If I didn't, in the predictable upwelling of post-race endorphins, wonder what more I was capable of, and if I would ever have the chance to find out.

Sometimes progression happens in small, almost inappreciable increments, one step after another, so subtle you hardly notice. Other times it requires a huge, terrifying leap. In rock climbing, the most difficult part of a route is called the crux. It's make-or-break. You have to reach for the next crimp with your hands, inch yourself upward to find a solid foothold, or you're stuck. Once you make the move, you've passed through. There are not so many crux moves in life, really, in the scheme of things. Looking back, you might have had five or ten such decisive turns, where circumstances swerve one way and change everything.

Not long after the half marathon, I convinced *Outside* to send me to Yosemite to write a story about the country's top female rock climber. Steph Davis was a year younger than me and split her time between the red rock spires in Moab, Utah, and the granite walls in Yosemite, where she lived with her husband, pro climber Dean Potter. Toward the end of my trip, she suggested we climb Half Dome. I'd been rock climbing maybe half a dozen times in my life. When I told Steph this, she just smiled her dazzling smile and said, "Great!"

On the six-mile hike from the trailhead, I tried to reassure myself that she did not mean I was actually going to *climb* Half Dome, the nearly five-thousand-foot granite crest that's the most recognizable landmark in the park. Perhaps she was going to haul me up—or, in climbing parlance, "jug"—the way climbers ferry gear up a steep pitch, using a complicated system of ropes and pulleys. I had no problem being carted up the mile-tall monolith if it meant not falling to my death. Or maybe she said "climb" when she really meant "hike." Plenty of regular people hike Half Dome every day.

But when we got to the base, I looked up at the face, as sheer as a skyscraper, with a lumpy ridge running down the middle like a serpent's back, and I knew there would be no walking involved. Steph pulled out an extra pair of rubber-soled climbing shoes and thrust them at me. "These should fit!" she said happily. Then she handed me a harness.

On rock climbing's difficulty scale, the route we were taking to the summit, named Snake Dike, is rated a 5.7, which is a beginning-to-intermediate technical route. It's the easiest climb on Half Dome. But it's also two thousand feet of exposed vertical rock. Following Steph's lead above me, I inched out on the route, panic-sweating through my T-shirt almost before I found my first foothold. We picked our way up the slab, Steph clipping the rope that connected us into bolts every twenty feet. Far below, the forest looked like the synthetic miniature pine trees Meg and I used to glue onto the model towns we built at Huntly, perfectly conical and painfully spiky. I couldn't look, but I couldn't not look, either. Never had I experienced such gorgeous, brain-addling vertigo. I was going to either puke or wet my pants.

"Don't look down!" Steph called from above.

"I have to go to the bathroom!" I shouted nervously.

"Just pull your shorts down and pee on the rock!" she yelled back. I've peed in plenty of places while running before—squatting in riverbanks, behind trees, between open car doors at trailhead parking lots, and once, accidentally, on top of a poison oak bush—but this was a new one. I jammed my feet into the dike and fumbled with my drawstring shorts. It was awkward to work around my harness, and my hands were shaking. *Please don't fall, please don't fall.*

An indeterminate number of hours later, we heaved ourselves over the smooth lip of Half Dome. We'd been alone all day, but on the summit we were surrounded by hikers as we unclipped from the rope and stepped out of our harnesses. Somehow it was more harrowing to stand on the top, peering over the edge at the whirl of ravens and wind, with nothing but air and rock below. I backed away on rubbery legs while the hikers eyed us suspiciously, trying to figure out how we'd materialized in their world.

I was just as dumbfounded. My body was trembling from the exertion and adrenaline, but my mind had disassociated from the effort hours earlier. This was the only way I'd been able to keep going. I'd had to mentally detach from the physical world and its untenable risks—those prickly treetops and the gaping sky beneath my flailing feet—and to operate purely as animal, moving from my arms, legs, fingers, palms, and eyes. To become automatic.

Now that I'd returned to my senses, my brain was trying to catch up to what had happened. What *had* happened? I'd just climbed Half Dome! This was the biggest, craziest physical achievement of my life so far, maybe never to be surpassed. You could do things you never thought possible, sometimes by *not* thinking. If I died tomorrow, I would be happy.

Steph and I hiked the seven miles back to the trailhead. Half Dome reared up above the east end of the valley, silvery and colossal, its summit curving gracefully like the snub nose of a dolphin. I felt my throat catch, my eyes sting. It had endured millions of years of weather and thousands of climbers just like me grappling up its indifferent face. I would never matter to it the way it would matter to me, I felt certain, for the rest of my life.

It was Father's Day, and I dialed Dad's number from a pay phone in the parking lot while we waited for the hikers' shuttle bus. I hadn't spoken to him for a while, and I was excited to hear his voice. The phone rang and rang. It was early evening in Virginia, and I could picture him on his tractor, mowing meticulous lines into his fields.

The answering machine picked up.

"Hi, Dad, it's Katie!" I said breathlessly after the beep. "I'm in Yosemite. I just climbed Half Dome!"

Dad was always the one I called first when I got home from an assignment or adventure. Mom fretted that I might slip and die or forget to eat, and she couldn't comprehend why anyone would want to camp out like a dirtbag for a story. But Dad had lived it. He *got* it. I knew that when we spoke next, I would tell him about the light reflecting off Half Dome's granite face, the breeze riffling my skin, the orange I peeled on the summit and shoved into my mouth whole. He would want to know these things. Not because I'd taken risks or overcome terrific doubt—plenty of others had done the same with more grace and skill than I had—but because he cared about all the parts that made up a story: the details and characters, the texture and arc.

What impressed Dad wasn't pure stunt or bravery, I knew this now. Nor did victory matter all that much—he wasn't an athlete and didn't think like one. Adversity alone didn't wow him; it had to be in pursuit of something bigger, less frivolous, weightier, something beyond pride and personal gain. It was about strength of character. I'd tried my best, kept my eyes open, and come home with a story to tell. This was exactly the kind of adventure that would make him proud.

8

Letters from Home

Dad at Huntly Stage, summer 1978

Between visits to Virginia, I have a birthday. It's October 30. I'm thirty-nine. I wander shiftlessly around the house, trying to pretend that I'm not waiting for Dad's call. He always comes through with a silly greeting or gift, something to mark the day. The year I turned ten, he baked me a birthday cake in the shape of a train: two long rectangular cakes for the engine, smaller round cakes for the wheels, a square cake for the smokestack. It was an old-fashioned locomotive, more *The Little Engine That Could* than Amtrak Metroliner. He frosted it with sticky chocolate icing and outlined the doors and windows in gumdrops. The caboose he adorned with lollipops. In the picture he took, I'm wearing a green "Super Girl" T-shirt and rainbow *Mork & Mindy* suspenders, surrounded by a handful of children I don't recognize, from neighboring farms. It was the only birthday I celebrated at Huntly Stage, and maybe only the second ever that I celebrated with my father. He was determined to make it a party.

How could that one cake outweigh all the other birthdays we were apart? I don't know, but it does.

This time, though, Dad doesn't call. He doesn't leave his usual message on my voicemail: "Happy Easter—I mean Fourth of July . . . wait, no, don't tell me . . . birthday?!" He doesn't send me a new book with a long inscription or a funny card with a smiley face beside his name. He's in the hospital. Two days ago, he was rushed to the ER in the middle of the night to have a catheter installed to irrigate his kidney for blood clots.

So much of my relationship with Dad has been conducted over the phone or by letter: weekly calls to New Jersey on his staticky party line at the farm, long conversations about school and sports; prearranged calls to a phone booth on an island near ours on Stony Lake, Dad closing with his usual goofy admonition: "Whatever you do, don't go near the water!" Phone calls about writing and photography. Phone calls asking for advice: *Hey, Dad. What digital camera should I buy? How do I hook up my stereo speakers? What's your favorite Stan Getz album?* Phone calls with good news: *Dad, I'm getting married! I'm having a baby!*

He mailed postcards from his various wanderings and letters from work on *National Geographic* stationery. By the late nineties, he was sending long, chatty emails on his America Online account, signing off with his trademark breezy farewell, "Later . . . Love, Dad." Now, though, he's stopped writing. In the last email I got from him, in mid-October, he concluded, "And now I'm off to La-La-Land."

When I call his hospital room, he picks up on the second ring. His voice is low and scratchy and rushed, as if he's been waiting all day for me to call so he could get right to the point—no birthday wishes, no preambles.

"This is a game-ender, Katie," he says.

"The catheter?" I ask hopefully.

There is a long pause.

"The cancer," he answers.

After we hang up, I drive to the Atalaya trailhead. Running is the last thing I feel like doing, but I make myself go. I need to feel the sun on my skin, to see the mountains in their same old place to the north and east of town, all their bumps and pleats, to run the trails I know by heart. I start off fast, so I don't have to think, but the tears catch me after half a mile and I lean over, crying so hard I can't breathe.

Now I know how this is going to end. There won't be any more letters or notes, no more chatty missives about the books he's reading or movies he's seen, no more envelopes scrawled in his handwriting. I see that I'm going to have to try very hard to hold on to the sound of his voice, the deep, throaty way he called *Gooood night, girls* through the guest room door, his pitch rising on the last syllables as Meg and I lay in our twin beds in the dark, and the way I could always hear his voice, even in his letters, ringing through the pages.

Of all the letters he sent, there's one I will never forget.

It was 2004. I'd been with Steve for four years, and he was impatient to get married. He lived rent-free in a caretaker's guesthouse in exchange for gardening work but spent almost every night at my place. He kept a toothbrush by the sink, frayed canvas work pants in the closet, and strong ground coffee in the fridge. We liked to joke that we lived together and his stuff lived in the guesthouse, but the joke had gotten old. Though I loved him immensely and liked him even more, I wanted a guarantee that what had happened between my mother and father wouldn't happen to us. I worried that I harbored some secret, genetic flaw that would doom my own marriage to failure.

I worked myself into a state of frenzied indecision, running up and down my mountain in the evenings after work, as though the answer might emerge from the trees and dirt, from the long views and the sweat sliding down my temples. Steve and I had arrived at a fork in the trail, a crisis of the heart: One sharp turn would take me away from him. It was not so difficult to imagine. After all, my impulse had always been to run. In some ways, it was easier than staying.

Soon, I told Steve whenever he hinted at marriage, trying to buy myself more time. *Soon.*

There was something I had to do first.

One evening, I got out my stationery and pulled a card from the box. I'd never been as good at letter writing as Dad, but I knew I had to try. I took a deep breath.

Dear Dad,
As you know, things with Steve are getting serious. I think he
wants to get married. But before we do, I'm curious to know what
happened between you and Mom.

There were certain basic facts I'd always assumed about my parents' divorce: that Mom had taken us away from Dad; that I was somehow responsible; and that our leaving had hurt him. I'd seen the way he said goodbye to us after each visit, the longing in his eyes. They were the saddest eyes in the history of the world.

Maybe if I knew why their relationship had failed, my own might have a better chance of succeeding. But now that the question was down on the page, I realized I knew nothing about what had happened. It was, and had always been, pure conjecture.

I paused, then signed, "I love you, Dad." I couldn't remember ever saying it so plainly to him, *for* him. I licked the envelope and slid it into the mailbox before I could chicken out.

The letter that arrived in the mail two weeks later was nineteen pages long. It was too fat to fold, so Dad packed it in a flat envelope, like a legal document. I tore it open. It was typed except for the first line—"Dear Katie," in black felt-tip pen—and the sight of his handwriting soothed me. This was my father, not a stranger. What could he possibly tell me that I didn't want to know?

"Okay!" he began. "Ready?"

The exclamation point was a good sign. Upbeat, nothing to be afraid of.

Before we wade in too far, it's important that you realize that the reasons Mom and I went our separate ways are not inheritable. They are not contagious. There is no "curse"!

He'd read my mind.

Hope fueled me, and I began to read. I could tell it was a fantastic letter, divulging and conversational, one adult to another. He had clearly taken great care to explain as much as possible, as thoroughly as possible. I'd asked for an explanation about his divorce. What he'd given me was an epic. His.

For much of his life, Dad explained, he identified himself as a loner. "I began to nickname myself the goodbye boy, because I seemed to be becoming increasingly skilled in finding ways to smile through endings." Later, when he was married, with a mortgage and two young daughters, he grew impatient with the routine demands of family life, and dreamed of a life of adventure.

The house on Legation was feeling too normal, too "what all people do." How could I singlehand around the world from there? The tug at the feet again.

I wanted to stop reading, but I couldn't stop reading. Everything had already happened—there was no stopping it now.

Dad began to look for diversions, and he found plenty of them in the halls of *National Geographic*: the far-flung expeditions and long evenings poring over negatives on the light table. "There was always more film to look at, photographers to call, research to do, text to write, assignments to be outfitted for." He and his "working-circle"—bosses and secretaries—"were so intensely together that we became our only friends." On the weekends, they rode their bicycles along the Potomac River. It reminded me of *Outside* when I first moved to Santa Fe, only it was Washington in the early seventies.

> *It's important to say something about D.C. and the Geographic in those days, because it was all part of a powerful (and then not terribly positive), yet exciting culture of the times. All across the nation the Vietnam war frenzy was boiling. Demonstrations were on the streets. Divorces were becoming a dime a dozen. And the new gospel was "If it feels good, do it." It was an extremely hedonistic, me-first time. But everything seemed out of control; there wasn't solid footing anywhere.*

I sat at my desk, feeling the years collapse on themselves. I was ten again, running the Fodderstack, trying to outpace my shame. I was seven, watching the train platform slide away with Dad on it, one palm raised in farewell. I was six, and the moving van was easing down the street. I was five, on my bike, leaving him behind. I was two, and he was—gone.

He'd been working up to something; I could feel it. Ten pages in, there it was:

> *One day at an office party, a colleague with whom I shared a secretary pointed out that she was interested in me. That was all*

it took, I am ashamed to say. It was traitorous, the only word for it. And it finished Mom and me. And it finished our time as a family. It's why I was never with you or Meg for all the day-to-day growing-up things. More than I miss having Mom as my wife—as I can, when I remember back to that "Y" in the road— I miss that. I will never know it, never can know it.

He was having an affair. Why had this never occurred to me? I'd believed my own suppositions for so long, so completely, that I hadn't ever considered it. I almost couldn't bear to go on. Neither could Dad.

I stopped writing for a couple days. Depressed. This is difficult, Katie. But it's also long, long overdue. My treatment of you was cruel and unbelievably thoughtless. I suppose I thought you were too young to notice. Isn't that absurd! Remembering that I once did that cuts the legs out from under me. And I'm not just remembering now, this instant; I remember that always. What do I stand on, except to say I'm sorry. You didn't deserve that.

I felt the room tilt, and the floor slant at a sickening angle. My head had detached from my body and was hovering high above, looking down at the page in my hand. Nothing seemed real. We had abandoned *him,* hadn't we? But no, it was Dad who left *us,* trading us for his secretary and an apartment on Newark Street. The story on which I'd built my childhood, maybe my very self, had been inverted.

He described the day we moved away.

There you were, playing on the street. You didn't know what your lives would be like, what your new home would be like, where I'd be. Were you bewildered, frightened? We said our goodbyes—for you, maybe, as if for just another routine night—and I drove slowly away, pounding the steering wheel because I didn't know

what to say. I turned the corner onto 31st and you were gone,
Mom was gone, the house was gone, a life was gone. It was the
worst moment of my life. There was nobody left.

So. I hadn't imagined it after all. The baffling, unforgettable sadness. It was all real. He'd felt it, too. Worse, he'd caused it.

"But, see," Dad continued, "you've done well, Mom has done well, Meg has done well, I've done okay." This somber appraisal of his life was somehow the most heart-wrenching line in the whole letter. Because I knew that no matter how badly he'd screwed up, I wanted him to be not just okay. More than okay. I wanted him to be happy.

When I finally got to the end, I was glazed in sweat and my pulse was racing. I felt prickly and wired, as if I'd just finished a hard run or had a bad scare. How could I possibly go forward from here?

Dad knew. It's what he always taught me to do, no matter what.

"Onward, onward, dear girl!"

I shoved the letter into the back of my desk drawer and tried to forget it existed. When Dad called a few days later to talk about it, I played it down with some crappy toss-off reply. I wasn't as much mad as I was embarrassed and disoriented by his honesty, and it seemed an additional, unnecessary humiliation—for both of us—to talk about it.

I felt duped. How had I missed the clues? The whole thing was straight out of *The Bridges of Madison County*: the roving *National Geographic* photographer who feels trapped by family life and succumbs to wanderlust. Dad loved to take solo road trips, and his favorite place was the Midwest, especially North Dakota, where there was nothing to break the horizon but silos listing out of wheat fields. With his angular cheekbones, he even looked like Clint Eastwood—a walking cliché! In hindsight, it was all so obvious.

I couldn't bring myself to call Meg. I didn't know if she knew or not, and either way it would be bad news. If she did know, it would mean Dad had already told her or she'd guessed or—even freakier to contemplate—she'd known *the whole time*. After all, she was nearly nine when we moved away, and, unlike me, she remembered Dad living at home. If she didn't know, then I would have to be the one to break it to her.

But it was Mom who blew my mind the most about the whole situation. I'd always known she was tough, raising us alone at first, managing a house, and juggling a job. Optimism was her weapon: *We're the luckiest girls in the world!* But knowing about Dad's betrayal for thirty years without giving anything away? She was a total badass—even Dad could see that. "When I think of Mom, I've always felt the admiration first," he wrote in his letter, "the absolute stand-back, hair-raising recognition of excellence."

A few weeks after I got the letter, I called Mom. I thought it would be easier to talk about it with her than with Dad; it wasn't her shame, after all. But when I explained what I knew, she didn't sound relieved, only rueful. Her version of events wasn't so different from Dad's. She told me that when Meg was born, she'd had a premonition that he wouldn't be around to raise her. The broken furnace a few years later, she said, felt like the beginning of the end. When he'd run off with his secretary, Mom had stayed silent not to protect him or even herself, but to protect *us*.

Now it finally made sense why she and Ron never talked about Dad after we moved to New Jersey. The subject was taboo, because it violated another one of Mom's favorite sayings: *If you don't have anything nice to say, don't say anything at all.*

Gratitude would have been the appropriate response, but I couldn't form the words—not because I didn't feel them, but because they seemed so flimsy and inadequate under the circumstances. What I needed was a word that said *thank you* and *I'm sorry* and *holy shit* and maybe even *what the fuck?* all at once.

My communication with Dad tapered off. It happened gradually, over a period of a few months, then a year. We'd go a few weeks between emails and phone calls, maybe longer, and when Dad did write to me, I didn't always respond right away. It was the closest I'd come to fighting with him, without saying a word.

I didn't *feel* angry. Was I? Should I be? Mostly I was confused. Did his actions change everything or nothing? Did knowing? It had been so long ago, and I couldn't just go back and rewrite my childhood. I got the impression that Dad had been waiting a long time to write the letter, that he had been composing his answers well before I or anyone else asked the question, and that it was a relief to at last break the silence. That maybe he was answering his *own* questions.

Gradually, the shock faded, but I still felt betrayed—for the girl I'd been at three, in my raggedy cardigan, with my raggedy sister, both of us so young and clueless. Mom had since told me that the real reason she cut our hair short was so that strangers would think we were boys and wouldn't take us. But we were so homely, even Dad had left.

Every so often, Dad would send a quick email to check in on me. "Hello," he'd write. "Allow me to introduce myself. Perhaps you remember me? I am your father. . . ." I couldn't help but smile. I didn't *want* to be mad at him, and I knew he wasn't fishing for forgiveness. He understood that it was more complicated than that. "Ol' Dad is going to get kicked down the stairs, I'm afraid," he'd admitted in his letter, "but, well, that's the way it is."

What he wanted, really, was for *me* to be happy.

"As for you and your relationship," Dad wrote on the last page, "talk, talk, talk, don't hold anything back. Don't be overly proud. Don't expect 'thrill' to carry you very far or very long. Make sure there's that bedrock affection and respect. Remember that you'll get old one day and need help. So will he."

I had to hand it to him. It was solid advice. Someday I was going to get married, and probably to Steve. But Dad's letter didn't erase my girlhood guilt or reassure me that I wouldn't repeat his mistakes. If anything, I was more worried now that I would. He and I were similar in so many ways. How did he know that we wouldn't be the same when it came to marriage?

My chest was tight, and I couldn't take deep breaths in the natural way you breathe, when the air loops from your belly all the way to your throat and circles back the way it came. That stopped happening; I couldn't make the loop. Running was the only thing that helped. When I ran up my mountain, I felt the knot in my throat unstick and my breath loosen. Endorphins flushed my worries away, replacing them with practical matters, like not tripping over roots and getting down by dark.

The fear came back while I slept. In the morning, my teeth hurt from clenching them all night, and I rode my bike to work, full of anguish, as if I were seeing the world, and the way people lived in it, for the first time. The lament that looped on repeat through my brain had many different, piteous versions but mostly went like this: *Someday soon, I will be married with kids, and I will no longer get to have fun or ride bikes or run up mountains. My carefree days are dwindling.*

"You want to know what happens when you get married?" I announced to Steve one night at dinner. "You get boring and drive a minivan." I knew this to be true because Meg, who was now married with two young children, had recently bought one. The thing she liked most about it, she'd explained, was that she no longer had to stick her butt into the street when she was buckling her kids into their car seats. That this was the pinnacle of maternal contentment depressed me beyond words.

Steve chewed his chicken and stared at me deliberately for a long time, as though trying to process the absurdity of what I'd just uttered.

Then his face split open into a full-lipped, dimpled grin. "Minivans are rad," he said.

I don't need to tell you what happened next. Steve and I got married at Stony Lake. After the ceremony, in a wooden pavilion overlooking the water, Dad toasted our happiness. "I don't know a whole lot about love—ask anybody!" He paused meaningfully, smiling at his inside joke. The guests chuckled; his self-effacing humor always went over well with a crowd. "But for a long time I've been thinking, *Whoa, Katie, don't look now, but THIS IS IT!*"

I glanced around the room, with its worn pine floors and shutters thrown open to the fresh air. I could hear waves sloshing under the dock below, a sound as consoling as my mother's voice, as old maybe as the sound of water in the womb. Everybody I most loved was there: Steve; my siblings; my four parents: Mom, Ron, Dad, and Lesley. Even Uncle Phil. It didn't matter how we fit together. There was strength in numbers, in all that love. You could never have too much.

The DJ put on "Thunder Road" and Steve swung me around in my bare feet. *So you're scared and you're thinking that maybe we ain't that young anymore. Show a little faith, there's magic in the night . . .* It was easy to love Steve if I let myself, to realize that, even if we didn't have all the answers or know with certainty that we would stay together, we could live as though we would.

It was dark by the time Dad and I danced slowly to the song he'd chosen, Joni Mitchell's "Both Sides, Now." It was the song I'd heard him play on the stereo many times, the one he'd quoted at the end of his letter to me:

I've looked at love from both sides now
From give and take, and still somehow
It's love's illusions that I recall.
I really don't know love at all . . .

Now I knew why he loved this song. The lyrics captured all of his contradictions—his ambivalence and regrets, his lights and his darks, his desire to see and his instincts to suppress.

Below the song lyrics, he'd given his own take on the song:

Illusions are fine, and they can certainly excite the brain, but it's on the ground where it really counts.

Then he signed it by hand, in thick, black ink across the bottom of the page:

I love you, too, Katie

Dad

9

The Things We Threw Away

Dad framing his barn, 1984

On a gloomy Saturday in early November, we clean out Dad's barn. He designed and built it by himself in the early eighties. On long summer evenings after his commute home from D.C., he'd climb onto the roof and pound nails until it got dark. Months passed, and then a year, but Dad just kept plugging away, board by board. He prized stamina and preparation over speed, and he built the barn as he lived his life, from a place of deep patience and exacting, sometimes exasperating deliberation. The barn was his own improbable midlife achievement.

It's stood there ever since, tall and proud, solid as a drum, with plain lines and wide wood planks, weathering from chestnut to distinguished gray. Downstairs in his workshop, he stores his tools, each hanging in its proper place outlined in felt-tip marker, nails and screws organized by size in plastic boxes. Bicycles with rusty chains, his yellow sea kayak, and dozens of signs he found, bought, or otherwise procured over the years. A week before we arrived, Dad called the local NPR station in Washington to arrange for them to cart off his green VW bus for donation.

Upstairs, the hayloft is a repository for everything he doesn't know what to do with. Dad is a collector by nature but a minimalist at heart, a contradiction that seemed to encompass fatherhood, too. Just as Meg and I were mementos from an earlier life, so, too, were the chunks of driftwood he brought back from Canada and his glass fishing floats from the South Pacific. Now that he's sick, though, the clutter has become a mental weight threatening to drag him down.

We don rubber gloves and face masks and climb the ladder in the barn. The hayloft holds it all: his whole life encapsulated in cardboard, everything coated in dust and dead stinkbugs. Dad wheezes up behind us, wearing a scarf and two coats, and lies down in a plastic lawn chaise we drag out from under the eaves. He is much thinner now, and very weak. The embolization procedure hasn't slowed the tumor's growth, and the cancer has spread to his lungs and bones. The doctors think they've found specks of it in his brain, and he spends most of his days buffered in a groggy opioid haze.

Dad is the arbiter of what stays and what goes. Thumbs-up means keep; thumbs-down, chuck. We discover a striped wool afghan blanket his mother, Mary, knit decades ago, and he presses it to his face, inhaling its stuffy scent. We paw through boxes, holding up

their contents to the light, like indecipherable artifacts from a forgotten civilization: cracked vinyl suitcases; the instruction manual
to Dad's first computer, a TRS-80 from Radio Shack; one badly
scratched Cat Stevens album; a ceramic chicken wearing a sombrero.
Meg reaches bravely into a plastic container and fishes out the
cracked antiquarian scuba mask and regulator from his dive trip to
Jamaica when he first met Lesley. Dad is efficient, good-humored,
and unattached. Almost everything gets the thumbs-down.

Dad's best friend, Philip, rented a dumpster for the day, and we
fling everything out the loft door and straight into the giant bin
with reckless abandon and great peals of laughter. It's satisfying to
purge the place of junk and foul stinkbug carcasses, but beneath
our productive zeal, we all know that saying goodbye to Dad's stuff
is merely a precursor to the much harder goodbye to come.

Dad's snoozing in the chaise when I pull a wooden frame from a
grimy box. It's a needlepoint rendering of a *National Geographic*
cover. In the picture, a man is riding an antique bicycle with a
giant front wheel. He wears a brown velvet jacket and matching
dapper cap; behind him is a blur of crimson-and-orange foliage. I
recognize the photograph right away: Dad took it.

"Hey, Dad," I whisper, touching his hand. "Look what I found."

He opens his eyes and reaches for the picture. "Nana made it for
me," he says softly, turning it over in his hands. The frame is warped
and waterlogged, the thread faded, but the date below the *National
Geographic* logo was still legible: September 1972. I wasn't even one
yet when he traveled to the Connecticut River Valley to shoot the
story. In the years after this photograph appeared on the cover, Dad
continued to take pictures on assignment. He was invited to Wyoming twice to participate in the Lakota Sioux's traditional Sun
Dance ceremony. He went to Alaska, where he hung off the side of
a glacier. He won Picture of the Year awards. But at some point the
scale tipped from photographer to editor. He was at his desk more
than he was away from it. He published less and didn't show or sell
his work.

"Oh, he had such potential," Mom used to say, long after they'd divorced, always with a twinge of disappointment. "I think he could have been quite recognized for his pictures." This was the one bit of commentary about Dad she allowed herself. She had helped him hang his first, and only, photography exhibit, in Essex, Connecticut, in 1963. The black-and-white pictures captured everyday life in the sixties—high school football players in a huddle, college students in cat-eye glasses, a dingy train chugging through an empty rail yard—but beneath the surface, you could see the loneliness and yearning of being alive—his subjects' and his own, too.

PHOTO: DAVID L. ARNOLD

Dad, Hamilton, New York, 1964

These photographs became part of his portfolio that got him noticed by *National Geographic*. But once he'd been hired, and even after he left us to pursue his photography without distractions, he backed off. Maybe he found photography too exposing. Maybe it was safer being the person behind the person behind the lens. I didn't understand it, really, but I could feel his longing for photography, the kind of nostalgia you feel for something that you no longer desire in a definitive way but miss abstractly. The thing you've outgrown but wish you hadn't.

Like marriage, photography was a loss Dad had backed himself into, even as he continued to make pictures constantly, for himself if not for publication. Of Meg and me, staged in a million different ways, of Lesley and the animals, of Huntly Stage in all seasons and his road trips and his friends. He carried the loss well below the surface. You wouldn't know it from looking at him—he had the prized career, a good marriage with plenty of independence, their beautiful farm—but you could feel it, the unfulfilled promise, like his bass violin, a subtle, steady backbeat to the rest of his life.

In a strange way, this seemed to suit Dad. He had never been flashy. He didn't need the spotlight. He didn't like show-offs or fakery. Maybe he was happy with the choice he'd made. Maybe the disappointment was mine.

I was on the opposite trajectory. I'd started out an editor and was becoming a writer. It was the thing I'd always wanted and had been too afraid to say outright. For months after my assignment to Yosemite, I'd been trying to get up my courage and quit my job to write full-time. *Outside* was like family to me. I'd grown up there, but I was about to turn thirty-five and the magazine's masculinity had begun to feel confining.

The trip had changed me. Clinging to Half Dome with a crazed and petrified glee, I knew I wanted to write stories in my own voice, in my own way—by living in them. Not to impress my father or my colleagues or anyone else, not because Meg had let her English degree languish and got her MBA, not because writing was fair game now. But for me.

In 2006, a few months after Steve and I got married, *Outside* asked me to write a profile of professional ultrarunner Dean Karnazes. Karnazes had written the bestselling book *Ultramarathon Man*, about his unlikely journey from a mildly depressed marketing professional to an endurance phenom, literally overnight. One night in 1992, Karnazes was partying at a San Francisco nightclub. It was his thirtieth birthday, and he was feeling old and disillusioned. He left the bar after midnight, walked home, snuck into the garage so as not to wake his family, took off his pants, changed into a pair of old sneakers, shoved a twenty-dollar bill into one shoe, and set off running in his boxer shorts. It had been fifteen years since he last went for a jog, but for seven hours through the night, he ran. When he got to Half Moon Bay, the sun was rising, his feet were mangled, and he could barely stand. He found a phone booth and called his wife collect to come pick him up. He'd run thirty miles, straight out of one life and into another.

In the years that followed, Dean almost single-handedly transformed ultrarunning from an obscure, quasi-psychotic cult of extreme athletes into a respectable pastime. There were many other ultra-distance runners who were faster than Dean, but it was Dean who brought ultrarunning to the masses. He was living, breathing, running proof that average runners could run above-average distances. Way above average. You just had to have the heart, and the willpower.

Now Dean was coming through Albuquerque as part of his bid to run fifty marathons in fifty states in fifty days. New Mexico was number 22—not a race but an informal 26.2-mile route through Albuquerque. I wanted to interview him while he ran, and when I called him to suggest this, he said, "Meet me at the starting line!" The longest I'd ever run was the half marathon, a year earlier. I had no business contemplating 26.2 miles. At most, I might run six or seven miles with him. Maybe—if the interview was going well—halfway. But I would definitely peel off early, I told him. Definitely.

Dean was short and compact and unexpectedly muscly, with a bushy head of coily brown hair and glowing bronzed skin that looked like it came from a bottle but really came from spending almost every waking minute outside. He looked more like a gym rat than a distance runner. He was surrounded by a small entourage of support crew, fellow runners, and fans, but when he saw me, he parted the crowd, pounded me on my back, and shouted, "Let's get after it!"

We set out at an easy tempo along the willowy banks of the Rio Grande. I'd slung my voice recorder around my neck and turned it on. His voice was even, never out of breath, despite the mile-high altitude. He told me about his boozy, life-changing epiphany and his rabid work ethic. Most days, he said, he ran thirty miles before dawn; on his hundred-mile overnight epics, he'd run through the drive-through at Taco Bell or order pizza to be delivered on a street corner and gobble the whole thing while he ran. At his marketing job, he cranked out sets of push-ups and sit-ups between conference calls. He'd written *Ultramarathon Man* almost entirely while running, dictating chapters into his recorder.

Dean had been on the road for nearly a month, but his enthusiasm pulsed off him in waves. Miles passed as we talked. We reached the halfway mark, at mile 13, and turned around to double back to the start. His inexplicable urge to keep going made me want to do the same.

Four hours after we'd started, the finish line came into view. There was little fanfare—just a white ribbon, which Dean broke with his barrel chest, and a few cheering onlookers, including his wife and two kids, who promptly hustled him into their camper van. Dean didn't have time to celebrate; he had to be in Tulsa by morning.

After everyone cleared out, I sat on a curb at the finish line in a daze. I'd just run my first marathon, by accident. It was like the Fodderstack, on steroids, all over again. When I looked up, white jet contrails zigzagged like chalk against the blue sky. I'd been looking at the ground for so long, watching my feet and the road as I ran, that I'd forgotten all about the sky. It had been there, huge and bright, all along. It was so easy to forget.

I understood then that I could stay where I was, waiting for something, a sign, and nothing would change. *I* wouldn't change. I would miss my chance. The idea that this might happen filled me with revulsion. That's not too strong a word. *Revulsion.* It had been ten years since I stood in front of *Outside*'s owner and rattled off the reasons he should give me a job. Where had that fearless girl gone?

I got to my feet and jogged a few blocks back to my car. My legs felt surprisingly loose and light, as though I could run all day and into the next, the way Dean did. It was ridiculous, really, to think this was possible.

But I knew it was. Dean had told me his secret to running absurd, inhuman distances. "Just run to the next tree, and then the next. You can always go farther than you think you can. You're stronger than you think you are."

The sun was bright and warm, and the streamers in the sky were beginning to fade, the planes soaring on to someplace else, like weird messengers of hope. I felt a surge of optimism, and certainty. I wanted go for everything in life, even if it scared me. Anything was possible; all the greatest things were still ahead.

Three weeks later, I quit my job.

It's late afternoon when we heave the last of the boxes out the hayloft door. Dad has gotten creaky and stiff from the cold, and Meg and I help him back slowly down the ladder. He shuffles across the grass to the overflowing dumpster, rests his elbows on the edge, and peers in, surveying the mountain of stuff bound straight for the landfill: the *Tea for the Tillerman* LP and the Mexican chicken and the decaying scuba kit. In one hand he clutches his needlepoint *National Geographic* cover, and in the other a stuffed moose wearing a Santa hat. His face is inscrutable, and for a long while he says nothing.

After I read his letter, I thought that he had been too afraid to commit to us. But now, after hurling the relics of his life out the barn door and watching them sail briefly through the sky—

suspended between flying and falling—I wonder if he hadn't also been afraid to commit to himself. Somehow this is even sadder.

I'm fighting back tears, but when I turn to look at Dad again, the corners of his mouth have curved up into a faint, almost sappy smile. He nuzzles the moose and then heaves it high into the dumpster, a go-for-broke moon shot, and alley-oops the warped needlepoint in after it. Then he turns on his heels for the house. He's let go of everything. Now he's free and clear for whatever's going to happen next.

10

The Short Goodbye

Dad and Maisy at Huntly, November 2010

When Steve and I fly out with both girls a few weeks later for Thanksgiving, the sun has gone into hibernation, and the trees on Rattlesnake Mountain are bare and spindly. Dad has pitched off a cliff since the Barnstorming. His skin is the color of dirty dishwater. He can barely eat or get out of bed, his photo project has ground to a halt. Twice a day, Lesley doles out his oxycodone and OxyContin in a Dixie cup, the plasticky rattle of pills momentarily rousing him from his fog.

Sometimes when Meg and I visited the farm as girls, Dad would drive us into Winchester to see a movie. He favored action flicks with rugged heroes and outliers, *Superman* and *Butch Cassidy and the Sundance Kid,* or slapstick comedies like *Airplane!* One of our all-time favorites was the comedy-thriller *Silver Streak,* in which Gene Wilder plays a befuddled book editor trying to save a runaway train. He wrestled villains on the roof, ducking beneath tunnels and narrowly avoiding decapitation while the cars rocketed along the tracks. Dad's cancer feels the same: out of control and on the verge of derailing us all with its terrible velocity, only not nearly as entertaining. Even I've stopped thinking I can stop it. Now we're just trying to minimize damage and get out of its way.

The day before Thanksgiving, we call hospice. Dad's oncologist has informed him he's not strong enough for chemotherapy; he has crossed some invisible brink from which he will not return. The hospice nurse squeaks across the wooden floor in her rubbery white shoes and settles herself in the rocking chair beside Dad's bed.

We all know what this means. Time's up. Hands in the air. She is the face of surrender. Dad lies flat in his bed and stares up at her with hollow eyes, and nothing about her expression says she is surprised, says she hasn't seen this a dozen times already, three dozen even.

The nurse begins asking us questions. Can he walk to the bathroom unassisted? How bad is his pain? We all start talking at once—everyone, that is, except Dad.

"Maybe we should stop talking and let Dad answer?" I suggest. The wide-eyed look Dad shoots me from across the room is one of pure gratitude.

"Okay," says the nurse gently, turning to him. "What are some of the things you'd like to see happen?"

Dad answers right away, as if he's been preparing for this question. "I would like this not to be the norm. I would like to make progress every day, even if it's only in inches."

A stunned silence fills the room. I glance at Meg out of the corner of my eye. Her pen is poised in midair like a secretary taking dictation, trying to decipher his comment. We all are. *Oh, Dad,* I think, *do you really think this is still possible?*

The nurse dips her chin in a barely perceptible nod. She does not say, "You are too weak to walk. There is no progress left to make." What she says is "We can make arrangements for someone to come to the house to help you with physical therapy." To the list of things Dad will need, she adds a portable toilet on wheels because he's unable to make it to the bathroom on his own.

The next day, a paunchy deliveryman arrives with the rolling toilet and parks it beside Dad's bed. Dad is awake and propped upright in his charcoal-checked flannel pajamas, which from a distance look like tuxedo loungewear. There are many things in life you do not want to witness; a man delivering a plastic toilet to your father is one of them.

To break the awkward, awful moment, the man gurgles in his thick Virginia drawl, apropos of nothing, "Four more days and this month is over!"

Later that afternoon, I find Dad alone in his room. I pull up the rocking chair and sit at the foot of his bed.

The first thing he says is "Where did you learn that?"

I hesitate for a second, not sure what he's talking about. "Learn what, Dad?" I ask, scooting closer.

"That thing you did yesterday when the nurse was here. Just *listening.*"

This time I don't have to think. "From you, Dad. I learned it from you." I can tell by the way he cocks his head that this has never dawned on him before.

Through the windows, soot-colored clouds scud across the sky, west to east, and a turkey vulture glides in long, unhurried circles. Through the ceiling, I hear the scrabble of claws on the shingles. It's Peacock. Now that it's cold outside, he's moved from his roost in the trees to the roof outside Dad and Lesley's bedroom window, where he sleeps most nights. It's warmer there and more companionable, the murmur of voices, bodies rustling around on the other side of the glass.

I pick up a magazine and begin reading aloud a story about Louisiana. Dad, listening alertly, interrupts me after the first paragraph to recall a *National Geographic* assignment he once had driving around the bayou, poking around jazz clubs with sawdusty floors, half-lit oyster shacks. He's roved so many places, all on his own, a whole distinct life without us. I find this oddly comforting. He's had so much to love in this world; it's a relief to realize maybe we won't be his greatest loss after all.

Dad's eyes flutter shut, and he slips away, no longer in New Orleans but somewhere far away, his voice slurred and slow. Memories spill out, stories I've never heard, like shards of glass catching the light, disjointed and brilliant: waking in the Adirondacks on the morning of his best friend's wedding—the drummer in his college jazz band—listening to the bride play violin beside a river, the notes drifting up on the breeze to the cabin where he lies in his narrow bed, his own thwarted commitment still on the horizon. His life has been beautiful, tortured, full of love and regret.

Then, abruptly, he's talking in full sentences again, his words as crisp as ironed sheets.

"Katie," he says, in his familiar, emphatic old timbre. "Make sure you listen to your body."

All spring, Dad had been listless. His muscles trembled when he pumped iron on the Bowflex, and walking up the driveway, he fatigued easily. But he hated going to the doctor, so he put it off. By summer it was murderously hot, day after day above ninety degrees, and he blamed his lethargy on the heat. He lay flat on his back on the lawn after the sun went down, wiggling his toes in the grass. One morning he saw blood in his urine. After months of procrastinating, finally he called for an appointment. "A kidney stone," his doctor declared. "Anemia," he said. "Take iron."

But things didn't get better; they got worse. A lot worse. The rain gauge registered a big fat nada. The grass was turning to straw. One of Lesley's horses kicked her and fractured her wrist, Uncle Phil fell and broke his hip, and Meg had started divorce proceedings. Still, Dad rallied against his fatigue, his mounting anxiety. Perhaps he knew but didn't want to know. Perhaps he thought he would just push through, until he couldn't anymore.

He says it again, louder now so I won't forget: "Don't ignore your body. You will know when Something's Not Right."

Through the window just above Dad's head I see a flash of feathers on the roof: Peacock, fixing his glassy black eyes on us, keeping vigil.

There are two baby monitors now. One for Maisy, one for Dad. Hospice brought it so he can talk through it and tell us what he needs when we're not in the room, though mostly what we hear is raspy breathing.

We live for the moments when he's cogent. There is so much to ask. Has he written down passwords? Does he want us to call his friends? What would he like? What does he need? These are easier questions to ask than *Are you afraid?*

All I can think about is having The Talk with Dad, the one in which he tilts his head in a sage, fatherly way and says, "Now, I want you to always remember . . ." and then proceeds to reveal the Secret to Life as he has come to understand it. I'd even settle for the kind you see in movies, when the terminal patient summons his loved ones to his deathbed, one by one, and, in a flood of truth telling, all the secrets come into the open and the person can die in peace.

Something like this happened in my mother's family long ago. Her grandfather, my great-grandfather George, had been an only child. It was a lonely life for a boy in small-town Ontario in the 1880s, so he spent as much time as possible with his cousins, a large, boisterous family of children whom he adored. He grew up to become a printer and a semi-professional tennis player and had five children of his own, the eldest of whom was my grandmother Peggy. When George was in his sixties and his mother was dying, she confessed that she wasn't his biological mother. She'd been unable to have children, she told him, so her sister had given her George, her last-born. The woman he thought was his aunt was really his mother, and the cousins he'd longed for his whole life were his siblings after all. The news devastated him.

I think about Dad's letter to me. I want to believe that I'm brave enough to finally talk to him about it, but what could I possibly learn now that would change anything?

On Thanksgiving, we roast a turkey and bake pies. Dad's friends Philip and his wife, Merrill, come for dinner, and we hold out a tatter of optimism that he will miraculously rouse himself and eat with us. But he stays in bed, listening to Brahms's *Requiem* on the CD player and slipping in and out of sleep, while we clatter around the dining room, hoping our forced cheer will drift up through the ceiling. It feels less like a celebration and more like a test. We're practicing how we'll do this without him.

After dinner, we take our dessert upstairs to eat with Dad. Steve carries two plates of pumpkin pie and I carry Pippa, zipped into her pale-pink fleece sack that helps her fall asleep. At two, she is a flash of legs and arms and teeth and white-blond hair that sticks up like a bird's nest and a pinhole dimple to the right of her mouth that matches Steve's exactly.

The moment Pippa was born, I knew I'd given birth to a wild animal. It wasn't just the intensity of labor, or that she'd arrived with the summer monsoons, lightning shredding the sky and rain gushing through the arroyos. She was a ball of kinetic power, barely contained in a seven-pound body. She had the face of an organ-grinder monkey, the oblong belly of a tree frog, and the limbs of a baby wolverine, taut and wiry, ready to spring. You could never simply hold her or she'd wiggle right out of your arms; you had to wrestle her.

My doctor, Ira, took one look at Pippa's baleful, inky eyes and exclaimed, "Well, she's been around before!" He had graying hair that hung in frizzy ringlets around his face and the shaggy beard of an aging Deadhead and insisted I call him by his first name. Beside me, Mom tittered appreciatively. The Episcopalian in her found this exciting, exotic even. No one she knew talked about reincarnation!

But Ira was right. Pippa had an immediate presence that seemed to have nothing to do with Steve or me. How I adored her fierce energy, her determined will. It terrified me a little, too.

We've been at Huntly two days, but I've been hesitant to bring her up to Dad's room. I've worried that she'll be frightened by the sight of him, so ghostly and pale, all bones. I've worried, too, about whether seeing them together will make the future without him in it seem painfully real. I might have kept putting it off were it not for Steve. "Take Pippa upstairs," he told me in the kitchen after dinner. "It's time." And before I could protest, he put her in my arms.

Now, standing in Dad's doorway, I pull her close and whisper into her ear that we are going to see Pop-Pop, and I feel her settle, a still weight in my arms, and I settle, too. At the sight of her, Dad perks up, swooning almost. I know it's partially the drugs, but I see in his eyes a flicker of wonder—for his progeny, for life continuing, for something, perhaps, that he can see but we can't. He reaches for Pippa, and I prop her up on the pillows beside him, watchful and grave. And Dad, who's never been religious, gasps, "She looks like an angel."

Late that night, after everyone's gone to bed, I change my flight to stay on at Huntly a few more days. When Meg, Steve, and Pippa leave for the airport the next morning, Dad insists on coming out to the patio to say goodbye. He's as skeletal as the trees, and it takes three of us to steady him down the stairs. Together, Dad and I watch them drive down the driveway and disappear out of sight, saying nothing. Dad's gotten more stoic with age and illness. I have the feeling that he's not holding back as much as holding in, conserving, keeping what little is left of his strength and emotions for himself, so he has some for the end.

After a moment he turns to me. His eyes are tired, his expression muted by pain, but he smiles faintly as he says, "Steve is a very good father. I'm proud of how you two are raising the girls."

His words aren't a surprise, but the fact that he makes the effort to say them, as preoccupied and increasingly incoherent as he is, moves me. Steve *is* a good father, such a different kind of father. I made a good choice. I married the right man. I was smart even when I was scared. Dad and I stand together in the late November afternoon, feeling lonely for our own reasons, saying nothing for a few moments. In the silence, I can feel his approval and admiration, his regret that he hadn't always been there for us.

After they're gone, the house feels so hollow, it practically vibrates. I sprawl disconsolately across the sofa bed in the TV room and listen to Dad rattle-snore through the monitor while Maisy hooks her fingers around her toes, gurgling happily. A month ago, she rolled over for the first time on the living room floor as Dad watched, bundled in blankets, witness to her unstoppable progression. Already I miss Steve and Pippa, growing more distant by the minute. I do not want to be separated from them, not even for a few days.

How, I wonder, did Dad ever let us go?

The next morning, Lesley and I take Dad to an appointment at the hospital in Warrenton. A friend recommended a doctor there who specializes in late-stage cancer and has arranged to meet Dad to see if he might be a candidate for chemo after all. It's a long shot, but Dad agrees to go, whether out of weary submission or his own last stirrings of hope.

It's the first of December. Rain streaks sideways, the charcoal sky sinking down on us. Just like the deliveryman said, a new month has arrived. Time is not on our side.

Lesley and I help Dad down to the car. It's just the two of us supporting his weight today, and it's much harder. We put him in the front passenger seat and I get in back, as I did for so many years as a girl, Maisy in her car seat beside me. The rain falls in dreary conspiracy with our mood. From behind, Dad is a hunched back, inconceivably still, facing straight ahead. When we turn onto the county road, he pivots his head slowly to look at the Blue Ridge Mountains, frozen and bare and beautiful. I can't see Dad's face, the pain of loss or fear scraped across it, but in the stillness of his shoulders, I know I'm watching him watch his world for the last time, and I know he knows it, too.

At the hospital, Dr. Ali is bright-eyed and boyish, younger than me, with a soft smile that puts us at ease. Dad summarizes his recent medical history, and when he's done he says, "Well, that's my sad story."

"I don't know if it's a sad story, but it's *your* story," says Dr. Ali. He's right. It *is* Dad's story. He's accepted it, and now it's up to us to do the same.

"How much time do you spend in bed?" asks Dr. Ali.

This is the question that sinks us.

"Almost all day," Dad says. No sugarcoating, no heroics.

Dr. Ali puts his hand on Dad's forearm and holds it there for an extra beat. It seems an act of exquisite compassion, in light of what he says next. "An infusion of liquids will hydrate you and help you feel better, but I'm afraid you're not a candidate for chemotherapy."

I sit with Dad in the chemo room while a nurse inserts an IV drip of saline solution into his veins. The vinyl lounge chairs are filled with patients in various states of infirmity, but Dad is by far the grayest and ghostliest. He pats my hand and says, "Thank you for all your prodding. Thank you for stepping up."

"I'm glad I could be able to," I say.

"I'd give anything to be in your condition again."

"I'm so sorry you have to go through this, Dad."

Soon Dad nods off, and I slip out to nurse Maisy. When I come back, he's been loaded into a wheelchair. He wants to come out to the curb to wait with me for my ride to the airport. The wheelchair, wide enough for two large men, dwarfs his shrunken frame.

I bend down and give him a long hug, feeling his bony shoulders and the heaviness of his fatigue and my own, such overwhelming weariness.

"I don't want to leave," I say.

"You have a life to go back to," he scolds me gently.

"I know, Dad. And you're part of it."

Merrill pulls up in her Volvo to drive me to Dulles. I sling Maisy's car seat over my arm and look at my father. Surely this won't be the last time.

I raise my hand, like I'm taking an oath. "I love you, Dad."

We've said so many goodbyes, but this is the only time I can remember saying those four words all in a row out loud. It always felt like giving too much away, like plunging into a November creek in nothing but my underwear, without even the bravado of a dare to hide behind.

Goodbye in train stations, Dad propping one khaki leg on the bottom step of the train, half in, half out, coming and going, always this way. Goodbye in front of the junior high. In airport terminals, back when you could walk passengers right to the gate; Dad always parked and came in with us, even when we were old enough to go alone. Goodbye in the driveway at Huntly, leaning through the open window for one final assessment. "Allllright," he'd say, in his dieselly rumble, preparing to send us off. So much contained in that one drawn-out word. *I love you. Be good. Be safe.*

It was the same repertoire every time: "Watch the median. Be careful pulling out on that blind curve. Don't drive too fast." Then he'd step away from the car and lay his arms by his side and we'd ease away and he'd raise his hand and hold it up in a prolonged, slow-motion wave until we were out of sight. Until we'd dropped down the steady pitch of the driveway, steering the wheels carefully through the gravel ruts, out to the main road, the scent of rotten apple hanging in the air. Necks craning *right left right* to watch for cars, obedient daughters to the end.

Goodbye now to the home hills on this sleeting day, tree branches bristling the hillsides like fur.

Then I am waving to him through the window and I am gone.

11

Darkness

Rappahannock sunset, 1998

I have this idea that once I get back to Santa Fe, I will be able to think more clearly. I'm not sure why I think this. Waiting for me is rambunctious two-year-old Pippa, who turns the bed into a trampoline the minute I start nursing Maisy. I'm behind on the laundry and deadlines. I haven't even started thinking about Christmas. But still I'm hopeful: Maybe when I'm out on my trails, I will flush the fear from my brain and the soreness from my body and I will figure out what I want to say to Dad while there's still time.

On the first Saturday in December, I run across a mesa a few miles northwest of Santa Fe. From the scrubby doubletrack trails of La Tierra you can see twenty miles to canyons on the far side of the Rio Grande, the earth wadded up like a napkin. Behind them, the buildings of Los Alamos National Laboratory dot the flanks of the Jemez Mountains, metal roofs gleaming in the sun. I pick my way along the rocky ground, not thinking about Dad dying or my aching neck or the worry that thrums inside me. I'm just listening to the pebbles beneath my feet and watching the rising sun bring the mountains to the west into sharp relief, when suddenly I feel my own relief.

I know what I'm going to say. Of course. *I love you, Dad, and I know you love us. But how could you have left us? HOW?* And what I want him to say to me. There's only one thing, really. *I'm sorry.*

I have to get back to Huntly soon so I can say it in person.

Two days later, the jangle of a distant ringing phone wakes me before dawn. It's the worst sound in the world. I leap from bed, sprint to the kitchen, heart in my throat.

It's Lesley.

"I think you should come," she says.

I hold the phone to my ear, filled with a horrible foreboding that this is the last day of my life I will wake up with my father in it.

It's Thursday, December 9, 2010. When was the last time I heard Dad's voice? A week ago on the phone, when he confessed, "I'm weak as a kitten." He was quiet for a while before he said, softly, "Is this because of some kind of character flaw?"

My heart splintered. This was it, the big question, the one he'd been too afraid to ask. Was cancer his payback, his penance?

"Oh, no, Dad. *No,*" I said quickly, trying to keep my voice light. But for a split second part of me wondered it, too.

The next night when I called, Dad spoke to me for only a minute before he said, "I have to get off the phone." He sounded lower than I'd ever heard him. On Tuesday, he was too groggy to talk.

Just yesterday morning, he snapped nonsensically at Lesley and Merrill, at his bedside: "Stop talking about pigs! You're supposed to be taking care of me!" To the hospice nurse who arrived later, he announced crossly, "I'm not going to try to sit up anymore. If I want to lie down, then let me!" He would have said this in the pinched, disapproving voice that he reserved for only the most trying of situations. This was the voice you never wanted to hear when you were growing up. The voice that sounded like it had been slammed shut in a door and then stretched thin like chewing gum. Sometimes it was deserved, but mostly it came out when he'd good and had it and needed space.

The nurse dutifully removed a bolster, helped arrange Dad's head and shoulders low on the pillow, and retrieved an anti-anxiety pill from her kit. The medication might make him woozy for a few hours, she told Lesley as she put it in his mouth, but then he'd pull out of it.

Dad didn't pull out. He just sank deeper into some distant, beckoning place. Now, Lesley tells me, he is unresponsive, his complexion wan and his breathing jagged, with a horrid, rattling cough.

"I should warn you," she says, "you might not make it in time."

I hang up and crawl back into bed beside Steve and whisper him awake with the news. What I do next I do without thinking: call Meg, call the airline, beg for a bereavement fare on the next flight out. Open drawers, shove clothes—my own and Maisy's—into a suitcase. Diapers, pacifiers, swaddle blanket. Set the day in motion, say our goodbyes, we're out the door.

Maisy and I meet Meg on our layover in Denver. Never have I been so glad to see my sister. Our flight to Dulles is delayed by an hour, and we frantically pace the terminal. I'm relieved when the airplane door closes and I have to turn off my phone. This means I won't have to know. Maybe we will get there in time. *Please let us get there in time.*

I press my face against the window as the plane takes off. Fresh storms have passed to the east, pasting the land white with new snow. Even the square farm grids seem softer, less precise, as though we're floating through a woolly sort of dream state. I pull out my notebook, open to a blank page, and begin: *Dear Dad.* All the words I've wanted to say pour out of my pen. I stop once, to nurse Maisy. Beside me, Meg is trying to read. So much has changed since we were girls on the train, but so much is the same. I'm still writing when we touch down in Dulles two hours later. With trepidation, I turn on my phone to check for missed calls and messages—none—and silently beg it to stay quiet.

Merrill's waiting for us at the arrivals curb. Still no news. An air of jubilation fills her car. He's not dead yet! As though by managing to outrun the imminent all day, we might be able to avoid it altogether, forever.

It's rush hour in the suburbs, and traffic is crawling. I glance impatiently at my watch. It's 6:10. If we'd been on our normal nonstop flights, we'd be at Huntly by now. Merrill tells us the last thing Dad said to her before yesterday morning. "I want the girls to be here when it happens."

These words have barely left her mouth when Meg's phone rings. The car falls instantly silent. In the backseat, Meg tells us, "It's Lesley." I stare at the wall of red brake lights in front of us so I don't have to see her face. She says, "Oh, Lesley. I'm sorry." *Sorry, sorry, sorry,* over and over and over.

When we pull up the drive, Huntly Stage glows garishly on its hill. All the lights are on, a too bright beacon over the fields. I'm filled with an intense foreboding. I've always been squeamish in emergencies, and I've never seen a dead body before. But when I walk into the house, I'm possessed by a sudden boldness. I say my hellos to Lesley and Phillip and go straight to Dad's room before I lose my nerve.

There he is, lying in bed, utterly still, a yellowed husk, cellophane skin, eyes half closed.

"Daddy!" I cry. "I'm sorry I didn't make it! I tried!" The words come of their own accord, from beyond thought or intellect, from a place so old—or young—inside of me. It's easy to call him Daddy, even though I haven't in decades, because he is. Still my father. It's not terror I feel, but a queasy sort of marvel. I am not afraid.

I climb up on the bed beside him, touch his hair, the deep hollow by his temples. I find his arm beneath the thin red cotton bedspread and place one hand upon his chest and feel only bone, no beat, his rib cage so thin. Already his skin is cooling, but his fingers look like they might grasp mine at any moment, and I expect to see an eyelid twitch or the blanket rise just a breath, expanding with his chest. But it doesn't. Not even a little bit. All the life that had filled his lungs and animated his body has been sucked out of him, whooshed away to another world.

He does not look like himself, and he looks exactly like himself. I study him closely, trying to make sense of the optical illusion. All his features are the same—his thin lips and droopy earlobes and straight nose. The difference is one of dimension: He's as flat as plywood. His face has fallen in on itself, an ashen mask, strangely naked without his glasses. Lesley took them off yesterday because they'd begun to rub sores on his nose. The hospice nurse gave him a bath while he slept and swabbed his mouth with Listerine so that he was tidy for the hard work ahead of him.

And yet the sight of his body in repose calms me. How many times have I stretched out beside him—his socked feet sticking up, his hands clasped peacefully across his stomach. Playing Morsel in the cabin he rented in Maine. My grandparents' condominium in Pennsylvania, the winter of 1980, where we lay on our backs on the shag carpet, watching Team USA beat the Soviets at Lake Placid.

Meg's trundle bed at Legation Street, where he read us *Time of Wonder* after our baths. Despite his overwhelming physical absence in my life, he's occupied an enormous, indelible space.

I can feel him here in the room with us, his essence intact and hovering somewhere just overhead. For a few moments more, at least, he will still be Dad, outstretched, with long lines and edges, knobby joints and furred and freckled knuckles.

"The end was peaceful," Lesley says, breaking the silence. Philip read to him aloud about the whaleship *Essex* while he lay unconscious, and she touched his feet to see if they were cold—the nurse had said that would be a sign that he was close—but they were still warm. In the late afternoon, as the light leaked out of the sky, she told him it was okay to let go, and he rattled one last inhalation, and she thought to herself, *That's it,* and it was.

My father is dead, but my body is making milk and Maisy is hungry, so I sit in the rocking chair by his feet and nurse her. It feels natural to do this, as I had all fall when he was sick. The angle from here is less flattering, though. I can see into him, into the space he's just recently vacated: beneath his eyelids, into his dark nostrils. His half-parted lips make a faint grimace, pulled upward by the jagged last breath. How does a body just *stop* after a lifetime of motion?

Later, after I've put Maisy to bed and Merrill and Philip have gone home, I go back into the room alone and lie next to Dad. His face in death is already familiar. I kiss his cheek and read him what I wrote on the plane, things I've wanted to tell him for days, weeks, years: *I love you. Your creativity lives on. You did your best. I've lived my life trying to make you proud.*

And I feel certain that he hears me and that I am not too late.

The undertaker arrives right on the dot of nine, in a gleaming black Yukon with tinted drug-dealer windows. It's bigger and more discreet than a hearse, and only slightly less sinister.

"I'm Chris," the undertaker says at the front door. "I'm so sorry for your loss."

He's portly, dressed neatly in a pressed black suit, with fair, thinning hair and a young face and a soft, kneading handshake. To think that as Dad lay dying, Chris was probably sitting on his couch, watching TV; then his mobile rang and it was time to get presentable. Someone has died. For Chris, it happens all the time. Maybe every day.

We lead him inside to the living room. He and his associate, also young and balding, settle themselves on the couch, like guests at a cocktail party, to discuss Dad's arrangements (or, as Dad would say, Arrangements). "Perhaps you'll be more comfortable waiting here while we remove Mr. Arnold from the bed," Chris says. This is gentle funeral-home-speak for *This is the disturbing part: watching someone manhandle your loved one and take him away for the last time.*

When they go outside to get the gurney, Meg pulls me aside. "You don't want to watch this," she whispers.

But I do. Dad's death doesn't scare me now. Maybe if I pay close attention, it will make more sense, maybe it will mean that I hadn't missed it after all, his very last act, that I was here, that I saw it and took notice, just as he always had. Because he couldn't.

I hover outside the room, listening to the shuffling and rearranging, the clack of a metal apparatus opening, quiet grunts of exertion. Then Dad wheels by on a gurney. He's in a maroon bag that looks like a giant felt overcoat, mohair maybe, oddly proper against his faded red sweatshirt, and the undertaker and his partner are moving fast for the door, as if they want to get out before we lose it.

As they push Dad outside, Chris places his business card discreetly on the table, patting it as he would someone's hand. "Call us anytime," he says.

I stand at the window for a long time, watching their taillights disappear around the curve of the driveway, not knowing whether to wave or cry. So I do both, tears streaming down my face, flapping my hand back and forth the way Dad always used to do, until the SUV is out of sight. Then I go into the kitchen and pick up Chris's business card. His name is typed in an ornate, swirly cursive, and below it, in the same dignified font: INTERN. I feel a smile tugging at my mouth. Dad would chuckle at this, being carried away by an apprentice mortician. He would not do this meanly or out of superiority, but because it was the best and most bizarre detail of this long, strange day—that one word, so unnecessary, really, yet so proud, so full of hope. For the first time in weeks, maybe months, I laugh.

In the morning, I wake to the strangest, most magnificent sunrise. I'd fallen into bed after midnight, too exhausted to close the curtains, and now, through the tall windows, the sun is painting the hills pumpkin, peeling back the whiskery frost layers on the fields. The trees are awash in a deep persimmon, the light glittery and bright. Then, just as suddenly, the day goes dim again, as though time is crawling backwards. If only it would.

It's snowing: Fine flakes drift from the sky, then fatter flakes, accumulating on the driveway, the lawn, the windshield of Dad's pickup.

Downstairs at breakfast, Lesley and Meg and I pick at scrambled eggs and toast. Lesley says, "I think we should make a rule that we are allowed to cry at any time." And she puts her head in her hands and begins to cry.

Later we drive to the funeral parlor, in Front Royal. Chris greets us at the door and ushers us into the beige sitting room, where he presents Lesley with a shallow bowl containing Dad's personal effects: his scuffed gold wedding band, which I'd never seen him take off, and his black Timex watch.

Lesley holds up the watch. "Would either of you like to have this?" she asks us.

It is too soon to think about wanting anything—except for Dad, still alive, all the horrid cancer scrubbed from his body, the last three months a do-over—but as soon as I see the watch's familiar glass face, I know that I do. I look at Meg and she's nodding. "You have it," she says. I put it on right away. The black leather band is soft and water-cracked in places, permanently molded in a semi-circle and, even on the smallest hole, much too big for me. But through the curve of the strap, I can almost feel Dad's wrist, the size and heft of it, the heat even.

Just moments ago, the Timex was strapped to his wrist. Just yesterday, his wrist was alive, veins and pulse chugging weakly, their last hours on the job. But now it's December 10, and Dad is in the refrigerated room next door. We enter one at a time to say our final goodbyes. His face is more sunken, his skin colorless and ice-chest cold and pulled tight against his head. Yesterday's farewell felt like running a race as hard as I could and leaving everything on the course. I said it all, as much as I had. Now I simply stroke his face, kiss his cheek. It is so much easier than I'd imagined, to touch him. He is still familiar, intimate, my father.

Afterwards, Meg and Lesley and I drive to the grocery store. Philip and Merrill are bringing us dinner, and we've agreed to provide dessert. As soon as we're inside, I know that we've made a terrible mistake. We stumble around the fluorescent aisles, tarnishing the sanctity of our final moments with Dad, shopping for cheap, store-bought baked goods. We're plagued by indecision: devil's food cake or coconut cake with garish frosting? Some kind of weird jiggly flan in a plastic container or ice cream? Do we want to bake brownies from a mix? In a silent, mutual rage, we settle on a fruit tart. The raspberries on top glisten in a vulgar, unnatural way, and I know we will never take a bite.

I push Maisy's stroller out through the automatic doors and into the pewter glare of the sun, which is trying to press through clouds, insistent but futile. I can still feel Dad on the pads of my fingertips where I last touched him.

This is the thing no one tells you about death. It's morbid and heartbreaking, but it can also be wondrous. Because we want to know where they're going, but we never will. Because it's so terribly final. Because it wakes us up to the world, at last.

On Saturday morning, after breakfast, I go down to the basement, looking for Dad. If he's still any place in this house, it's his office. Six weeks or more have passed since he last was here, and it is stuffy and dim, warren-like. One window lets in weak, indirect sunlight above his desk, which is eye level with the lawn. He really *could* watch the grass grow. The room smells exactly as it always has: of felt-tip markers and tired rubber bands, manila folders where he stored his contact sheets, dusty Updike novels and cycling guides; of him.

For a long while, I sit in his swivel chair, spinning slowly, scanning the room. Papers and pictures are strewn about on his desk and stacked in orderly piles on the floor and shelves. Almost everything is labeled, though for whose benefit—his or ours—it's impossible to tell. It's systematic chaos, the domain of someone who devised a meticulous organizational system but ran out of time before he could finish. Dust motes slant through the shaft of light, and the air feels oppressive, heavy under the weight of memories and faded ambition, and also devotion.

I kneel on the floor, opening file cabinets, looking for nothing in particular, and for everything. His drawers are full of old family photographs, writings, letters, research. In one is a small wooden box labeled HAIKU! in his uppercase handwriting, the beginnings of an old book project from the 1960s that he never finished. He was going to pair his black-and-white photographs with haiku by the great Japanese masters. The box is filled with index cards, each with a thumbnail picture and a handwritten verse. One stops me cold:

If they ask for me
say: He had some business
in another world
    —SOKAN

On the carpet next to the cabinet sits a tidy stack of small black hardbound notebooks. They are identical, each about the size of a paperback. On the cover of the first one is a title typed in bumpy red embossing tape: LISTENING TO MYSELF. I pick it up and flip open the pages to the middle. The thick black ink looks fresh, but the date on the top of the page says otherwise: 1975.

His diaries.

I skim quickly. He has left Legation Street and is dating a woman whose apartment he frequents on Idaho Avenue. He hardly ever mentions Meg and me by name. We are "the kids," and his girl-friend is identified by her first initial, "A."

The secretary.

She sometimes spends the night at his apartment on Newark Street when we're there. In the morning, Dad leaves a box of gra-nola for us on the kitchen table, along with notes, one of which he's saved. "Have some crunchy munchy!" reads the paper, in the neat, oversize penmanship meant for little girls who have only just learned to read. "There's milk in the refrigerator, please don't wake me up until after 8 o'clock. Daddy needs his sleep!"

Stuck between the pages, miraculously unfaded, is an old snap-shot of Dad holding Meg and me on his knees at a playground, and a woman, presumably A., kneeling beside us. She wears round glasses and a kerchief around her neck. I have a bowl cut and baby thighs. We are all smiling, and A.'s face is abstractly familiar. She has lived in the recesses of my three-year-old's memory all these years, a sense of wrongness and disloyalty shrouding her like an aura. "Idaho Ave."—even Dad's reference is casual, shorthand, anonymous, elongating the distance between us.

Meg and me, Washington, D.C., 1974

I read on. It wasn't a simple trade-off: us for A. It might be easier to bear if it had been. Caught between his old life and his new one, Dad was conflicted about both, desperate to make his relationship with A. a "decent and good one, so that the terrible damage I did when I walked out could at least have led to some good." But already it was foundering. "A's and my relationship seemed to be crumbling faster and faster under the irrevocable weight of my doubts and the bitter hard kernel in the midst of it all . . . that our adventure together began as novelty for me, not as love." I can see exactly where this is going, even though I already know the ending. How impossible it would be to salvage something solid from the ruins.

His tone is too tormented to read it all at once, so I flip erratically through the pages, afraid of what I might find. Dad writes about loneliness and "storms," his blackest moments—here the ink is darker and the grooves of the letters deeper, the actual outlines of despair—the choices he made that he feared would "ruin my life, Betsy's life, the kids'," the pressures that drove him away and the gutting isolation of being gone.

I turn pages, forward and back. One line jumps out at me: There among the blur of words is my name.

I admit there were many factors contributing to my withdrawal from the family even in the early stages (including my deep resentment of Kate) . . .

I have to read it twice to make sure I didn't imagine it. My head is thudding and dizzy, and a hot, childish shame rises on my face, the shame of being caught doing something wrong but not knowing what. I was only three that year. What had I done, besides being born? Besides breaking Dad's bass violin? Besides confining him further to his role as father?

I glance over a few more lines, hoping he'll elaborate or take it back, but there's no explanation, nothing more to go on. I close the notebook, put it back on the stack, and press my head into my hands, trying to catch my breath, trying not to faint.

I think about the guilt I carried for so long, assuming the divorce had been my fault. And then, when I was grown, the shame I felt for thinking this. *Get over yourself! How could a three-year-old have been responsible?*

Well. Here was my proof, straight from the source.

I'd been right all along.

I'd wanted to tell Dad that I forgave him. I didn't understand his choices, but maybe I could forgive him. I'd been working up to this for weeks, years maybe. And when I got to Huntly and found him so flat and still, I showered him with sudden forgiveness. He was human; of course he was. Even now, after finding this terrible diary entry, I don't take it back.

That evening after dinner, Meg and I sit at the dining room table, working on his obituary. We're leaving in the morning, and we hurry to finish, reading lines aloud to each other. "He lived his own life and inspired others to do the same," I say. Only now I know another part of the story that goes: *He was a selfish bastard and he hurt a lot of people. He was a great father to us and a shitty husband to our mother and I love him still.* This part will never change.

There's another thing I wish I'd said: *I'm sorry, Dad. I'm sorry I wasn't around as much lately. I'm sorry if you thought I didn't care. I'm sorry I never answered your letter.*

Four days before Christmas, I fly back to Huntly with Maisy to help Lesley plan Dad's memorial. On the night I arrive, there is a lunar eclipse, the moon a spooky ball of molten rust swallowed by the earth's shadow. It's the first total eclipse on the winter solstice in more than four hundred years.

Dad's in a black metal box on one end of the kitchen counter. It looks like a cross between an oversize recipe box and one of those portable hard drives designed to survive nuclear explosions. The label eliminates any doubt: "This box contains the cremated remains of David L. Arnold, cremated on December 15, 2010," followed by a long serial number. Lesley and I have to reach over him to get our coffee mugs from the cabinet.

The next morning, I borrow a pair of Lesley's Wellies and tromp out to the barn to keep her company while she feeds the horses and cats.

"Where's Peacock?" I ask.

"Oh," she says, sounding confused. "Didn't I tell you? He's dead. I found him frozen on the floor of the barn three days after David died."

I'd hoped this might be the end of the long season of anguish and, now that Dad is gone, something inside of me would lift and I might find some relief from the pain of grief.

But of course it is only the beginning.

PART TWO

Shadows

I am frightened all the time. Scared to death. But I've
never let it stop me. Never!

—GEORGIA O'KEEFFE

12

This Is the Way
the Mind Works

Blizzard at Huntly Stage, 1984

In January, Steve and the girls and I fly back to Virginia for Dad's memorial. We fill the house with photographs by him, of which there is an impossible number to choose from, and pictures of him, which are scarcer: the elusive photographer caught on film. He is riding a tractor, paddling his kayak. He is a three-month-old with grave eyes and a grandfather holding his newborn granddaughter. A computer on a side table plays a loop of videos Dad made over the years: Huntly Stage in springtime, Meg and me running the Fodderstack, his life, and ours, flashing by on the screen.

His Rappahannock friends come over and his former colleagues from the *Geographic,* some of whom I remember from when we were girls. We drink wine and tell stories; then we cue up the Biggs on organ and crank the volume so high the floor starts to shake and it's impossible to separate myself from the music, to feel where I stop and it begins, and where Dad stops and I begin. He still seems three-dimensional, with height and girth and green-flecked eyes. It's easy to pretend I haven't lost him for my whole life, just for a little while, and that once the novelty of his dying has worn off, he'll walk out of my memory and back into this world, camera bag slung over one shoulder and that same old grin, always.

We're so busy, there's no time to go down to the basement. It's just as well. I can't stop thinking about Dad's notebooks, but I can't bear the idea of reading them. Instead I sort through his clothes. His half of the closet is still full. There's his red down vest, a lop-sided stack of sweatshirts; khaki work pants and dress pants; a faded *Outside* T-shirt; and an itchy snarl of ragg wool socks, too many to count. On the top shelf, next to a step-on scale, is a small spiral notebook. Only the first few pages are filled—a list of dates and numbers, in Dad's handwriting. It's his weight, recorded every day for three weeks, beginning in late August: 180 pounds. The trend was down. By his last entry, the day before his diagnosis on September 16, he'd dropped eight pounds. The rest of the book is blank. There's no need for words. The numbers say it all.

Is this what it feels like to finally grow up?

Moving to New Mexico hadn't made me a proper adult. Neither had marriage or even motherhood. I still called Dad when I needed advice. Mom flew out when I got my wisdom teeth pulled and birthed my babies. But losing a parent feels like naked, permanent vulnerability, full exposure to the elements.

Back in Santa Fe, the muddle of motherhood reels me back in. There are many days when I don't have the energy to make the bed, when yolky breakfast bowls languish all day in the sink, when time passes in a swirl of teething, nursing, napping.

When they hear the news of Dad's death, friends and acquaintances murmur their condolences. Some tell me it takes a year to grieve the death of someone you love: four seasons, all the anniversaries. This is meant to be a comfort, as though there's a beginning and an end, and once twelve months are up I'll magically be done. I've said the same thing to friends. But it's not comforting; it's panic-inducing. Who gets a whole year just to grieve? What a luxury it would be to mourn without interruption, like a nun cloistered in a whitewashed room in Italy, with stone floors and a view of a blue lake far below. If this were possible, maybe the sorrow really *would* pass in twelve months. But grief isn't glamorous. It's not a fantasy. It's ordinary and mundane, all tangled up with real life. It *is* real life.

Before Maisy was born, when my stepsister, Amy, asked me what I thought would be harder, going from no babies to one or from one to two, I replied confidently, "Zero to one." I'd already made peace with round-the-clock breastfeeding and seriously curtailed freedom. If I wasn't so tired, if I didn't feel like I had needles poking into my eyeballs, I would think my naïveté was funny. I did not imagine Pippa, my darling, irrepressible wolverine, scratching my face to get my attention. I didn't imagine how many times in a day this girl would shriek *No!* I didn't realize it was possible to be so exhausted—bleary, hungover, comatose, *wrecked*—and still wake at first light, buzzing with nervous energy.

Motherhood is a kind of schizophrenia. No one will tell you this beforehand, just like no one warns you that breastfeeding is hard to figure out and hurts at first, or about later, when the feral animal baby bites you with her razor teeth. But it's true. Both are an agonizing ecstasy. The terrible feeling of separation, the longing embedded in your body when you leave your baby—even when you were frantic to get away, to go for a run or even to the grocery store (such outrageous liberation!), even when getting away was the only thing you could think of, the very second you're gone, you want nothing more than to be home. You are two bodies wrenched apart. Love is almost unbearably physical. In this way, it is not so very different from grief.

I'm so relieved to have left the stupor of cancer behind in Virginia, the papery stinkbugs slinking everywhere, the pain calcifying in my body, that at first I rarely cry. I actually think: *I'm handling this!*

But grief is cunning and persistent, determined to find an outlet, like water. It channels through my whole body, filling every crevice and joint, following the path of least resistance, like an incoming tide on the mudflats that long-ago summer in Maine, rushing the sand until it's deep enough to drag me under.

One morning in January, I'm awoken by a dull throb at the base of my neck. It's been sore on and off since the summer, when I was breastfeeding Maisy seven times a day. I'd written it off as normal overuse, but now, in my half-conscious state, Dad's words come back to me, a voice from beyond. *Pay attention to your body. You will know when Something's Not Right.*

Fear pools in my stomach and rises up through my throat. How have I not realized this until now? The ache between my shoulder blades is cancer, a rogue tumor on my spine, compressing my nerves, spreading by the minute. It's so obvious. I must be dying, too.

Even when I tell Steve this, sobbing at the terrible irony, and he says, "It's probably just our saggy old bed," and even when we go out and buy a new mattress and my neck pain subsides literally overnight, my anxiety doesn't. Resourceful and nimble, it just switches targets. My healthy body is riddled with aches and unfamiliar sensations and strange blemishes I've never noticed before, proof that I've been stricken by disease. I listen with fascination and horror to stories of others people's illnesses. It doesn't matter if they're people I know or complete strangers. It doesn't matter that cancer isn't contagious. If they have it, so do I.

Every few weeks, I'm dying of something new, sometimes several things at once. My tingly scalp must be a brain tumor; my chronically chapped lips, melanoma. My symptoms defy logic and reason. I can conjure heart palpitations, numb fingers, and aching kidneys with a single thought and then lock them into my body until I'm sure my days on this planet are numbered. Is this what an anorexic feels like when she looks in the mirror and sees fat when in fact she is all taut skin and angular bones? I see Dad's concave temples transposed onto my own head and think, *That's it. I've got it, too.* Some days, many days all in a row, the illusion of illness is all I can think about, a twisted distortion that no one but me can see.

I've come back from death only to find it has followed me home.

To be a new mother is to live in a bubble. You can see out into the real world, but you're buffered from its sharp edges by a gauzy brain haze. It's like running above the clouds high on the mountain. It's clear where you are, but the quilted sky sequesters you from life far below.

The bubble is created partly by fatigue, partly by awe and adoration, and partly by hormones. Inside the bubble, all that matters is the bare necessities: eating, sleeping, changing diapers, surviving, loving. As in childbirth, your body knows instinctively what to do.

The baby bubble is evolutionarily essential. It's what keeps you focused on your baby so that you don't accidentally leave her on the side of the trail, where she will get eaten by coyotes. It's what tamps down your ambition, temporarily disables your ego, frazzles your short-term memory so that you aren't tempted by work or deadlines or other nonessential distractions. This doesn't mean you're not working harder than you ever have in your whole life. You are. But the bubble dulls the perceived effort. You're so exhausted that you're unable to fully grasp how exhausted you are. Thank God for that.

Inside the bubble, time is elastic and the days are outrageously full, as though you're moving at half speed. For a while, you are. The membrane that separates you from the rest of humanity thins as time goes by. Occasionally you'll think you've popped out the other side, but you're really still in the bubble, peering wishfully into a blurry world. Then your baby starts teething and stops sleeping and under you go, swallowed again. Resistance is futile. And in spite of everything, you'll miss this when it's gone.

I know because everyone tells me so. Strangers feel compelled to stop me in the grocery store, their eyes growing misty when they see my darling precious lovelies, one or both of whom may be fussing in the cart. "I have two babies of my own," they shout over the din. "They're eighteen and twenty now! It goes by in a flash!" The thought of this makes me want to weep, both in despair that they're right and dread that they're wrong. What if I am forever being spit up upon and tormented by fatigue? What if I blink and my babies are gone?

After Pippa was born, I stayed in the bubble for fourteen months. Coming out was like stumbling out of a movie theater in broad daylight, squinting at the sun. Who am I? Where am I? Life and all its busyness had carried on without me.

Now I live in two bubbles. A bubble within a bubble: mourning and motherhood. Like the baby bubble, the grief bubble is a protective shield, strange and disorienting, only darker. Living in my double bubble is not an entirely bad thing. It means I cannot get worked up over distant threats like an earthquake or tsunami, a nuclear leak in Japan or air strikes in Libya, unless of course I am thinking about the Future, capital *F*, as it pertains to Pippa and Maisy. And then I lie awake in bed at night, feeling the panic inch into my throat, and wonder, *How will our daughters live in this world?*

Nothing drives home mortality like motherhood. When you care for a wrinkled, helpless creature who depends on you for everything, from whom you are inseparable, you realize that you absolutely cannot, must not, die. And then you watch your father die and you realize that you absolutely will. And someday so will they. Just not now, please. Not for a very, very, very long time.

Nights are the worst. Steve falls asleep instantly, while I lie there, stewing in gruesome scenarios until eventually I get up and swallow a baby aspirin. (Mom, who rarely takes medicine, swears they are a cure-all.) Sometimes even this backfires. "Steve!" I whisper one night. "I think the aspirin is stuck in my throat. Do you think it's like . . . burning a *hole* in my esophagus?"

He turns to me, eyes brimming with fake alarm. "Yes, right this *very minute!*" He checks to make sure I know he's kidding, then scoffs, impatiently, *"No."*

Another time I wake to the faint shrill cry far off in the tunnel of my ear. A baby, but which one? Dazed, I stumble down the hall. All is quiet. Then, faintly at a great distance, the piercing wail. Not in our house; not human. Outside in the arroyo, coyotes. Pulse racing, I creep back down the hall.

Sometimes I startle awake, fearful that in my delirium I've brought Maisy into our bed to nurse her and I forgot to put her back, and now she lies tangled in the sheets near our feet, suffocating. I slide my hands around, feeling for her in the dark, and jab Steve with my elbow. *"Where is she?"* I ask frantically.

His voice rises from the bottom of a deep cave. "Who?" he mumbles sleepily.

"MAISY!" I cry.

"In her crib."

I've sweated through the sheets, and I curl my feet around Steve's, breathing in time with him, until I fall asleep.

In the light of day, when I ask Steve if he ever feels afraid, he looks at me blankly, as though the thought of coming home to find an ambulance flashing in the driveway has never once crossed his mind, as though he doesn't live in abject terror of our daughters choking on grapes or becoming entangled in blind cords. I do the worrying for both of us. Early puberty, terrorism, the pimple in Steve's belly button, leukemia, breast cancer, Pippa skiing into a tree, divorce, car accidents, avalanches—they come fast and furious at all hours of the day.

In my bubble, I vacillate between despair for tiny perfect bodies going wrong and awe that everything is exactly right: Maisy rearing up on chubby cellulite knees, about to crawl, toothless pink gums, hair coming in like peach fuzz; Pippa's round toddler belly pressed into mine. I crave my girls; I long to be on my own. I love them fiercely; I miss my freedom. I want to write, I want to sleep. I am desperate for Pippa to stop pinching me, for Maisy to start sleeping through the night, but I don't want them to change. *Ever.* Motherhood is madness, the craziest kind of love I've ever known.

Santa Fe is swarming with natural healers of every stripe, and as the months go by, I consult them all. Am I experiencing sympathetic grief-induced hypochondria, post-traumatic stress from the shock of losing Dad so quickly, an almost midlife crisis? It's all of them. A perfect, terrible storm.

I become my own lab rat, a one-woman experiment. I quit sugar, cold turkey. I see an acupuncturist. Once a week for a month, I drive to a subdivision on the edge of Santa Fe. A yellow-haired woman I've never met before, Janice, leads me into a room with mystical accents where she teaches me how to tap on my temples, my forehead, under my eyes, my clavicle, while chanting. It's a method called Emotional Freedom Technique, or EFT, she explains, and it's designed to purge trauma from my psyche by replacing the negative memories in my head with positive ones.

We sit facing each other on chintz chairs and I try to copy Janice as she taps. Forehead, eyes, temples. Forehead, eyes, clavicle. It reminds me of the old clapping games Meg and I used to play—*Miss Mary Mack, Mack, Mack. All dressed in black, black, black*—except that the words are woes: *I am afraid of dying I am afraid of dying I am afraid of dying because . . . I am afraid of living I am afraid of dying because . . .*

I'm tapping and chanting, and at the same time I'm thinking of what this is costing me and how embarrassing it is to divulge my most private fears to a total stranger in a broomstick skirt, and what a racket she's running because surely this whole thing is a scam, a kind of creepy brainwashing. And even as I'm thinking this, I know I'll come back next week and maybe even the week after. That's how desperate I am.

In the middle of our third session, Janice abruptly stops tapping and tugs at my arm. She makes a dramatic shushing gesture with her cracked coral lips and points out the window. A few feet away in her backyard, a cat squats along the fence line. It's tawny and plump, with inquisitive ears and speckled fur, nearly camouflaged against the winter-faded bushes. It watches us as we watch it, but when it stretches to its feet, I can tell by the way it moves, with both sureness and secrecy, that it's not a house cat. It's a bobcat, wild and alert, the way I long to be.

When the session is over, I can't get out of there fast enough. The bobcat has broken the spell. I won't go back again.

In one corner of his office, Dad kept a small display of cameras. There was his small, blocky Kodak Brownie; an early-model manual Nikon with a cracked leather strap; several scratched light boxes and dusty lenses. Eventually, Dad joined the modern world with the purchase of single-lens reflex Canons and, reluctantly, digital SLRs. He never had an iPhone. His preference was always for simple manual equipment that required you to do the thinking.

The simplest device of all is the camera obscura, in which a small hole or several holes let light into a dark chamber. Images of objects outside the camera appear upside down and backwards, scrolling across the top and sides of the blackened chamber like a movie reel running in reverse. Looking into a camera obscura is like being inside a grainy, slow-motion home video on rewind. The smaller the aperture is, the sharper the image; the larger it is, the blurrier and more abstract, as though the events you're seeing are happening to you and not happening to you at the same time.

This is what it feels like to be inside my brain.

I try yoga, hoping the dim lights and quiet postures will calm me, but when I bend backwards into bridge pose, my neck feels so exposed, I think I might die, as if I'd been guillotined in my last life. The instructor speaks in an exotic French accent that's almost impossible to understand. I think she's saying, "Open through the kidneys. Feel your kidneys. Soften your kidneys." I don't know exactly where my kidneys are, nor can I feel them, but the mere mention of them makes me think of Dad and his cancer, and I turn my face away from the teacher so she won't see me sobbing silently through the rest of the class.

I get a massage to release my tense muscles, but the masseuse lectures me about developing a spiritual practice, which only makes me tenser. I go see a German Pilates trainer for a private lesson to strengthen my core so my back won't hurt so much. The instructor, who specializes in a method called Contrology, has oily brown hair and sits cross-legged on a wood-and-metal apparatus. "The Reformer is modeled on a hospital bed," he says loftily. "With traction. See the springs?" He doesn't offer me a seat, so I sit on the floor, aware that I'm hunching my shoulders, that I'm soft and weak around my middle. He demonstrates the exercises and I perform them with the trepidation of the scrutinized. They are harder than they appear on the little black-and-white diagram taped to the wall.

"Lift, lift!" he says. I raise my arms, but he barks, "Not your *arms,* your core! Separate!"

I don't know what this means or how to do it, but I do not want to separate; I want to be whole.

"Drop your shoulders, drop your shoulders!" he yells.

"I'm trying!" I say.

"Try *harder!*"

I am paying this man to berate me, blowing my modest inheritance from Dad on *this*. I want to cry, but instead I retort, "Hey, cut me some slack." My insubordination surprises both of us. When our time is up, another client comes in and the German trainer is sunny and cheerful, as if the abuse of the past hour didn't happen. He says to the man, "What's the news?" and calls him Jefe, and there's no trace of his German accent.

When I tell the trainer I won't be back, he smirks in triumph, as if to say he knew all along I wasn't tough enough. I don't tell him the truth: that trying harder to be in control, to keep my grief at bay, is the last thing I need.

I call Bob, my Rolfer. Rolfing uses a form of deep tissue massage to manipulate the body's connective tissue, or fasciae, that surround the muscles, bones, and organs. I found Bob thirteen years ago, after I hit a tree while learning to snowboard and broke five ribs in my back. My left leg was shorter than the right from the impact, and my whole body curled around itself like a misshapen *S*. After my fourth session with Bob, I dreamed I was running, and when I woke in the morning and went out for a jog, my first in months, my body was full of lightness, released from its crooked pain. Bob put me back together again after childbirth, dug a knot out of my Achilles tendon following my half marathon, and even did craniosacral therapy on Pippa when she tumbled off my foam roller and got a concussion. Does it get any more Santa Fe than that?

Now I climb onto his table in my clothes and tell him about my aching neck, my fears that I might be dying, too. Bob is in his sixties, bald, with the tranquil, Yoda-like manner of someone who exists in a near-constant meditative state. Rolfing gets a bad rap for being obscure and excruciatingly painful, massage's evil doppelgänger, and while Bob does occasionally go after me with his elbow and puts his whole weight behind it, most of the time he uses a mysterious alchemy of light, precise pressure and energetic healing.

Sometimes I can't feel his touch but can sense it from the frisson of energy pulsing back at me.

Bob doesn't talk much when he works, but he does talk to himself. "Oh, there we go," he'll murmur soothingly when he feels something essential but invisible shift into its rightful place. This time, though, Bob is silent, and I drift in and out of sleep, thinking about Dad, when he lay on a massage table, for the first time in his life, in the last month of his life, after he had given up but before we had. He was too sick to be massaged, so the therapist ran her hands above his body as Dad dozed beneath the thin sheet. After a while, I feel my mind drift above the table, hovering over my body in a strange and dizzying, but not unpleasant, way, in two places at once.

A magpie calls shrilly through the window, and I fly back into my body. Bob's hands are cradling my neck so tenderly that I want to cry, but I wipe my eyes with my sleeve, because I don't want to embarrass him, and because I'm afraid that once I start, I might not be able to stop.

My days are so full of appointments, I barely have time to run. It's winter at seven thousand feet, and the trails have turned into luge tracks. I strap spikes onto my sneakers and labor up my mountain alone. Through my sneakers I can feel my toes trying to curl into the frozen ground for purchase. Even when it's fifteen degrees, I dress lightly: tights and a wind jacket with a layer or two underneath, thin gloves, maybe a hat, maybe not. It's surprising how warm you get when you run uphill.

My favorite time to go is during or right after a snowstorm, when I'm the first one up the mountain. It's harder and slower breaking trail, but the powder muffles my footsteps and makes the trail feel new and forgiving, cocooned in white, the snow still fluffy and not yet hardened into icy pitches. I run straight into the storm, doily flakes falling as fine as mist, the squall whitewashing the sky, my eyes streaming tears in the cold wind. I don't notice that my feet are soaked and my socks are clumped with ice balls. I don't register anything but the tips of the piñon branches gleaming with snowflakes, the ravens spinning overhead, black as coal against the sky, and the woolly cloud world enclosing me.

Some days it's so cold that my muscles slug along like a car engine that's been sitting out overnight in sub-zero temperatures, the gearshift gluey and slow. Skin-cracking, nostrils-sticking-together cold. The world is hard and splintery, and my legs and arms are out of sync. By the time I reach the top, I've finally warmed up, maybe too much, because my skin and clothes are damp with sweat and I freeze on the way down. Someone has chipped me out of a glacier from the last ice age. At the car, it takes me five tries to fumble the key into the ignition, and my hands are so frozen I can barely steer. When I get home, I stand in the hot shower for twenty minutes, letting the water drum down, get out and wrap a scarf around my neck, boil water for tea, and sit in front of the woodstove, coaxing flames from tiny, worthless embers. Still I'm shivering.

It's only after the hypothermia and endorphin rush wear off that my worries come rushing back. I've developed a tightness in my chest that I'm sure is a congenital heart condition. Mom's chain-smoking father died of a heart attack at fifty-eight, and her older brother suffered a fatal aneurism at sixty-one while jogging on his treadmill. In a scene straight out of the movies, Dad's father keeled over from a coronary at Meg's wedding and died two days later. He was eighty-six.

According to Mom, there's a bad heart in the family. "The Minnis heart," she calls it, referring to her father's genes, in an ominous, accusing tone, as though the same ruined organ has been handed from one generation to the next, like a Christmas fruitcake nobody wants. Mom had her heart tested and supposedly she doesn't have it, but I worry that it skipped a generation and is coming for me.

Every few months, Mom sends me articles about the health risks of high-intensity exercise to the heart. *F.Y.I., dear! I thought you'd be interested! Xoxox,* she writes. I skim them dutifully, uneasily, then email her back with studies asserting the opposite: *Look, Mom! Running proven to make you smarter! Running may add as much as seven years to your life!* I know this is our way of talking about love and running without actually talking about love or running.

In February I go see my doctor. Ira retired, and I've known Dr. G. for only six months. He listens patiently while I tell him my long sob story about Dad and all the ways I, too, might be dying or about to die, potentially right this very minute. He takes my vitals and hooks me up to the EKG monitor while I study his framed diplomas on the wall so I don't have to see the bad news written all over his face.

Instead he turns to me, smiling. "It's normal," he says affably, unhooking me from the machine. "Have you thought about antidepressants or anxiety medication?"

I shake my head. I've always been wary about taking drugs or medicine—not because I'm tough but because I'm scared. I'm afraid that they'll cloud my mind and I'll feel as though I no longer belong in my own body.

"I'd like to try other things first," I tell him.

I take St. John's wort capsules and vitamin B to calm my nerves. I dose myself up with tinctures of the homeopathic Rescue Remedy, which is made of flower essences but, by its acrid taste, mostly alcohol. I swallow the smelly brown Chinese herbs that my acupuncturist gives me. They ease me into a nice, soft sleep, but I have to try very hard not to think about a friend's thirty-eight-year-old yoga teacher who went to India, experimented with Ayurvedic herbs, contracted a mysterious illness, and died six months later.

A few weeks later, I go back to the doctor's office. My fingers are tingly, and I have to keep pinching my arm to make sure it's not going numb from a stroke. Ann, the physician assistant, looks at my chart, then hooks me up to the EKG again. When I sneak a peek at her watching the readout, she's shaking her head.

Oh, God . . . please, *no*.

Except she's smiling.

"If you could sell these numbers to people, you'd be a millionaire," she says. "It must be all the running—you are so healthy."

Then, almost as an afterthought, Ann says gently, "You know, at the root of all anxiety is a fear of dying. Maybe this is a good time to become friends with death. We are all going to die."

This is simultaneously the most sane and the most insane thing I've ever heard. *Of course, of course, of course* I'm afraid I'm going to die. That's the problem! But *making friends* with my own mortality? The thought of it makes me shudder. I'd be banging down the doctor's door every other day.

She must see the panic on my face, because she continues. "You know how I do it? Meditation. I've been practicing for twenty years, since I was your age."

I nod. I can almost feel the tweezers in my chest loosening a little.

"It's hard work and takes practice," she says. "It's not peaceful and quiet, where you get to turn off your brain. You see what your mind is doing, racing and worrying. In the beginning, this can be quite painful."

But she looks so calm, so not crazy. Maybe she's right.

My pain and fear leach into everything, like cancer cells run amok. At the first sign of a new symptom, I leapfrog over all the plausible explanations and the possible ones, too: the ones that aren't exactly pleasant but won't necessarily kill me. In the span of a day, sometimes a few hours, my imagination takes me all the way to the far end of probability, to the worst-case scenario, to incurable, fatal.

I can't look at Facebook, because people get sick or die there all the time, right in front of your eyes, and they're all too young. I get a sore on my tongue and I worry for a week that I have a rare form of tongue cancer, but then I forget about my tongue because my jaw has begun to hurt and someone I heard about on the news had a rare form of jaw cancer. My brain is a lazy Susan of incurable diseases. Spin it and see where it stops! I'm so porous, I can catch a fatal illness from a radio report, from a single line in a newspaper article, from a novel, from a passing mention of someone else's sickness. I even get what the dog has—my chocolate Lab, Gus, who survived bone cancer and getting his leg chopped off and beat the vet's odds by four years but who is really, finally dying this time, of lymphoma. Which of course I have, too. Somehow my grief has gone all wrong. I'm so preoccupied imagining my own death that I've stopped mourning Dad's.

During my nanoseconds of sanity, I recognize that this is my way of holding on to Dad a little longer, and that my anxiety is an unconscious defense mechanism gone awry, paranoia short-circuiting my grief so I won't have to feel sad. On days when I emerge from the anguished fog, I know I'm lucky. Nothing is really wrong. We are all healthy. I think of others who are truly suffering and I am ashamed, and this only sends me deeper into anxiety.

"Are you ever afraid that you're dying?" I ask Meg one day on the phone.

We call each other more often now, sometimes for no reason—not like when Dad was sick, to compare notes or to strategize, but just to check in.

"Not specifically, no," Meg replies agreeably. "I worry about other things, but not that." By *other things* she means: single-parenting two small children, holding down a full-time mega-stressful job as a CEO, and navigating her own thorny divorce. She's so much tougher than me.

Every few weeks, I call or email Lesley, who, after the frenzied buildup to the memorial service, has gone quiet. There's so much I wish I could ask her, just like there's so much I hadn't asked Dad in his final weeks: *Are you afraid, or curious? Are you sad?* I wish I'd done his dying better, for both of them. I hadn't gone to Huntly enough, and when I had, I'd been in such a hurry to get home and sandblast the sadness off my body.

Mom is mourning in her own way, too. After Dad got sick, she mailed him a funny movie on DVD to cheer him up, with a short note. "The girls have turned out so well," she wrote. "They are your legacy. You should be proud." He never responded. She sent Meg and me money to pay for our flights to Virginia. And I can tell now, by the way she asks after the farm and his photographs, that it's hitting her all over again: Dad missed his opportunity, with his pictures and with us.

I don't tell Mom or Steve or Lesley about my imaginary tongue tumor, because I don't want to worry them or sound like a maniac, but also because I am superstitious that saying the C-word out loud will make it so. Nor do I dare write about it in my notebooks, because it would be only a matter of time before someone found them, in a plot twist too fantastic to be believed, and tsked mournfully, wiping away a tear, *She was too young. Too young.*

The irony, of course, is that my anxiety takes me away from Steve and the girls every day. I'm short-tempered, easily distracted, too busy wondering if I'll survive to know Pippa and Maisy as teenagers to see them as they are right now, at two and a half and not quite one. At night, after they're asleep, I realize my error and sneak into their rooms and watch them, trying to memorize their soft, breathing bodies, their musky night smells, their limbs stilled for now and so small, but not for long.

On my better days, I shriek into a pillow; on my bad days, I yell at Pippa to *Stop whining!* when I give her five dried cranberries and she asks for ten. Her face when it crumples just about destroys me. I am the worst mother on the planet. Which becomes its own, new worry. Maybe they'd be better off without me.

The pressure builds until eventually the panic spills out of me in a torrent and I lie in bed next to Steve, sobbing that I'm going to die. *"Please take care of the girls,"* I wail. Steve does not know what to do with me. "There is nothing wrong with you," he says, exasperation creeping into his voice. But he is not in my brain. He is not in my body, feeling that *something's not right*. And doesn't he know that telling someone not to worry does not make them not worry?

I train him to say five words: "Everything's going to be okay." I know it's trite and, in the long term, patently untrue, but there's something about the way he says it each night before bed, in monotone, like a robot, half asleep under the pillow, one hand patting mine, that makes me feel the teensiest bit better.

"Really?" I say. This is his cue to repeat it.

"Yes," he sighs. "Everything's going to be okay."

One winter night, after the girls are asleep in their cribs, we're lying on the sofas reading magazines. Steve has the latest issue of *National Geographic* spread out on his lap and is eating vanilla ice cream straight from the carton. He's trying to get all the last bits of melted drippings from the bottom, attacking it with such diligence, like it's his only concern in the world. *Scrape, scrape* goes the spoon.

Is there any more irritating sound in the history of humankind?

"Check this out," Steve says, passing me the magazine. It's open to a picture of a man whose arms were torn off by lions in Tanzania.

Scrape, scrape.

Steve shakes his head solemnly. "Next time you think you have it bad . . ."

I nod and furrow my forehead, trying to look appalled. "That *sucks*," I say, and does it ever, but secretly I'm relieved. I'm not going to Tanzania anytime soon, which means chances are slim that I'll be mauled by wild African lions. Here at last is one thing I don't have to worry about.

————

Dad comes to me in wispy, passing moments. Usually when I am doing something else. (I am always doing something else.) Often when I'm driving.

There's an intersection in Santa Fe, diagonal from the state capitol and a neighborhood grocery store, where you can look straight up the Santa Fe River canyon into the watershed. The city's drinking water comes from two reservoirs that collect snowmelt from the Sangre de Cristo Mountains. The watershed has been closed to recreation since the 1920s, to protect it from wildfire, and so it remains a largely untracked swatch of forest just a few miles from town.

Within the watershed, in the layered canyons behind Picacho Peak, there's a small mountain in the shape of a pyramid. I've tried to decipher it from other vantage points in town, but the mountain looks this way—exactly triangular, a perfect emoticon for a mountain—only from this exact spot. Sometimes when I sit waiting for the green, I wonder what lies up there that I cannot see. Mountain lions, trees scarred by lightning, old sheepherder paths, trails that Kit Carson once roamed. And I wonder who else sees this and is wondering the same thing.

My desire to run there isn't as strong as my desire to keep wondering.

This is where I'm stopped one afternoon when I feel Dad in the car with me. I lean over and rest my forehead on the steering wheel and sob. It feels so good to cry. So easy. How long has it been? But my tears stop almost as soon as they begin. Through the windshield, the pyramid rises, steadfast in its place, even when I can't see it and don't understand it.

You can't speed grief. The light turns green, and on I go.

13

Breaking Down

Student, Wittenberg University, Ohio, 1958

Time skids by. The ice luge melts into mud and spring winds howl, blowing dust in through the windowsills. Damp ground becomes sunbaked dirt. The girl looking back at me in the mirror isn't a girl anymore. She's thirty-nine. She has dark circles under her eyes, deepening crows'-feet, and sparse, dull hair. She's nothing like the girl who stood with one hand on her hip a million years ago, grinning confidently at the camera.

My running is erratic. I have good days and bad days, and many days when I can't get out the door. It's nearly impossible to establish any kind of routine. Pippa goes to daycare twice a week; our nanny comes the other three mornings, but I'm still nursing Maisy, so I have two hours, three at the most, to be out of the house. I write and run on the edges of the day, stealing time whenever I can find it.

The only fixed point in my schedule is a weekly hike with my new friend Natalie. I met her a few weeks after Maisy was born, but I knew her before that, the way that people in Santa Fe and around the world know Natalie Goldberg. I knew she was a Buddhist who lived in town and had written a book called *Writing Down the Bones,* sort of a Zen writer's bible, and that she taught writing the same way she taught meditation: as a mindfulness practice. I'd seen her once, strolling near one of the local Zen centers, and a thought popped into my head: *Someday we're going to be friends.*

Then Maisy was born and I had two babies and I took a break from freelancing and my writing consisted of frantic, illegible scribbling in my notebook. Occasionally I would think of Natalie, walking so serenely down the middle of the road. If only I could sign up for her next retreat, but I was doubtful that I could pull it off while breastfeeding a baby. I was waiting for a sign.

A week later, I was walking on my trail, with Maisy strapped on my chest, when there, like an apparition, was Natalie. She was coming toward me down the trail, head bowed contemplatively and hands clasped behind her back. She wore baggy cotton pants and shirt, and her short dark hair poked out from her sun hat. She was nearly past me when she looked up and did a double take.

"Is that a baby in there?" she demanded incredulously, pointing at the canvas baby carrier. Natalie has lived in New Mexico for thirty-five years, but she still has a Long Island accent and the unapologetic bossiness of a schoolteacher.

"Yes," I said, nodding sheepishly. I had that awed feeling you get when you're in the presence of a real live guru, mingled with the peculiar shame of being a new mother who's pretty sure she's botching the job.

Natalie scowled at me. "Is she suffocating? Can she *breathe*?"

Maisy was pressed against my sweaty T-shirt, and I could tell by the slow, contented cadence of her inhalations and exhalations that she was already asleep.

"Oh, yes, we do this all the time," I said, trying to sound casual, confident. I hiked through two pregnancies and the whole first year after Pippa was born. I'd been spit up on, sweated on, wailed on, snowed on, and stormed on, but so far we'd always come back alive. "She's napping—see?" I said, unsnapping the sun cover so she could peer in at Maisy, eyes closed and panting lightly through half-open lips.

Natalie nodded brusquely—I could tell she wasn't convinced. She left without a goodbye, and as soon as I got home I called the Zen center and signed up for the class.

The next time I saw her was a month later, on the first day of the retreat. She was sitting on a folding chair at the front of the Zendo, and she pointed at me and called out loudly, "Oh, you're the woman with the baby!" The other students, clustered silently around her on their meditation cushions, turned and stared. I nodded, feeling self-conscious and shaky. That very afternoon, I'd learned that Dad had cancer.

After the retreat, Natalie and I started hiking together. We walk the same trail every week: two miles to the top of 8,500-foot Pica-cho Peak and back down the way we came. I strap Maisy to my chest, and we climb in silence and at our own pace, the distance between us gradually increasing as we wend our way through a narrow canyon, past a stout ponderosa leaning into the trail, and up a series of switchbacks to a granite overlook where Natalie stops to sit and meditate against a tree. I keep walking to the top, Maisy asleep in her carrier. Then I descend and meet Natalie, and we talk the whole way down. This is our ritual, and we seldom deviate.

Natalie's a teacher in her public life, so she doesn't necessarily want to be a teacher on a Tuesday morning on the side of a mountain. This is fine with me. I've decided that I'm not going to grill her for meditation pointers, even though clearly I should be doing it more—well, doing it, *period*. Instead we talk about food, about traveling, about Dad, about writing. We joke that our hiking will save the world, but I know it's saving me from myself, from my obsessive fears and imaginary ailments. Each week, Natalie listens as I catalog my latest disease. She's kind enough not to state the obvious: that clearly I've gone bananas. Nor does she try to placate me with empty reassurances. She only murmurs a little, so I know she's listening, and then she pauses for a long time before saying something enigmatic like "You need to know death in order to blossom fully. Life is so full for you right now."

The weird thing is, I know she's right. I *do* feel full. Full of sadness, love, and my father; of writing that feels alive even while I'm sure I'm dying.

"You have your whole life to grieve," she goes on, her voice squawky and soothing at the same time. I don't have to cram all my sadness into one manic year—I can pace myself—but the idea of spending my days in perpetual mourning sounds awful. As with most things, I'm in a hurry. I want to get it over with as fast as possible.

My anxiety comes and goes like clouds blowing in from the west, wispy and innocuous at first, the wind building until the storm is directly overhead. It flattens me for days or weeks at a time with its charcoal skies and sideways rain. It is a meteorological event. I don't have a say in the matter.

Every now and then, the storm eases and I burst out of my bubble. These are the days when I look back on the past six months and think, *Wow, I was so fucked up*. I think this means I've broken through to the other side, but I haven't, not yet. I'm still just a temporary visitor in the land of normalcy. It's only a matter of time before the maelstrom whips around and sucks me back in.

One warm morning in late March, I brush my hair and put on one of my slightly less moth-bitten sweaters and ride my bicycle to the coffee shop a few blocks away, to meet with a man named Alan, for whom I'd done some writing in the fall. He'd hired me to prepare a report on the sorry state of public school education in Santa Fe. I'd met him between trips to Huntly Stage, to go over my findings. Now he wants to thank me for my work and see how I'm doing.

The sight of him brings it all back: the creaky dying-ness of the fall, the decrepit grief plastered all over my skin. I think about the emails I sent him from Virginia, how composed I thought they sounded, how professional. *My father is dying but I expect to be able to send you my research on time.* I'd been so sure I was keeping my shit dialed. I was too busy to be sad! But I can tell by the way he's looking at me now, with sincere pity, that I hadn't, not at all. I'd been in the storm then, and I'm *still* in the storm.

Alan lowers his head and glances around the room. "After my father died, I talked to him," he says. "It helped me a lot."

I force a smile and avert my eyes. It's nothing he's done or not done, but I can't look at his face without Dad dying all over again. I thank him for his condolences, wish him luck with the research, and pedal away.

I find my healers the usual Santa Fe way: word of mouth through the New Age grapevine. *So-and-so knows so-and-so, who tried such-and-such, and it worked!* Always when I get a new lead, my first response is great hopefulness. It's only when I arrive for my first appointment that I become nervous. What if this person's a nutjob? I shouldn't spend so much money. I should be more discerning, but if I were more discerning, I wouldn't be in this situation in the first place. I would know the difference between other people's suffering and my own.

My latest hope is a woman named Abby, who practices somatic therapy, which helps patients tune in to sensations in the body as a way to reduce stress and anxiety and overcome trauma. Intensely shocking or upsetting experiences disrupt the nervous system, Abby tells me at our first appointment, and the irregular buildup of stress hormones manifests not just with worried thoughts but with physical discomfort—everything from muscular pain to dizziness to digestive troubles. Increasingly, somatic therapy is being used with success to treat veterans suffering from PTSD.

In my case, the shock of Dad's diagnosis and the speed with which he died coincided so closely with Maisy's birth that I didn't have time to acclimate to either. All the fear and joy and grief are still whipping around inside me, like a traffic jam of emotions. This, Abby says, creates bottlenecks of physical pain in my body, including my perpetually stiff neck and sore back. The tingling I've been feeling in my fingers and toes and scalp isn't a tumor or a stroke. It's my confused energy looking for an exit.

Abby begins asking me questions about Dad, and every few minutes she says, "Notice what you're feeling in your body." I name them aloud: buzzing shins, an uncomfortable pinch in my neck, thoughts spinning through my brain like buzzards circling the farm. She gives me a few simple deep-breathing exercises.

In the first one, she instructs me to turn my head and look over my left shoulder. Then, very gradually, I turn it back until my chin is pointing over my right shoulder. The key is to move as slowly as possible. "Pretend you're doing it in your sleep, and that your head is floating lightly on your neck," she says. "Can you feel your breath deepen?" I can.

Next, she says, I'm supposed to yawn.

"Really?" I ask.

She nods. We're conditioned to think that yawning in public is rude and should be suppressed, but it's actually one of our bodies' best ways of releasing stressful energy. "Let your mouth hang open and your chin go slack," she instructs me. "Tuck your chin slightly in toward your neck. This will trigger the familiar yawning sensation. Then open your mouth wide, close your eyes, and let the yawn come. If you're really feeling it, stretch your arms above your head."

Yawning is reflexive, but yawning on command in front of someone you barely know is very awkward. I try to close my eyes, but I can feel Abby watching me, and I'm too self-conscious to let my mouth fall open. What if I have spinach in my teeth?

She must sense my discomfort, because she says, "It helps to try this alone at first until you get the hang of it. You should feel free to make whatever expressions you usually make when you yawn, whether it's squeezing your eyes or hunching your shoulders."

Before I go, she asks me to tell her about a moment of joy from my day. I think and think. I can't think of anything. How can this be? I have a nine-month-old baby who laughs constantly and a bright-eyed two-and-a-half-year-old who's learning a new word almost every day. I leave her office determined to pay closer attention.

The next morning, after breakfast, I read to Maisy in the playroom. She sits on my lap for two pages, then squirms off, an inchworm nosing her way across the floor. I open my mouth and wiggle my chin. Maisy studies me and does the same. The yawn starts tentatively, like it might not happen, and then it does, rippling outward, cracking my face wide open, taking over my whole body. I waggle my arms sideways, above my head; the yawn is a deep sigh filling me with air. I pick Maisy up, and together we twirl around the room. She squeals and flaps her arms. I know she is happy. *I* am happy. It is so easy, I can't possibly forget.

The days pendulum back and forth, and my moods with them: peaceful, elated, enraged. Anger is unseemly when you have babies. They are precious and beautiful and they mean no harm, and I am lucky to have them. But I am not really angry at the babies, and I am not really angry at Steve, though sometimes when I look at him, all I can think is *You got me into this.* No, the anger is voluminous, an ancient, collective rage that's bigger than me, bigger than Dad and his duplicities, maybe bigger than even anger itself.

By May I've reached a breaking point. On the recommendation of a friend, I make an appointment with a family psychotherapist named Kate. Her specialty is mindful parenting, which combines Eastern meditation with traditional counseling. At our first session, she hands me a questionnaire. When I'm done filling it out, she sits in her wing chair and studies my responses. I stare out the window. The questions on my lips are the same ones that always come to mind when I'm at the doctor's: *How bad is it? Am I going to make it?*

When I meet her eyes, she smiles kindly. "You have moderate perinatal mood disorder," she says. She explains that it was most likely brought on by an ill-timed alchemy of grief, fatigue, and hormones.

Now I finally have a name for the weird, surging fury, the listless blahs, the screeching impatience, the simmering rage, the occasional overwhelming urge to run away. Kate gives me strict marching orders: nine hours of sleep a night. Do whatever it takes and take whatever it takes to catch up on my sleep.

She shows me how to use my five senses to relax when I'm feeling anxious. "What do you smell, see, hear, taste, feel?" she asks. "Go through each one of your senses and name them, one at a time." This will ground me in the present moment, which is not nearly so terrifying as the future.

In other words, pay attention.

Oh, that. I'd forgotten.

Then she says, "And I want you to lower the bar. It's okay to be a B parent. It's okay to be okay."

This is harder to swallow. I'm hardwired to strive. Okay wasn't always okay in our house. Yet I know she's right: Even now, when I'm killing myself to overperform, there are many days when I barely muster half-assed.

"When you find yourself impatient or angry, what are you resisting?" she asks. "Can you shift from the moment you wanted to the moment that is?" It sounds so straightforward, but I know that this will be the work of the rest of my life.

At the end of May, Steve and the girls and I fly to upstate New York to bury Dad's ashes. His plot is next to his grandparents', in a cemetery near Oneonta, where my great-grandfather was president of Hartwick College after World War II. Lesley is there, and Meg and her kids, and Merrill and Philip. Even Uncle Phil has made the trip from Wisconsin, where he's lived for the past decade, accompanied by his house mother. At sixty-nine, he's stooped and frail and seems in a daze. He did not get to see Dad before he died. "Is that Dave in there?" he asks, rapping his cane on the ground.

Dad's hole is so small, and he is so small in the small carved mahogany box that his friend Philip made by hand. When Pippa bends down to place white roses on the urn, I think about all the things she'll miss about her grandfather and won't even know she's missing: lying with him in the grass, shooting rubber-band airplanes into the sky. And I think about all the times I've left Dad, but especially the last time, scooping his ashes into a plastic ziplock bag in the kitchen at Huntly Stage, the strange weight of them, how chunky and granular they were. This leaving feels anticlimactic. The box is too small to hold all of him.

The next morning in the motel, the girls wake before sunrise. I hide under the covers, hoping they'll go back to sleep, but Steve gets them out of their cribs and lets them wrestle around in an impromptu boxing match on the bathroom floor. Pippa is winning, Maisy wailing.

"Shhh," I hiss, afraid they'll wake the neighbors through the thin walls. Then I think that maybe if I don't move, they won't see me in the bed, won't cry *Mama,* won't need me for five minutes more. It dawns on me that maybe this is what Kate means by okay.

"Someday we'll laugh about this," I groan to Steve from beneath the comforter.

And Steve, in a pitch-perfect tone of weary resignation, in a display of perfect, lovable Steveness, replies, "Might as well be today."

Later, as I'm changing Maisy's diaper, she kicks her pudgy legs in the air and tries to roll off the table. She isn't in a rush or perturbed or sad or impatient or distracted or exhausted. She's just there, smiling and doing her best to squirm and strive while I do my best to hold on. This time I don't even have to try: I yawn, big and wide, showing all my teeth. For a split second, my mind empties of all worries and I imagine a day far in the future, when I look back and remember this time as crazy and wonderful and maddening, maybe even magical.

Might as well be today.

14

The Thin Edge

San Juan River, Utah, 2011

N ow that I have a name for my condition—postpartum anxiety—
I can feel it lifting slightly. Three million women in the United
States suffer from perinatal mood disorders every year. I'm not
crazy, I'm not alone, and there are steps I can take to feel better.

I develop a sleep system: I drink a mug of chamomile tea before
bed and turn my computer off by 9 p.m. I wear wax earplugs (never
rubber; they fall out) and a memory-foam eye mask that molds to
my face and blocks all light. A humidifier purrs white noise in the
corner of our room. Swaddled in my night cocoon, I can't hear the

dogs' toenails clicking across the wood floor or the coyotes yipping or the girls cooing in their sleep, but I can hear them crying. When they do, I elbow Steve and he gets up without a grumble.

Even by twenty-first-century standards, I know I lucked into a highly evolved member of the male species. Steve cooks. I do dishes. We take turns going grocery shopping. I breastfeed, he changes diapers. He takes out the trash, I do the laundry. I work part-time at home, he works full-time outside. I bought the house, but for now he's paying the bills. He plays Frisbee in the evenings, I run in the mornings. Our division of labor isn't exact, and it isn't completely equal—if anything, Steve's doing more right now—but we balance each other's blind spots.

I know this is mostly because of Steve, but I like to think it has just a little bit to do with Dad, too. "I feel compelled to give you my standard advice, about fathers," he wrote me in an email a few weeks before Pippa was born. "Make sure they feel included. Don't forget about them!"

Sometimes when Natalie and I walk, the subject of meditation comes up in passing. We talk about it casually, the way we might discuss the omelets we ate for breakfast. I've learned, for example, that in Zen Buddhism, meditating on a cushion on the floor is called zazen. When she was in her thirties, Natalie sat cross-legged in zazen for so long that she did permanent damage to her hip. Now she's become looser with her practice, meditating in a chair, leaning against a tree, lying in bed. The few times I've tried zazen since Dad died, I either started crying, fell asleep, or became so filled with a nameless wrath that I wanted to run, screaming, from the room.

When I mention this to Natalie, she says, "That's normal. You might like walking meditation better. Watch me—" and she clasps her hands behind her back, bows her head, and walks slowly down the trail, more slowly than I've ever seen her walk, more slowly than seems humanly possible. With each step, she presses her foot into the ground, rolls through to her toes, and lifts it up again, one foot after the next, swaying a little as though dancing to the world's slowest beat.

"Breathe deeply and feel your whole foot on the earth," Natalie says, without turning around. I try to copy her. I think I might fall over, but I'm also aware of the pine needles and pebbles beneath the soles of my shoes and the way the air glides in and out through my nose, in time with my feet. We walk quietly like this for a few minutes, and then Natalie says, "Okay," and snaps back to her regular gait, like she has places to go. It would have taken us hours to make it down the mountain at that pace, but I like the idea that I might be able to achieve the same results as sitting—relaxation and peace—without actually having to sit.

A few years ago, Steve built a flagstone garden path around our house, and sometimes when the girls are sleeping I do laps in my bare feet. Steve and I call this going around the world. In my last life, before babies, I went to Africa and hiked over an eighteen-thousand-foot pass in Nepal and waded fast clear rivers in Patagonia and climbed ocean cliffs in Thailand. Now I walk in circles through our backyard. There's something about the narrowness of possibility, the small effort required of me, that I like. I don't have to think about where to go or what to do or what to wear; I just walk out the door. Sometimes I pause outside the girls' bedroom windows and prick up my ears like a fox, listening for sounds of stirrings, feeling like a ghost in my own home.

One evening a few days later, when Steve is out playing Frisbee, I practice walking meditation on my way around the world. The stones are smooth under my feet, and I try to remember how Natalie did it: land on my heels, roll through my arches, press through my toes. Repeat, repeat, repeat. It usually takes me less than two minutes to complete the loop when I'm walking slowly, but now I try to stretch it to five or six.

"Walking is a way to taste impermanence," Natalie told me on the mountain. At the time, this made no sense to me: Who needs to taste impermanence when you're drowning in it? But now, as my mind empties of worry, I become aware of the breeze that will never repeat itself, another day in our daughters' lives gone beyond our grasp, clouds drifting east over the mountains, their exact pattern impossible to duplicate, and I almost understand what she means. Impermanence is everywhere, the only true constant.

Kate, the mindfulness psychologist, gave me strict orders to REST. I wrote it down in my notebook in all caps and underlined it twice. Lying low at home until the panic passes would be the normal, sane person's response to acute anxiety. Unless, of course, you're me, in which case you will go anywhere, do anything, and try anything to escape it.

For example, the river.

Friends of ours have invited us to join them on a rafting trip down the San Juan River in southeastern Utah. Some men give their wives jewelry after they give birth, but when Pippa was born, in 2008, Steve bought us an inflatable raft. It was thirteen feet long and bright blue, the color of the New Mexico sky, with a pair of long yellow oars. My "push present," we joked, was a boat. But it wasn't a joke, really. Steve and I had been doing river trips together around the Southwest since we met, paddling whitewater and running up side canyons, and we wanted to raise our girls the same way, outside, in the landscapes we love most.

When Pippa was ten months old, the age Maisy is now, we took her on her first river trip, for five days down the San Juan, fifty-six miles of easy Class I and II rapids. I'd been in full freak-out mode beforehand, but when we got to the boat launch, I saw a family with a baby draped over a cooler, sound asleep in his life jacket. The mother, in faded nylon river shorts and tanned bare feet, was loading gear onto the raft with one hand and feeding her toddler crackers with the other. Relief flooded through me. Maybe we weren't insane after all!

"How old is your baby?" I practically screamed.

She glanced up and smiled reassuringly. "Ten months." Then she added nonchalantly, "This is his second river trip. We took him last fall, when he was four months old."

The memory of that mother comforts me—for about one second. Pippa, at nearly three, is as curious and energetic as ever; she will require constant watching. Maisy is still nursing, and both are in diapers. Diapers! What was I *thinking*? Who takes not one but *two* babies on a desert river? What kind of mother does this? A terrible, deranged mother, that's who.

I stew over doomsday scenarios: Maisy falling overboard into the muddy water and vanishing forever. Pippa flipping out of her Pack 'n Play crib and sleep-crawling in the middle of the night. Bee stings, rattlesnake bites, sunstroke, hypothermia, flash floods, concussion. Appendicitis! I'm pretty sure I've imagined every possible catastrophe until I drive to my friend Sandy's house to borrow a satellite phone, in case of emergency.

"Better bring a mosquito net," Sandy says. "You wouldn't want the girls to get West Nile virus."

A couple of days before we leave, I put Pippa and Maisy into the car to pick up some final supplies. I've spent all morning sorting piles of Pirate's Booty and applesauce and a small mountain of organic, whole-grain snacks, but in my agitated state I'm convinced we need more. Even if going rafting isn't the most irresponsible idea ever, there is absolutely no way it will ever be worth the logistical toil of packing.

I'm at a traffic light, waiting to turn left, when I freeze, overcome by all that's happened and all that might. I can't go on. Cars zoom this way and that, careening in and out of lanes, the world raging on, indifferent to loss and full of vast, unspecified terrors. We could be rear-ended and sent spinning into oncoming traffic; I can almost feel the impact. My skin tingles as though my body has turned itself inside out and my nerves and veins are exposed. When the light turns green, I turn around and drive home in the slow lane the whole way. How desperately I want to keep us all safe, but I see now that it's impossible. Maybe the adventurous life we love is nothing more than danger in disguise.

At home, I call Meg in distress. "This is total insanity," I say. "I can't do it. I'm going crazy."

I've always relied on Meg for levelheaded advice, but this time she sounds rattled, like she thinks I've gone off the hook for real. "I've never heard you like this," she says. "Maybe you should cancel."

I tell her I'll think about it and hang up and call Dr. G., secretly hoping he'll advise me not to go. Instead, he says longingly, "I love the San Juan this time of year." He writes me a prescription for Xanax and phones it in to the pharmacy. "Bring it to the river just in case."

This time I fill it.

The night before we leave, I go around the world. One lap, then two, and still my mind is whirling with what-ifs. On my third loop, I stop at the peach sapling we planted a few weeks ago on what would have been Dad's seventy-fourth birthday. In the soft breeze, the leaves are waving back at me like little hands. I lie down in the dirt and look up at the branches, fighting back tears.

"The river trip's tomorrow," I sob out loud. "Should we go?" I'm not blubbering to the tree, exactly, but to Dad, and it seems not unreasonable to hope he might be able to hear me, and then it is not a stretch to discern what he might be saying back. *You're doing the right thing. You're doing a good thing.* I can almost hear his low, calm voice reminding me how important it is to let kids play outside and get dirty and not have every minute jammed up with Stuff and Things to Do.

As surreal as it seems to be hallucinating my dead father, I don't feel as unhinged as I did moments ago. I'm talking to Dad and he's talking back, and just as Alan had told me in the coffee shop, it *does* help. When it seems like I've said my piece and he's said his, I go inside to finish packing. The trip has a momentum of its own, and it's already begun.

River canyons in the Southwest are among the last places in the country where cellphones don't work. The walls are too steep, the sky in between too skinny. This is a large part of the appeal—to unplug for days at a time. Unless, of course, you have a new baby and are in the grips of grief-induced postpartum anxiety. Then it's a nervous breakdown waiting to happen.

At the boat ramp in Mexican Hat, the river is high and silty, the color of baked beans. Just downstream, two thousand cubic feet per second of snowmelt funnels through a rapid. I look at Maisy, dozing in her car seat under the shade of our umbrella, and try not to hyperventilate. *I see the brown river. I smell the damp, sweet willows on the banks, I hear the rush of rapids. I taste fear, sharp in my mouth, and eggs from breakfast. I feel the sun on my shoulders. I am here. I* am. Then Steve pushes off and the river catches the raft and pulls us out of the eddy and into the canyon.

Eddies are pockets of calm water surrounded by moving current; they form when an upstream obstacle like a boulder or a logjam blocks the downstream flow. On higher, faster-moving rivers, the boundary between the main current and an eddy is often strong and clearly visible, a sloshing, foaming pleat, on the inside of which is flatwater that curls upstream like a gentle whirlpool. It takes effort and will to punch through these eddy lines and reach the calmer water. This is called eddying out. Sometimes, though, you may blunder into an eddy by accident, suddenly stalled and moving in the opposite direction from where you're trying to go.

I have paddled pushy rivers where the current roars along like a freeway at rush hour and the eddies are practically nonexistent, and quieter rivers where the eddies are tranquil pools. I have watched as the seam of conflicting currents flipped a friend's kayak in an instant. Sometimes you long to be in the eddy so you can catch your breath and rest. Other times you are stuck in the vortex, trying to break loose.

We make our first night's camp on a grassy bench above a wide beach. Before dinner, I climb to a small knoll above camp to test the satellite phone. I dial Mom's number and wait. The screen flashes the same spinning icon, trying to connect. I look down on our tents, pitched in a line well back from the water's edge; I can't see them, but I can hear them—kids' happy voices rising above the rush of the river. I study the phone. Nothing.

Above me rise two-hundred-foot limestone cliffs, part of a geological formation that was deposited three hundred million years ago when the riverbed was a shallow sea. The canyon walls are too tight to let a signal in. The phone doesn't work. If we need to get out in a rush, we'll have to row fifty miles downstream to the closest road.

I repack the phone in its case and follow the faint trail back to camp. One of our friends is baking lasagna in a cast-iron Dutch oven, another is playing guitar, and Steve's drinking a beer. It's a scene so benign, I know it must be true.

Morning brings the relief of sunrise, of survival. The river is still brown and fast, thick with sediment, but my worries have begun to fade. Cut off from real life and the incessant stream of bad news, of people I know and millions I don't know dying of cancer, I can finally let go of my fears.

For five days, we row the turbid water downstream, our bare feet on sunbaked mud that has cracked into slabs like pieces of a puzzle too big to decipher. Above us, the canyon walls have been varnished by millions of years of wind and rain and sun. Each layer of rock corresponds to a different epoch—youngest upon oldest—giving the impression that we are looking back in time, seeing the past exposed in every crack and fissure and flake.

Maisy and Pippa, San Juan River, 2011

We know this canyon so well, but it's never the same river twice. The water chugs on, draining from its source high in the San Juan Mountains, two hundred miles upstream. So much has changed since our first float. Each trip marks time. We're older, the girls are older. The water appears infinite, unstoppable, but this, too, is a false constancy. Someday in the future, the San Juan will not be a river, but a dry bed. I know this, but I don't believe it, not completely. We drift with the current, at its pace, hearing the canyon wrens warbling our passing, feeling the hot air waft down on the wind, and I remember how it feels to be happy and filled with hope, in spite of the unknowns, or maybe because of them.

A year before Pippa was born, I'd gone back to Yosemite on assignment to write a profile about climber and BASE jumper Dean Potter. In the two years since I first met him with Steph Davis, he'd gained notoriety. He'd used a bow and arrow to shoot a rope over Delicate Arch, the famed Utah landmark, and climbed it, rogue, at first light. He BASE-jumped off cliffs with a parachute rigged to his back and walked "highlines," tightropes rigged hundreds of feet off the ground, between rocky spires, sometimes without a safety harness. If he fell, he'd have to catch the line with his hands and pull himself back onto it; if he missed, he'd almost certainly die.

That week in Yosemite, I camped out on the floor of a shack belonging to one of Dean's climbing buddies and tagged along with him to his favorite climbing routes and jumps. BASE jumping is illegal in the national park, but Dean and his friends jumped at sunset, when they were less likely to be spotted by rangers. He called his risky pursuits "the dark arts" and told me they were a conduit to a heightened state of awareness. He said he felt most alive on this fine line between life and death, where there was little margin for error. But he didn't want to die doing these things. He wanted what all adventurers want: to live, so he could *keep* doing them.

In my free time, I ran alone through Yosemite Valley; the Merced River glittered in the midday sun, and El Capitan and Half Dome rose up on either side. The trails were soft with pine needles, and my feet made no sound. In the hushed forest, I became acutely aware not just of my surroundings but of running itself: fast, full of awe and strength and possibility, something more to me than sport. Maybe, like writing, like Dean's climbing and flying, it was a way of being awake in the world. The notion was there in a flash, and then it was gone. Some things you can't hold on to, like my long-ago helium balloon. You just hope they come back.

On my last day in the park, I stopped at the Mariposa Grove of three-thousand-year-old sequoias. The trees were so old and huge, I could feel life radiating from their massive trunks, the steady, ineffable pulse of time. They were the largest living creatures on earth, anchored to this exact spot for millennia. It seemed disrespectful to run, so I slowed to a walk, moving my fingers across their gnarled bark, their living skin, aware that I'd stumbled into something lasting and almost holy, the thin edge where time slows and then expands and all your senses fire in unison. It was here, Dean had told me, that his mind stopped its relentless, pesky spinning—"brain-rattles," Dad called them in his letter—and the world with all its fears went quiet.

It was the summer solstice, and the full moon was rising in my rearview mirror like a ripe apricot. Summer had begun, but something else, too: the conviction that anything is possible—huge, audacious, unfathomable things—when you live on your own thin edge.

Man on a tightrope, early '60s

PHOTO: DAVID L. ARNOLD

By our fourth day, the San Juan is a different river: wide, slow, and lazy, all the urgency drained out of it. We've cleared Government, the last Class III rapid, and now the river has nowhere to go except to Lake Powell and Glen Canyon Dam, twenty miles downstream. The river is quieter, no longer rushing whitewater but a low, steady swish. It's the sound of time passing, of land forming and disintegrating, of a world in constant motion.

Everything is simpler on the river: Keep the kids safe, don't get too much sun, take off your watch and live by the light. My cotton sundress is filthy with mud and marshmallow residue, and I've stopped worrying about getting out of the canyon alive. Now I don't want to leave. The river isn't the threat, after all. It's the cure, nature's antidepressant, better than the unopened bottle of Xanax in my bag.

On our last night, we set up our camp chairs in a circle on a beach. The stars come out like a shaker of salt tossed into the night sky. Kids streak along the sand, waving glow sticks. A sliver moon hangs above the canyon rim in the hood of darkness. I feel Dad here, too, his familiar deep voice drifting on the down-canyon breeze. *Well done, old girl.*

In a few months, I'll turn forty, but here between the walls, my hair caked with silt and my shoulders freckled from the sun, I feel young for the first time all year. I think of people my age who want bigger, more beautiful houses, high heels, new haircuts, the best schools. I just want *this:* to move my body until it's tired and dirty and write stories and sleep outside and love my girls and Steve as long and hard as possible. I know this as clearly as I know there's no way of knowing anything, really. I'll have to fling myself forward, with equal parts conviction and ease, just like the river.

If I'm going to die, I want to live.

15

Resolve

Crawling over the Fodderstack finish line, 1982

It's the last day of December. The year is over, and somehow I'm still alive. Maisy turned one and weaned herself, learned to walk. All the first anniversaries of Dad's illness arrived and passed. I've endured the hypochondria and loneliness, the moments of pure lunacy, the teething and tantrums, the bewildering fatigue, the hammering headaches and night sweats and the certainty of imminent death. I've eddied out, in writing and life, swirled in endless panicky circles in my mind. I've run up mountains and floated rivers and mourned my father. I've felt all the elation and terror of being human on this planet.

None of the things I thought would kill me have killed me yet. With this realization comes an inkling of something familiar and pleasant but very, very faint. Optimism.

That night, after Steve and the girls have gone to bed, I sit in front of the woodstove in the half-darkened living room, listening to Dad's favorite K.D. Lang CD. I haven't taken it out of the stereo since I brought it home three weeks after he died. In two hours, it will be a new year, the second without him.

Helpless, helpless, helpless, K.D. and I sing plaintively. But I haven't been helpless. Isn't that what the past year has taught me? That I knew what I needed: mountains and rivers and motion and love. That I asked for help and accepted it and that I also helped myself.

I pull out my notebook, and at the top of a blank page I write, "2012 New Year's Resolutions." Suck the pen tip, trying to dredge up my old ambition. A memory floats out of the cobwebs of my brain, the shape of something I once wanted, and maybe still do: to be bold and adventurous, and wild every day.

I think for a moment and write, "Train for and run a 50K ultramarathon."

Ultrarunning is defined as any distance over a standard 26.2-mile marathon. The "shortest" ultramarathon is fifty kilometers; from there, race distances typically increase to fifty miles, a hundred kilometers, and a hundred miles. Participation in ultrarunning has quadrupled in the past ten years, with more than eighty thousand Americans competing in more than twelve hundred ultra trail races each year, including the notoriously brutal Hardrock 100 and Western States 100-Mile Endurance Run, events that make obstacle races and road marathons seem like warm-up runs.

Many ultrarunners describe their transition to ultra distances as coming out of nowhere: Dean Karnazes ran thirty miles to Half

Moon Bay on his thirtieth birthday; the vegan ultra athlete Rich Roll, overweight and unhappy on the verge of turning forty, went out for a spontaneous twenty-four-mile jog. The urge to push your body beyond its known physical limits doesn't originate from rational thought. It's too unruly to fathom. If you pondered it logically, you would see it for what it is: pretty much insane. Rather, it arises from within, from the voice in your unconscious that knows that you long for bigness and are capable of achieving it, even if you haven't the foggiest idea how.

I've been making New Year's resolutions for years, mostly unsuccessfully. Sometimes I focused on ordinary and slightly embarrassing personal habits I ought to have mastered ages ago, like flossing every day and not biting my fingernails. Other years I went for lofty personal mantras—don't micromanage my career so much!—that I could never quite figure out how to execute. Sometimes I chose single words ("true!"), which buoyed me in the beginning of the year but were soon overshadowed by more mundane mantras like "What's for breakfast, Mama?" I was not in the business, however, of setting audacious, pit-in-the-stomach objectives that required concrete steps to achieve.

Two months ago, I turned forty. I was pregnant or breastfeeding, and sometimes both, for four years straight. For the past twelve months, I've been terrified of my own body, certain I was dying. Why on earth would I want to run long distances alone through the wilderness?

But the unconscious mind isn't linear. It doesn't travel neatly from A to B to C. It circles and spins, doubles back, detours and switchbacks and jumps ahead—months, decades, lifetimes even. I hadn't thought about Dean Karnazes in years. The idea *came out of nowhere*—my own disorienting, eddied-out nowhere.

One of the ideas of Buddhism is that between the polarities in your life, there is an unseen third thing, a way to sidestep the suffering and contention. Natalie had mentioned this in passing on our hikes, but I always felt like I was listening to her with cotton stuffed into my ears. I'd hear her words, but I couldn't make sense of them. She cheerfully admitted that, most of the time, she couldn't, either. "If I had sixty more years, I still would hardly know anything," she sometimes said.

I've always been torn: between my two fathers, two mothers, two homes, New Jersey and Virginia, Northeast and Southwest, water and desert, suffering and joy. I could live or die. I could be a good mother or a good writer. Between the worry and the love, the heart-break that my babies will someday grow up and leave me and the fear that they will never sleep through the night, my insatiable urge to go and my longing to stay, there's a middle way, a third thing building. I just don't know what it is.

It's the same with children. Sometimes Steve and I arrive at a moment when it seems that maybe we're finally getting a grip on parenting. But no sooner do we congratulate each other than the girls stop napping and redouble their addiction to their pacifiers. I've read that in very young children, regression is a sign that they may be on the brink of a major developmental change, like learning to walk or talk. The brain is so busy conserving bandwidth for the big leap that other systems go haywire.

Maybe the swirling turmoil of the past year has served a purpose after all. It has led me here, to the harebrained notion to run thirty-one miles. The resolution flies out of my mind and onto the page. The words stare back at me from my notebook like a proclamation. Like the craziest thing I might ever do, and the one thing I absolutely have to try.

The third thing.

Deep down, I know that running has the power to save me. Only it won't be enough to run up my mountain for an hour in the evenings while day turns to dusk. I need something huge enough to swallow my intractable grief, a goal that requires total commitment. I need to go farther, longer, deeper.

The next day, I give Steve a piece of paper with the words "My athletic goal for 2012 is _____" written on it. He never makes New Year's resolutions, and I haven't told him about mine. He reaches wordlessly for a pen, pauses to think, and bends his left hand around the paper, humoring me. A moment later, he gives it back. In his scrawly penmanship, he's written, "Run a 50K ultramarathon."

I stare at his resolution to make sure I'm not imagining it. It's the exact same thing I wrote. The coincidence is uncanny. It's been so long since we shared a goal beyond parenting, beyond just getting through the day, yet somehow we're still in sync.

"You know what this means," I say, handing him my paper. "Now we have to do it."

Then I tape our resolutions to the refrigerator so we won't forget.

Fifty kilometers is thirty-one miles.

Thirty-one miles is only five miles longer than the marathon I'd accidentally run with Dean five years earlier. If I have to, I can always walk the last five miles.

Aside from Dean's can-do mantra—"Just run to the next tree"—my only training advice comes from a professional ultrarunner named Darcy Piceu, who lives in Boulder, Colorado, and whom I'd recently interviewed for a magazine story. Darcy has a young daughter and a full-time job. She told me that the only thing that really matters when training for an ultra is your long run each week. She ran for six or seven hours every Saturday, trading childcare duties with her husband, who was also an endurance athlete. During the workweek, she said, as long as you get in some "short" runs, you'll be fine. I figured Darcy must know what she was doing, because she'd finished fourth overall at the toughest mountain ultra in the country, the Hardrock 100, in the San Juan Mountains of Colorado.

Ultrarunning is one of the rare sports in which, at the highest level, women are physiologically capable of beating men; ultrarunners of both genders call this getting "chicked." The longer the distance, the greater a female runner's advantage. In the nineties, ultra legend Ann Trason won the women's division at Western States 100 fourteen times; she twice came in second place overall and finished in the top ten eleven times. While there's plenty of anecdotal evidence of rampant chicking in the sport, there's little hard science to explain why females fare so well in extreme endurance. The most widespread speculation is that women's innate ability to withstand the ardors of childbirth also enables them to keep going for hours in other pursuits, even when they feel that they will surely perish from the effort.

My own labor with Pippa lasted thirty hours, an ultramarathon of childbirth. I subsisted on Popsicles and contraband energy bars Steve smuggled in when the nurses weren't looking. People kept handing me giant plastic cups of water and begging me to drink. I declined an epidural; I'd decided to do it naturally, as my mother had with me. ("I don't remember *any* pain!" she reassured me, with a straight face.) The pain was outrageous and unrelenting, huge horizontal waves that crested and broke, only to rise again almost immediately. Steve and my birthing coach, Simone, slumped on plastic chairs while searing blades of agony tore me in two. A living, breathing creature was trying to claw its way out of me.

"I can't do this," I moaned.

"You *are* doing it," Simone corrected me. "The only way out of this is through it."

I burrowed in. *You're stronger than you think you are.*

Finally, at the end of the second day, Pippa scrabbled into the world. I held her and looked around the room, marveling at how different it appeared. It was much smaller than I remembered. The walls pressed in, and the bed was narrower and seemed to be oriented in a different direction, though I knew it hadn't moved. I felt like I'd been away on a long journey, traveling vast distances, when in fact I'd been here all along. It was my mind that had left—it had to, to escape the torments of my body.

I tell myself that if I can withstand thirty hours of labor, then surely I can run for six or seven. This shouldn't be consoling—almost anything is easier than a day and a half of natural childbirth—but somehow it is.

For a few weeks, I bask in the glow of our resolutions on the fridge, as though simply writing them was noble enough and we don't actually have to go through with them.

These are the darkest days of winter, and I'm a creature of light. My body wants to sleep and ski and bake chocolate chip cookies—anything but start training. By late January, though, I can't take it anymore. Procrastinating is harder than running.

First we have to choose a race. Steve and I agree that it needs to be in New Mexico; neither of us wants to drive a long distance to run a long distance. This narrows it down: There are only a handful of 50Ks in the state, and the closest is the Jemez Mountain Trail Run, thirty-one miles through the backcountry above Los Alamos. It's in late May. We have four months to train, just barely enough time.

I start with a rolling six-mile run along the railroad tracks south of town. The Rail Trail follows the Santa Fe Southern Railway twenty miles from downtown, through bristly grasslands and a scattering of subdivisions, to the whistle-stop of Lamy; thirteen of these miles are dirt. In the summer, the railway operates a tourist train, but in the winter the tracks are quiet, just the jackrabbits, a few mountain bikers and dog walkers, and sometimes one of the Kenyan marathoners who live and train in Santa Fe.

Santa Fe's elevation of seven thousand feet is widely considered the sweet spot for high-altitude endurance training: It's high enough to condition your body for the thin air of mountain running, but not so high that you dramatically compromise your speed or aerobic output. The Rail Trail is five hundred feet lower, though, so it's usually clear of snow when the town and mountain trails aren't; it's also relatively flat and thus fairly fast. Some days I feel like I'm bounding along like the Kenyans, and only when I turn around do I realize that the wind has been at my back; now it's howling in my face. (Note to self: If you can't feel the wind, it's probably behind you.) The wind can be awful out there.

I run five days a week, rarely more. I don't keep track of my pace or my mileage, and I'm not following a training plan. Though there are plenty of regimens floating around the Internet for free, something in me rebels against the obvious. I want to listen to my own instincts, not someone else's. I've never been a very good follower.

The year we moved to Summit, I joined the Brownies. I was in second grade and had no aspirations to be a Girl Scout, but I signed up for the junior troop because I liked the brown uniforms with the sashes, pinned with badges. I imagined my own wide sash drooping and jangling under the weight of them as I walked alongside the other girls.

But when I put on the uniform for my first meeting, the perky brown cap sat uncomfortably atop my brown bowl cut, and my brown knee socks itched in my dull brown penny loafers. Even the penny was brown. A terrible, unforeseen monotony. I looked in the mirror and saw that I looked just like every other Brownie in every other town across the land—the world, even. This unsettled me. I did not want to look like every other girl, and I was ashamed that I'd made my mother spend money on the uniform, which I knew now to be unremittingly drab. I longed to be on my blue bicycle, streaking home from school, wind strafing my face, exactly me, unlike anyone else.

Mom went with me to the meeting. Outside the school, we paused by the bike racks and looked up. Above us, a jumbo jet was cresting the last ridge on its descent to Newark Airport. It was lower than any plane I'd ever seen, and it hung in the sky, bloated and silvery and eerily silent. Somehow it was not moving, as though it were tethered by a thread. I could see the jet's black wheels already lowered for landing, and I could imagine the people's faces looking down through the oval windows at the low-slung brick school and the bikes all crammed together with their rat traps and little tin license plates, at my own awestruck face looking back. Mom sputtered with disbelief and joy, squeezing my hand in hers. She always had such an amazing capacity for delight.

Who else had seen the plane? It was possible that we were the only ones. And already it was gone, coasting east. Watching it disappear from sight, I knew I didn't want to be a Brownie anymore. I went inside because I said I would, but then I relinquished my uniform and never went back. These weird wonders, they didn't last. But if you kept your eyes open, instead of just following along blindly, you could catch them.

My only real plan is to increase my longest run by fifteen to twenty minutes each week. It's an inexact science, but at this rate I figure I'll be up to four or five hours by May. I vary my routes so I don't get bored. I run up Atalaya and along sandy arroyos and only rarely on the road. I prefer slow, long runs to speed work, and hills over flats. No two weeks are ever the same.

Grief has its own topography, jagged and unpredictable. In the beginning it was like dragging myself up a vertical face, the surface loose and slippery, trying not to slip backwards into darkness; then there were the brighter days when I skimmed along the rolling flats in the bright sun. As the first anniversary of Dad's death approached, I felt like I was running fast downhill, picking up speed toward a date I'd been anticipating all year. I didn't want him to be gone that long, but I was restless to put the pain behind me and finally feel better.

There's a fine line between coasting and crashing, though, and by early December time had begun to accelerate too fast, sweeping me along with it. On December 9, I was frantic all day. I felt as I had a year earlier, that I was rushing to get back to Dad before he died, as if there was a seam in time into which the past twelve months had disappeared and if I hurried I could slide back in and change the ending. All afternoon I checked my watch obsessively. It was 5 p.m., then 5:30. The urgency was futile. Dad had been dead for a year, and he would always be dead. His deadness would grow until he'd been dead longer than he'd been my father, and dead longer than he'd been alive.

Then the digital clock blinked 6:10, and he was gone all over again. The past irreversible, the future unscripted, as always.

By late winter in northern New Mexico, the ponderosa pines begin to smell like butterscotch. All it takes is a few mild days in a row for the sap to start flowing. You can press your nose into the trees' thick skin and know that spring is coming. The sweet scent of sap mingles with fallen needles, warmed by the sun, and snow-soggy trails drying into dust. By summer the needles will have begun to crisp like a million tiny bonfires lit along the trail. For now, though, they smell sweet, like hope.

I run with the weather, moving higher as the days warm and my mileage increases. The high point of the Jemez 50K is ten thousand feet, and I need to acclimate my legs and lungs to the altitude. I run to nine thousand feet beneath ponderosas along Tesuque Creek, hopping boulders and shimmying along ice-slicked logs. By early May I can make it to ten thousand feet, sinking into patchy foot-deep snowbanks in the shade, scratching my shins on the crusty, dying drifts until they bleed.

Steve and I trade off, make deals. When he runs, I stay home with Pippa and Maisy; when I run, he does. Sundays are the only exception, when our friends take the girls so we can run together for a few hours—the most time we've spent alone together outside since before Pippa was born. Mostly, though, I train alone, on weekdays when he's working and the girls are at daycare. I don't want to take up family time for something that feels self-indulgent, maybe even frivolous. This is classic mother's guilt: the persistent worry that we should be caring for someone besides ourselves, tending to the daily details, being there just to be there. No matter how fast and strong I feel when I run, my guilt dogs me like a shadow.

Some days, I don't want to go. I'm sluggish, sucking wind, slogging uphill at a turtle's pace. The voice in my head is sharp and loud. It says, *Running is selfish. You should be at home with the girls.* I think about my babies in someone else's care, not so far away that I can't be with them but far enough away that I'm not. I bend over and put my hands on my knees and stare at the ground, longing to turn around, not because I'm tired in my legs, but because I'm so tired of leaving, of being left.

I don't turn around.

On the last day of March, nine weeks after I started training, I run the Rail Trail alone, nine miles out and nine miles back. Eighteen miles. It's my longest training run yet. The spring wind blows tumbleweeds against my ankles and grit into my teeth, and by the end my legs are sore and heavy, but I can't stop smiling.

A funny thing happens: The more I run, the less I think about the race. I'm not training to race; I'm running to live. What I crave, what propels me out the door, is the same thing that always has: the strength in my muscles, my beating heart, my brain lulled by motion, the wonder all around.

16

Into the Heart of Fear

Dad, self-portrait, early '60s

There's one question that people always ask me about running alone. It's the same question they ask me about taking young children down whitewater rivers or into the backcountry. I know their question because it's also the one I ask myself. *Aren't you scared?*

The answer is: Absolutely.

I'm scared almost every time I run.

I'm scared of getting lost and getting hurt and of being attacked by animals, wild and domesticated—even livestock. Dogs that lunge out at me from yards; cows grazing in backcountry meadows, staring at me with their mean, blank eyes when I sidle by in the bushes, daring me to pass. They're just cows, I chide myself, feeling foolish, but they are large and lumbering and ten times my weight, and they could mow me down in an instant.

I don't worry about lone coyotes—at forty pounds, they're too small and skittish to do any harm—but packs of coyotes, though rarely encountered, are unpredictable. (A solo female hiker was killed by a pack in Nova Scotia.) Rattlesnakes are uncommon in Santa Fe; they don't do well above seven thousand feet, or so I thought, until I leapt a pair of mating rattlers in the middle of the trail. Now I keep my eyes down.

Lightning exists in its own category of horror. On summer afternoons, heat rises from the desert and slams into the mountains, forming monsoon thunderstorms. There are more ground strikes in New Mexico than in almost any other state. The temperature can plunge twenty degrees in five minutes, and dry arroyos turn to raging rivers. I've been in the high country when the lightning strikes were so close that white flashed behind my eyelids and the thunder roared from inside my ears. I've seen the long serrated scars on ponderosa pines, their bark flayed open from top to bottom. When I run up high, I leave early in the morning so I'm off the bald peaks by early afternoon; I always keep one eye on the sky, trying to remember what to do if I get caught above the tree line. Do I squat with my shoes on, or take them off and crawl under a rocky outcropping? Or do I sprint like hell for cover?

Of all the objective risks, though, mountain lions scare me the most. They're not as big as black bears—adult males can weigh up to 180 pounds, to a bear's 300—but they're much stealthier. They prowl silently through the woods and can leap forty feet in pursuit of deer, coyotes, and rabbits; sometimes they even wander down the arroyos and into town. As the saying goes, you might have never seen a mountain lion in the wild, but they've seen you. Black bears galumph around eating berries, almost endearing in their shagginess, so big they can't hide. But cougars are wily; cougars *sneak*. When I run, I scan outcroppings for movement, listening for rustlings. I can't shake the feeling that I'm being watched.

Statistically, the biggest threat to a woman alone on the trails isn't lightning or wild animals, but people. I know this because I *am* a statistic.

It was November 18, 2008, a Tuesday, 4:15 p.m. Pippa was four months old and weighed ten pounds. I strapped her onto my chest and walked alone into the foothills on a trail I'd run countless times on my own. I'd hiked throughout my pregnancy, and walking was the only thing that could reliably put her to sleep. At the trailhead, I nursed her in the front seat while her spindly legs kicked the gearshift. Then I laid her on the hatch, wrapped her like a burrito into a cotton insert shaped like an oversize tortilla, buckled the baby carrier around my shoulders and waist, and shoved the entire package inside. She was still so small that she faced forward, legs sidesaddle, her chin to my chest. She almost always fell asleep before I even left the parking lot. The only trick was that I couldn't stop, not even to tie my shoe, or else she'd wake up and start fussing to be fed; breastfeeding her on the side of the mountain intimidated me more than climbing the mountain.

On that day, however, it wasn't Pippa's usual nap time. As I walked up the switchbacks to the top of the hill and began descending, her marble eyes flicked open and shut, watching me watching her. I could hear hikers behind me on the trail; the sun was still up but wouldn't be for long. If I hustled, I'd make it back to the car before it set.

I was a quarter mile from the parking lot when I rounded a bend and saw a man ten feet away, coming toward me. He had a shag of graying hair and wore shorts and a sweatshirt. His legs were deeply bronzed, the kind of tan you get when you live outside all year long and not on purpose. Homeless tan. I recognized him right away—a sixty-something guy Steve and I often saw trudging up the side of the road, carrying a plastic grocery bag in each hand. Shorts Man, we called him. We assumed he bivouacked in a camp on the edge of the forest with another homeless local we referred to as Duster Man, for the ankle-length oilskin coat he wore winter and summer, along with a coonskin cap.

My brain made a series of instant calculations, like a slot machine spinning. Because I'd seen him before, he was familiar, and because he was familiar, there was no reason to be afraid. And because there was no reason to be afraid, I raised my hand in greeting and kept walking toward him.

Only . . . there was something weird. Shorts Man was missing an arm. One arm was swinging next to him the way arms naturally do, but the other was gone.

Just as my brain struggled to recalibrate, the arm appeared. It had been behind his back. This was a grand, if momentary, relief. He had an arm! And the arm was—

The arm was throwing a rock.

Shorts Man was eight feet away from me. The rock was the size of a grapefruit. It wobbled at first, as though in slow motion, suspended by air and time and disbelief, and then, as my brain adapted, assumed terminal velocity straight for my head.

It hit me right above my left temple. My knees gave out. As I fell, I instinctively pressed my hand to the baby carrier and pulled Pippa toward me. My first emotion wasn't fear but outrage: *I cannot believe this fucker just threw a rock at me. At my* baby! *On the trail! This can't be happening.*

The blood dripping into my eyes was proof that it was. I lay in the dirt, but I couldn't stay there because—

He was running toward us.

The slot machine spun. Cherries, oranges, sevens. *Fuck, help, stop.* Nothing aligned, and then it did. *Get up. Get up. Get up.*

I staggered to my feet and began to run. Straight uphill, off the trail, smacking piñon branches with one arm, cradling Pippa's back with the other as he chased me. Someone was screaming so ferociously it reverberated off the hills. The person screaming was me.

I took one fast glance behind me. Shorts Man was nowhere. I'd dropped him. A couple of hikers ran toward me, screaming, "We're here! What happened?" and staring with horror-movie eyes. I looked down: There was blood splattered across the carrier and the canvas sun hood that covered Pippa's head. She had not moved a muscle or made a single sound during the attack. Had she been hit, too? I pushed back the flap and there she was, staring up at me without blinking. Unscathed. Like a baby bird in a nest that instinctively knew it must keep absolutely still and silent to survive.

The hikers escorted me down the trail, one on either side, and called 9-1-1. Shorts Man had vanished into the trees. "You're lucky it didn't hit your temple. It could have killed you," the paramedic told me in the ambulance on the way to the hospital, where the ER doctor would give me four stitches and Pippa a clean bill of health.

This is what I didn't say aloud but couldn't stop thinking: The rock was the size of Pippa's head. What if it had struck her instead of me?

A few days later, the man was caught and arrested. He'd been living in a tent in a thicket of trees just off the trail, adjacent to a neighborhood. Residents sometimes gave him rides and glassed his camp worriedly through binoculars from their kitchen windows. On the morning of the attack, he'd suffered a schizophrenic break; he thought his body was on fire and crawled into the creek to put it out. He was hiking back to his camp when he came across me and became paranoid that *I* was going to hurt *him*. He pleaded guilty to assault and endangerment of a child, both felonies, and was sentenced to twelve months in the county jail.

After the attack, I stopped hiking with Pippa. I stopped hiking altogether. Even when I pushed Pippa in her stroller on the sidewalk downtown, I flinched when someone approached us abruptly. When I started missing the trails too much, I called friends to go hiking with us.

A year later, in November 2009, I got pregnant for the second time. Pippa was sixteen months old, and so rambunctious she no longer wanted to be cooped up in the carrier, so I hiked alone once more. The man who'd attacked me was still in jail, I reasoned. What were the odds of the same thing happening twice?

I walked up Picacho almost every day, carrying a small vial of pepper spray Steve had bought for me. When I got to the summit, I sat on a rock and looked for ravens. They were my sign that everything was okay: with the baby inside me and the trail that would lead me home. I'd hear them first, their wings whooshing above the piñons, cawing as though through a mouthful of pebbles. Then I'd look up and see them rise on the thermals, onyx against the clear sky, whirling and chortling and dive-bombing one another, but never in malice, and a calm would come over me. They knew nothing of the turmoil on the ground. They dipped and soared, the embodiment of fearlessness and freedom.

There's a difference between fear and anxiety. Fear is a response to a known threat; it emanates from our cerebral cortex, the center for rational thought and the only part of the human brain able to distinguish between real and imagined danger. Anxiety, however, is dread of a perceived or imagined threat, of what *could* happen; it is anticipatory, not actual. It originates from the amygdala, which triggers the classic fight-or-flight response, which has kept us alive for millennia. It is the voice inside of us that says that man on the trail doesn't look right. Turn around. *NOW.*

During periods of prolonged stress or trauma, the amygdala's warning system can become too sensitive, overriding the cortex. It's increasingly difficult to switch off the fight-or-flight impulse and distinguish between real threats and imagined disasters. Flooded with the stress hormones cortisol and adrenaline, your body exists in a state of constant anxiety, immobilized in clammy terror, battered by intrusive thoughts. The worries feed on themselves, magnifying until you're locked in a vicious cycle of perpetual alarm.

Running long distances doesn't erase my anxiety, but it does help me manage it. Caught up in the physical effort, I detach from the circuitous worry in my brain. There are practical hazards that require my attention, like looking for bears and not tripping over my own feet and pitching off a cliff. At night, I no longer lie awake in a state of hypervigilance, convinced I'm dying. I'm so exhausted, I fall asleep as soon as I turn off the light.

And while I still fret about invisible diseases, my body tells a different story. My quads are taut, my glutes more defined. I can run uphill with a friend and talk without huffing too noticeably. My skin is clear and has a healthy glow. The circles under my eyes have faded; the frown creases beside my mouth are less pronounced. Running is both cure and proof of the cure. If I can run twenty miles and come home and take the girls to the park and finish a story on deadline, I can't possibly be dying of cancer.

From a young age we're conditioned to suppress fear. This has always been my strategy. I feigned bravery in front of Dad at all costs. I put myself in the crosshairs of risk to prove I wasn't a wimp. I worked in an office of macho guys, where vulnerability in the wilderness, in writing, and in life was discouraged.

But trying to repress fear is counterproductive. It only makes it worse. Fear itself isn't good or bad. It's our resistance to it—our fear of fear, our *anxiety*—that makes us suffer so. The trick is not to run from it but to follow it. "Make friends with your fear," Natalie sometimes says. "What's beneath it?"

This was the same thing, more or less, I'd heard when I went to

Utah earlier that winter with my friend Mary. We'd signed up for a skiing clinic led by former world champion Kristen Ulmer, but it wasn't your typical sports camp: We wouldn't learn downhill technique; her coaching was all mental—by training our minds to be more expansive and present, we would become more confident on and off the mountain.

On the first day, I rode the chairlift with Kristen and two other participants. She gave us a scenario: Envision our absolute worst fear; close our eyes and imagine it happening. I'd done this so many times already that the image came easily. Losing one of the girls— this was without a doubt the absolute worst thing. As I sat there with my skis swinging above the powdery slopes, I pictured unthinkable loss. I *felt* it. My eyes stung and I started to cry. It was so painful, but for once there was nowhere to run. I just sat there, sobbing quietly.

Finally Kristen spoke. "Breathe in your worst fear and breathe out the possibility of ever letting go of that fear." This is not what I wanted to hear. I'd come to Alta to exorcise my anxiety once and for all, to burn it out of me in one go, or, if not, then to squelch it as best I could. Bad idea. "If you ignore your fear," Kristen continued, "it becomes like a sullen teenager, raging in the basement, tearing the place apart. It becomes anxiety." She had faced so many of her own fears—perilous couloirs, avalanches, mediocrity, failure. There is never any end to the fears. The trick is to move toward them, not away.

Running is as good a way as any to try. I'm alone with the voices in my head for hours at a time. I can study my anxiety for patterns; I see its ragged, wily persistence. I greet it with a halfhearted wave as I would someone I've known a very long time but am not entirely happy to see. *Oh, you again.* Some days my worry is more acute and sometimes less, but it's always part of the package: inescapable, chronic, not so very different from love itself. The crux is to live as big as you can, to love it all even when you stand to lose it all.

On the first of April 2011, my cellphone rings. "This is the Santa Fe County Adult Correctional Facility," a woman's voice says.

I cannot fathom why she might be calling me. I think, *Is this some kind of April Fool's joke?*

She says, "I'm calling about a case that may be of personal interest to you."

Great, I think, my confusion turning to irritation. *Who got arrested? Steve?*

She continues: "I'm notifying you that Bill B___ was released today." She explains that my attacker is free to go where he chooses, that his psychological treatment has ended, and that if I have trouble with him in the future, I can file a restraining order.

I know he probably has no memory of the attack and wouldn't be able to pick me out of a crowd. "Thank you for letting me know," I reply, and hang up. There's nothing else to say.

Now Bill is back in the world. Some days I pass him in my car on the street. He is browned by the sun, still limping with his stiff-legged gait, still carrying his grocery bags. He is favoring one bad ankle, and he looks older, less threatening and more vulnerable. Sometimes I see him skulking along the perimeter of the playground where I take Pippa to play. He's no more than twenty feet away, his eyes lowered, and I recoil instinctively and look away to let him pass. To let myself, and my fear, pass.

I have to recalibrate again. In my new hierarchy of risk, running is safer than hiking, because it is faster. I can get away more quickly. After my terrible encounter with Bill, I understand things about myself that I've known but never quite trusted: That I can run. That I am fast. That my body and mind will always know what to do. And that running isn't something to fear. It could save my life. It already has.

I don't go back to the trail where it happened. I stay in my mountains, where the slopes are steeper and less accessible. These hills are farther from town and do not border private property, and to some people the remoteness might make them seem riskier, but in my logic, this makes them safer. I learn to count cars at the trail-head. More cars means more people to help me if I need it. But the wrong cars—sketchy vans with boarded-up windows or pickup trucks with little wooden shacks listing on the bed—are worse. I go on instinct. Sometimes when I drop into a hollow by the creek or run off the back side of Atalaya into shadows and something about the light or air feels wrong, goosebumps rise on my forearms and I pick up two small rocks, just in case.

A certain amount of fear in the wilderness is healthy. It keeps you alert. Like your lungs and your legs, courage is a muscle you can train; I have strategies for mitigating risk. I always tell Steve where I'm going. I never run without my cellphone (though I'm often out of range) and my pepper spray. Sometimes I take my friend Blair's seventy-pound Rhodesian ridgeback, a breed that originated in Africa as lion hunters.

I rehearse what-ifs in my head. If I see a mountain lion, I'll yell and hold my pack above my head to make myself look less like prey and more like a predator. I will wave a stick in its face; never, ever run; and fight back if I have to. If I come upon a bear, I will back away slowly. If I fall and twist my ankle crossing the creek, I'll soak it in the cool water and then hobble out to the nearest trailhead. If, on a desolate two-track dirt road where pickup trucks routinely rumble by with gun racks, someone pulls over and comes after me, I know what to do, because I've done it before. I'll run.

I run the same trails every week, committing them to memory, pushing a little farther and higher as the weeks go by. Each time I come home safely, I feel more comfortable. I know this is flawed logic. Animals and people are erratic, and risk factors shift with the weather, the season, the day. Past performance is no guarantee of future results.

I have so many scars. The pink ripple on my knee from falling on Atalaya, the nearly invisible *x* on my forehead where I got rammed by an old-fashioned metal chairlift at a ski resort in West Virginia when I was five. The divot in my chin from when I took a surfboard in the mouth off the coast of Mexico, the pale white line on my right heel from when I was ten and waded barefoot through a river and sliced it open on a rock.

But this scar I can't see or feel. It's hidden beneath my hairline. The doctor sewed it so neatly, it may have vanished entirely. The scar that remains is in my mind. I will never again not think about risk. I will never again take my safety in the wilderness for granted. Yet each time I ask the questions—*Am I taking too great a chance? Should I keep going?*—the answers are always the same. The answer is no. No, I will never give up my trails for fear. That would be an even greater risk.

And the answer is yes. Yes, I still love this world and its wildness, *for its* wildness. And for mine.

17

What I Carry

Old Rag Mountain, Virginia, 1983

Sometimes when I tell someone I'm training for an ultramarathon, a look of incomprehension crosses their face. "Oh, God," they shudder. "What do you *think* about when you run for so long?"

What *don't* I think about? I think of everything, all the most boring, banal things. I think about whether my legs hurt and what I ate for breakfast and if my Achilles are sore and if the pain is real or just imaginary. I think about whether I'm hungry, and the stories I'm writing and people I have to call, and what Pippa and Maisy are doing right that very minute—I always think about the girls. I think about mountain lions and whether I'm pushing too hard or not hard enough and whether my heart is going to beat right out of my chest. I think about grocery shopping and how I wish I were a better cook and about bills I've been avoiding and whether our joint bank account is running low on money and if I need to make dentist appointments for the girls, and am I shirking my duties by running and is Steve's patience wearing thin? (Probably.) I think about Mom—would she be worried if she knew how much I was running? (Yes, definitely.) And I think about whether I will ever be ready for the race.

The unofficial motto of ultrarunning is "relentless forward progress." This doesn't mean that ultrarunners never stop; it just means that when they do, they start running again. Over the course of a three- or four-hour run, I usually pause a couple of times to tie my shoes or eat a snack. Sometimes I stop to pee behind a tree or take a picture or jot a few ideas with the pen and index card I stash in my pack. When I run up the mountain at sunrise, I always stop at the granite ledge on the summit and breathe in the day. I might stretch or do sit-ups in the dirt, but I am careful not to dally for more than a few minutes; otherwise, my muscles might get tight or my sensible thoughts will come rushing back, the ones that say, *You've gone far enough. Aren't you bored yet? It's time to go home.*

Of all adventure sports, trail running is the simplest. Unlike triathletes, runners don't need a carbon-fiber road bike or a wetsuit. It's not like mountaineering, which requires a rack of gear and a partner on the other end of the rope. You don't need a gym membership or the latest moisture-wicking nylon shorts. You could be the person running down the side of the road at noon in a black track suit and a *Rocky* scowl, sweating profusely through soggy cotton, and this would be fine. Because all you need is the willpower to go out the door on the days when the last thing you feel like doing is going out the door. All you need to do is start wherever you are and take the next step and then the next, a few more every week.

But there's a limit to going light, even in running. The farther and longer you go, the more you have to carry.

Ninety minutes is widely considered the threshold for how long an athlete can perform moderate aerobic exercise without eating and drinking. Our bodies store glycogen in our muscles for fuel, and most runners typically have enough in reserve to go for an hour and a half before their energy flags, their muscles fatigue, and their brains become fuzzy—in the endurance world, this is known as bonking. Beyond the ninety-minute mark, the typical runner needs approximately two hundred calories an hour; every body is different, of course, and how far I can run without refueling depends on the day, the weather, the trail conditions, and what I've eaten in the past twenty-four hours.

I experiment with carrying different foods. Sports bars pack a lot of calories in a small package, but they can be chewy and hard to digest when you're trying to eat on the run (and forget about winter, when they freeze solid and practically rip your teeth from your gums). Energy gels belong to a category of food product—emphasis on *product*—that, as an endurance athlete, you can't live without but desperately wish you could. The first time I squeezed one into my mouth, I thought I was going to barf it right back up. It had a sickly sweet vanilla flavor, a translucent tint, and a gloppy consistency. The tiny plastic packets contain a few squirts and about ninety calories of almost pure sucrose. I want to hate them, but the sugar goes straight into my bloodstream like a jolt of electricity.

Most of the time, I stuff a couple of Gu gels down my sports bra for easy access. (It helps to have the chest of a thirteen-year-old.) When I get home, my mouth is slathered with a thick, sugary film, and I have to peel the crusty empty packets off my bare skin. This is a little-known hazard of ultrarunning: You will get into the best shape of your life, but you will rot your teeth out in the process.

Hydration is a trickier formula. I carry water in four ten-ounce plastic flasks in a nylon waist belt. The belt has a tiny front pouch in which I can fit my car key and maybe an extra Gu. In two of the flasks, I drop an effervescent electrolyte tablet, which helps replace the sodium and potassium lost when I sweat. The third and fourth flasks I fill with plain water. On my longest runs, I carry two iodine pills in a plastic baggie, in case I run out of water and need to refill from the stream; the iodine gives the water a grimy, metallic taste but kills parasites like giardia that could make me sick.

I carry a bear bell attached to my pack and my pepper spray, and often I clip my iPod to my pack and thread my earbuds under my T-shirt so the cord doesn't slap my face. There are some in the trail running community who frown upon running with music, but for me it's a trifecta of happiness, the ultimate mood boost. When I'm outside, moving through nature, listening to songs I love, I become more, not less, attuned to my senses, my surroundings, and the physical sensations in my body. I'm not fussy: I'll listen to almost any song with a good story and a steady beat. Slow, fast, pop, rock, rap, folk, Bob Dylan, Alicia Keys, Lucinda Williams, Eminem, Ryan Adams, the Boss, even deep cuts from Dad's college jazz album. Country songs are the best for the long, grinding middle miles: Someone's always down on their luck and clawing their way back.

I carry all these things, and I carry my body: five feet five inches and 112 pounds. The body I've always had, except during my pregnancies, when my hips vanished for four years. Both times, my body came back to me as I came back into my body and began to run again. My waist slimmed, my hips reemerged, my shoulders and chest narrowed, and my quads and calves became leaner. Even my feet, which had grown half a size during pregnancy, got smaller as the muscles in my arches grew stronger.

It is not a burden to carry my body, because my body also carries me. This is the way it has always been. And I carry love and fear and the cancer that killed Dad, his regrets and mistakes, his loyalty and his infidelity. And always the wondering: *Why?*

Now, when Meg and I talk about Virginia, we no longer say "When are you going to Dad's?" or "We should book our flights to Dad's." By mutual agreement, undiscussed, of course, we say "Huntly." It isn't his anymore.

In late April, we fly to Huntly to clean out his office. Outside, everything is alive again: dogwoods and cherry blossoms blooming pink beside the house, the fields a carpet of green. This is the busiest time of year for Lesley's horse-breeding business, and the day we arrive, a new foal is born, a gangly chestnut who suckles her mother and paces skittishly in her stall. I don't feel the raw agony of grief as much as the dull ache of loss. Dad's absence has a permanence now, like a lump in the throat that won't go all the way down.

He's been dead for sixteen months, but his basement looks like he's just gotten up to get a cup of coffee—still disheveled, only dustier. Lesley has to walk through the room every time she does laundry and, though she's been patient, I can tell it's beginning to weigh on her. More than once she's reminded us that his papers and memorabilia are ours for the taking. "Yerdad"—this is what she's always called him in emails or notes—"wanted you to have everything."

First we have to finish his photo archives. Before he died, Dad estimated that he'd cataloged 90 percent of his pictures, and we promised him we'd try to track down the remaining images. They could be anywhere, in any form: contact sheets in the dozens of white binders on his bookshelves; black-and-white prints in his filing cabinets; negatives in plastic tubs in his old darkroom; digital files on his thumb drive in his safety-deposit box, the key to which has gone missing.

We follow clues around the room like we're on one of the scavenger hunts Dad used to make for us outside, trying to think as he would have. When we get stuck, all we have to do is look and the answer is there in front of us: on a Post-it note scrawled with obscure explanations—sticky notes from the grave!—or in an email to Jenna, an assistant who'd been helping him with his archives right before he died. The synchronicity is so eerie it's almost funny. *When in doubt, choose the obvious,* he seems to be telling us. *The answer is in front of you if you open your eyes and slow down.* Even in death, Dad is half a step ahead of us. We leave nearly everything where we found it, like a crime scene investigation. It seems reckless to dismantle the room, lest we trample the trail of crumbs he's left for us.

After a while, Lesley clears her throat and says loudly, "Well, I've got work in the barn," and gets up to go. I know the foal is mostly an excuse to leave us alone with Dad's things. Meg and I sit on the floor, opening file drawers filled with family memorabilia and speckled black-and-white photographs. From the back of one I pull a leather-bound baby book. Pressed between the pages is a wallet-size parchment-paper envelope containing a lock of fine black hair.

"Oh, my God," I say, holding it up gingerly for Meg to see. It's the first hair of my newborn father and the very last remnant of his physical self. Fingering the silky strands is like touching a ghost, the invisible soul of someone I never knew: Dad as an infant, his original self, blinking and yawning, wet head and clutching hands, the baby who would become a man, my father, and someday die.

I put the baby book back in its file and wander into Dad's old darkroom. When he and Lesley bought Huntly Stage, he set it up in a small walk-in closet next to the laundry room, but after a while he stopped using it. Cameras were going digital, and it was easier to get his prints made at Kmart in Front Royal, like everyone else. Eventually he converted the darkroom back to a storage room. The shelves at eye level are stacked with wrapping paper, gift boxes, and old family photo albums I've seen before, but lower down are dozens of plain plastic containers I haven't. I open one. It's stuffed with eight-by-ten black-and-white photographs in white envelopes. Many are landscapes—wintry hills and deserted college campuses—but there are whole folders of young women: close-up portraits in profile, serious eyes, demure smiles, glossy dark hair swept back to one side.

In 2004, when I called Mom about Dad's letter, she told me about their first year of marriage, when they were living above a carriage house in Connecticut and Dad was taking pictures for *The New Era* and building his portfolio. On the side, he made portraits of women. It was all still innocent, Mom insisted, but I thought I could detect a trace of uncertainty in her voice. Now, seeing their eyes stare back at me in the half-light of Dad's basement, imagining them staring back at my father, it seems like the start of something.

Dad, Wittenberg, Ohio, 1958

Below the plastic tub is a carton labeled BETSY. Inside are dozens of letters, hundreds perhaps, exchanged in 1962, the year my mother and father were courting, each penned on thin sheaves of stationery. In girlish blue handwriting, Mom writes about engagement parties and wedding plans. Dad's earnest replies are typewritten and many pages long.

Beside it on the shelf is another box, and another and another, each one labeled neatly with a name. Names I don't recognize: Laura, Mary Lou, Nancy, Pam.

I know who they are: the women Dad loved before he loved us and the women he loved after. And maybe even *while* he loved us.

The goodbye boy.

I feel my cheeks redden for my father; for myself, for discovering his most intimate writings; for Meg, in the next room, who doesn't know; and for Lesley, upstairs, who probably does. It would be so easy to snap the lids back on and walk away.

"Meg!" I call, before I change my mind. "Check this out!"

She comes in and rifles through the cartons for a long time without saying anything.

"Did you know?" I ask, afraid of her answer.

Meg nods. "Since college. Dad told me when we were driving somewhere. I didn't want to hear it when he was telling me, and afterwards I wished I didn't know." Twenty years she's known, and she kept it to herself. I'm not mad, just surprised, though of course I shouldn't be. We are expert stuffers, she and I, raised by the best.

"Do you think Lesley knows?" I ask.

"I don't know. She must. How could she not?"

The boxes are a map through a minefield, and the letters are the mines, tidily organized and left for anyone to trip.

I go where I always go when I need to breathe: outside, in bare legs and sneakers, letting gravity pull me down the hill. I smell Dad in the sweet scent of spring grass, growing anyway, without him. I imagine him pulling away in his pickup, feeling content, distracted, overburdened, but alive. Maybe he would feel his aliveness, or maybe, in his haste, he would take it for granted. But this also would make him alive, and human. How I wish he had one more afternoon, one more chance to choose.

At the bottom of the hill, without thinking, I veer off the driveway, climb over the split rail fence, and cut across the tall grass. My instinct is to walk, and, rather than push through my reluctance like I usually do, this time I gladly give in to it. My body registers where I'm going before my brain does. I'm trying to find the old footpath through the woods to a grove of pines on the hillside. We followed the trail as kids, scavenging along in hot pursuit of the clues Dad set for us, one slip of paper leading to the next. The pine tree grove was the lone clump of green in an otherwise colorless winter skyline, and though it consisted of only six or seven trees, when we stood beneath the boughs, looking up, it felt much bigger. In summer it was harder to find, as the entire slope was awash in green, and you could traipse in circles, looking, and when at last you found it, it was as though you'd chanced upon a hidden, magical place.

I angle across a low slope, scanning the edge of the forest for signs of the path. In my distant memory, Lesley buried her black dog, Jason, in a grave on this hillside after he'd been shot by deer hunters. I walk slowly, following a damp creek bed uphill, beating my way through barberry bushes, scraping my shins on brambles, looking for any trace of footprints or indentations on the ground or trampled leaves—anything.

Nothing.

The longer I search, the more insistent I become. Years ago, Dad carved a sign and hung it from a tree in the woods. He inscribed it with a quote by Stephen Vincent Benét: *When Daniel Boone goes by, at night | The phantom deer arise | And all lost, wild America | Is burning in their eyes.* Dad would regale us with stories about the wandering woodsman as we walked, and the sign seemed to rear up out of nowhere, and never in quite the same place as I remembered it. I found this mystifying and a little spooky, as though the ghost of Boone were still out there, flitting between the shadows in his coonskin cap, somewhere just beyond sight.

When I get to the pine grove, or what I think is the pine grove, my shins are bleeding. It's not a grove of trees but a pair, and they are shorter and spindlier than I remember. It's been two years, at least, since Dad walked these woods and thirty-five years since I did, and the trail, wherever it was, has long since grown over. I keep walking downhill, toward the pasture, knowing I won't find the sign. It's been reclaimed by the trees, or maybe it never existed. Maybe I'd imagined it.

At the meadow's edge, I slop across the creek in my sneakers, rinsing the blood from my ankles, and duck beneath the thick cover of persimmon trees. I feel Dad in the space between sun and shade, where the sunlight strafes the branches, filtering through the narrow openings in the trunks like tuxedo stripes. There are so many questions I want to ask him. *Talk to me, Daddy,* I whisper. But the only sounds are a gust of wind lifting the leaves and my blood drumming in my ears.

When I get back to the house, I leave my shoes by the back door and tiptoe guiltily down to the basement alone, as though I'm snooping where I'm not supposed to. Everything's so neatly organized and labeled, I know Dad wanted us to find it, but what, if anything, did he want us to *do* with it? There's no answer scrawled in his handwriting, just all the boxes beckoning.

Sitting on the floor, hugging my knees, I skim a few of the letters. There are letters to and from the girl he'd known when he was younger, with whom a relationship would have been, for countless reasons, taboo. His first true love in high school, with whom his parents feared he was too serious —the one who got away, the one he pined for on and off for fifty-five years. The college girlfriend in Ohio, with sultry eyes, who'd gone off and married someone else. The red-haired temptress in Washington. "A." from Idaho Ave., for whom he'd left his marriage but who, in the end, he couldn't love.

The correspondence is enthusiastic and erratic. He's saved not only the women's letters to him, but copies of his letters to them. He'd done the same with his letters from his parents, Uncle Phil, and his college bandmates. I'd seen the folders on his computer with all the emails he'd batted back and forth with Meg and me over the years. He wanted to capture both sides of the conversation, the whole picture.

With some of these women, there are long periods of silence and then contact resumes, sometimes many years or decades later. Occasionally, there is the suggestion of a meeting—never, seemingly, fulfilled—but just as often the talk is of grown children and grandchildren, music playing and charity work. These women had creaky knees and retired husbands. Why did he feel such fondness for them? Had he told them he was sick, or did they think his silence was another unexplained chapter in their sporadic communication? I wonder briefly if I should write and let them know, but even as I'm composing the email in my head—*I'm David's daughter. I'm sorry to inform you that he passed away. I found his letters to you*—I know that I won't. Not because I don't want to hurt them, but because, if I'm honest with myself, I do. Let *them* wonder now.

Only one of the women he'd loved was my mother, and he had loved her imperfectly, disloyally, and he had been afraid to stay and afraid to go. So in the end it had been her decision. Mom had wanted me to know this, when we talked about Dad's letter. She didn't sound recriminatory, but she wanted to be clear: *She had chosen.*

Mom outside the carriage house, Essex, Connecticut, 1963

It was the Friday of Memorial Day weekend, May 1974. Meg and I were sitting on the front steps of the house on Legation Street, waiting for Dad to come home from work. We were singing, *When*

Daddy comes marching home again, to the tune of the Civil War bal-lad "When Johnny Comes Marching Home." We sang this song so often for him that we knew the words by heart. Over and over we belted out the chorus, the volume and force of our *Hurrahs!* becom-ing ever more insistent because Daddy was late and the long week-end stretched before us. The dogwoods and azaleas bloomed riotously beside the front door, and we pressed our bare knees to-gether, and we sang and we watched until finally his dark green Triumph convertible rounded the corner on 32nd Street and slid to a stop at the curb.

We are tapping our bare feet in time with the tempo. I remember the beat, low and slightly mournful at first, then rising steadily to a hopeful crescendo.

Dad climbs out of the car and crosses onto the sidewalk.

"When Daddy comes marching ho—"

Here the fragments of memory dissolve—the sweet pink blos-soms, the rhythm and the words of the song embedded where so many memories live, beyond conscious remembering, not in the brain but in the body. My toes curling around the concrete steps, fingernails chipping anxiously at the peeling black paint on the railing. The happy expectancy of waiting, wondering. *Where is he?!* eclipsed by the deep thrum of worry: What's *wrong*?

All of it subsumed by what happens next.

Inside, Dad says to Mom, "I want to go to Charleston for the weekend." He would have blurted this, fast and reckless. That he wants to go with A., his secretary. He hasn't thought it through, not all the way. He just wants to go. The way he says it, not a question—like he can leave and come home again after. As though nothing will have changed. As if my mother would put up with this. A terrible, callous miscalculation.

Because of all the scenarios Dad might have imagined, this was not one of them. My mother rewriting her story, *our* story. Chang-ing the ending.

Mom tells him that if he goes to Charleston, he can't come back.

This is the last straw, it's over. She is sure. She has to be. She has us to look after, and herself.

This is the moment we'd been barreling toward and away from our whole lives, a stone tossed in the water, rippling outward in waves. Dad wants to go to Charleston with another woman, and not even his daughters singing for his arrival can change his mind.

How could we not have changed his mind?

And so when I run, I also carry Dad's letters and notebooks, stacked where I left them, so many still unread, on the floor by his filing cabinet. And I carry the other version of my life. The one where Dad opens his mouth to say "I want to go to Charleston" but hears our chirpy baby voices singing and says instead, "I'm home."

Sometimes Dad comes to me when I run. He arrives not as a voice or a thought but as a sensation, a faint waft of air on the skin. The suggestion of memory. It's almost always when I am running down-hill toward home, back to my girls and Steve, waiting for me. There are no words, just a feeling: *I'm here with you.* And he is, but not for long. Only a few steps and, just as abruptly, he's gone, swirling off to whomever or wherever he goes next. He has no form, no per-manence. He is air and light. He is memory and love and regret. He is joy in the running. And he is joy.

These are the days Dad carries *me*.

Three weeks before the Jemez 50K, I'm running through the pon-derosas when I feel a sharp pinching, like a chicken bone lodged in my throat—the clammy certainty that something is going terribly wrong and that I or someone I love is about to die. I gulp at the air, trying to slow my choppy breathing, and take inventory: The girls are at preschool, Steve is at work. I'm safe on this trail. The sky is blue, the trees are sweet with sap. My legs are strong, my heart is beating. *Everything's going to be okay.*

Instinctively, I begin to whisper, "Dad, let me go! Let me go!" I look around furtively, but there's no one in sight. The only sound is my voice. It grows louder and more animated with every step. I've been carrying his illness and his angst, his guilt over leaving, his inability to stay, but I don't have to anymore.

"Dad, I'm letting you go! I'm letting you go!" I'm shouting now, my pace quickening to match the cadence of my words. "Your sadness is not my sadness, Dad! Your story is not my story. I am not you, Dad. I love you and I'm letting you go!"

I know that if I keep running, I will shed my pain, which is his pain, also, and send it out into the trees and the wide New Mexico sky, and I will break through.

PART THREE

Upward

Let the beauty we love be what we do.

—RUMI

18

Plunging In

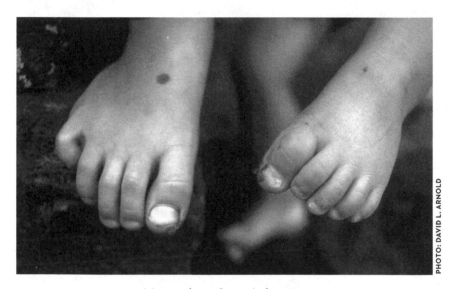

Meg and me, Stony Lake, 1973

Mornings start early in our house. They start whether Steve and I are pressed tightly together in sleep, the cat curled into her spot on his left hip, or I'm tiptoeing down the hall to light out for a run. I swear the girls have sonar: They can't possibly hear me above the din of the white-noise machines in their rooms, but they can *sense* me. Pippa's door hinges creak open, the whole of her spilling into the kitchen. "Mama, I'm hungry!" I slice her a banana and remind her to let Maisy and Steve sleep. Then I slide out the back door and into the unimaginable good luck of dawn.

When I come back, it's an assault of small bodies, dogs barking,

Steve asking, "Do we have a grocery list started?" But I'm always more here after I have been there. After a run, when I'm tired and content, the world seems shiny and full of hope, and I see that the commotion I found exasperating only yesterday is now the very thing I love most. I sit on the front porch with both girls, listening to the scrub jays chattering in the poplar trees, wishing spring would last longer, that Pippa could stay three, maddening and precious, with seashell ears and wise old eyes, forever.

For my last long training run before the race, I get up at first light and meet my friend Blair at the Winsor Trail. The Winsor climbs 3,700 feet in ten miles, all of it singletrack, from the village of Tesuque to the Santa Fe ski basin. From there you can keep running seven miles and another 2,300 vertical feet to the summit of 12,600-foot Santa Fe Baldy or drop down to the alpine Lake Katherine. You can follow the Winsor up and over the back of the range into the Pecos Valley or run north through the roadless, remote Pecos Wilderness and the spiky, thirteen-thousand-foot Truchas Peaks and nearly the whole way to Taos, almost entirely on trails.

In its first three miles, the Winsor dips and rises over small, sandy badlands, climbs steadily under cover of two-hundred-year-old ponderosas, and fords Big Tesuque Creek eleven times. Only three of the crossings have narrow wooden bridges. I always go back and forth: Should I keep my feet dry by balancing on slippery logs or stepping-stones and risk turning an ankle, or just run right through the water and suffer the consequences of cold feet? I usually opt for dry shoes, especially on days like today when the creek is running fast and high with snowmelt.

The air is still cool, not yet sixty degrees, and though my bare arms have been pumping hard, like my feet, they're rubbery and cold. In a meadow filled with wild irises, I unwrap an energy bar for breakfast and give half to Blair. No one's awake but us, and the silence is thick, enclosing us, wrapping us in the forest.

We run for four more miles, above where the trail leaves the creek, up a steep, rubbly pitch, through a second meadow, to my favorite stretch, rolling easily along a ridge. I float through the dewy morning, over pine needles. My body is light and loose, as though no effort is required of it, and time is without measure or meaning.

When we reluctantly turn around, the trail is still deserted and all ours. This time, I don't think; I run right into the frigid creek, plunging up to my shins. In a few miles I'll be home; there's no longer any reason to keep my feet dry. Yesterday the water was a curling cornice of snow hanging off the side of a mountain; today it's falling over itself in a rush to the Rio Grande. It fills my shoes and puddles inside my socks. I crash through the pools, ignoring my numb feet, the sharp stab of cold between my toes, skipping and sloshing the whole way down.

This is runner's high: the rush of mood-enhancing endorphins winging through my bloodstream, filling me with confidence and pleasure. The longer and harder I run, the more intense the rush. Sometimes runner's high lasts for hours, sometimes into the next day, and it makes me want to do crazy, exuberant things like buy a new car or invite all my friends over for dinner even though we have nothing in the fridge.

But this is the first time I've experienced such a prolonged runner's high *while* I'm running. In his book about running, Sakyong Mipham calls this the second, or lion, phase of training, named in honor of the Tibetan snow lion, which represents "delight, discipline, and auspiciousness." In the Lion phase, running comes more naturally, and it's naturally more joyous. You're in better shape, and your technique is more proficient, so you don't have to think as much when you run. This enables you to tune in to your surroundings and experience what he calls "panoramic awareness."

Ten days before my first ultramarathon, my mind is strong and calm and my body is ready. All I need to do now is remember this feeling.

The night before the race, Steve and I drop the girls off at a friend's and we sit on the terrace, eating two helpings of pasta each. I've laid out my race gear and organized my pack, but when I get into bed, I'm so jittery I can't fall asleep. When I finally do drift off, I dream that we've missed the start and are so far behind we need to sprint to catch up.

At the starting line in Los Alamos, a couple hundred runners mill around in the dark, checking their race bibs and fiddling with their packs. I'm trying to look natural, as if showing up before dawn to run thirty-one miles is something I do all the time, while simultaneously scanning the crowd to assess the competition; everyone looks serious and very fast. Ten minutes before the start, Steve and I stash our down jackets in the car and huddle together, shivering, my heart ricocheting against my ribs.

Then the official yells "Go!" and I forget to be afraid. Steve and I go out together at the back of the front pack. The sun is rising as we leave the dirt road for a singletrack trail that drops into Los Alamos Canyon. Within the first mile, the leaders begin to spread out, and it no longer feels like we're racing, just running together.

In the hurried last moments before we left the house, I stuck a pin Lesley had made for Dad's seventieth birthday onto the front of my waist belt. It's a close-up photo of Dad's face beneath the words "Sensational 7-0!" He's wearing his red sweatshirt, and his smile is so huge it shows all his teeth, reminding me to keep going but not take myself too seriously. For the first few miles, I hear the pin clanking against my waist belt, and every few minutes I reflexively reach down and pat his face.

Somewhere after the first aid station, at mile 5, I graze my waist pack with my fingers. *Shit, shit.* The pin is gone. Steve is in front of me and runners are strung out behind me, and the trail is narrow and bordered by prickly scrub oak and cacti. I'll never find it. It's pointless to try. Better to leave Dad where he lies, in the silty Jemez dust, on a rolling stretch of trail I know he'd love.

In the early miles, the course traverses canyons and foothills at the base of the Jemez Mountains. Steve lets me set the pace, his feet clopping behind me along the hard-packed dirt trail. We are running easily enough to keep up a conversation, which consists mostly of Steve announcing the Latin name for every wildflower he sees: *Lupinus argenteus, Castilleja, Penstemon.* I let his words hypnotize me and feel my body moving all its parts in the right order: feet, legs, arms, repeat, inhale, exhale.

By mile 7 or 8, we begin to catch up to people and pass them. They are the tail end of the fifty-mile race, which started an hour before us. The runners are jogging the flats and the downhills, but as soon as they come to an incline, they decelerate to a walk, hiking them casually, as if they're just out for a stroll. It hadn't dawned on me that walking might be part of ultrarunning, but I see now that it has a purpose, especially in mountain races like this one: It conserves energy.

Just ahead of us is the longest and toughest ascent of the day—a six-mile, 2,500-foot climb to the summit of 10,440-foot Pajarito Mountain. As the pitch gets steeper, we slow from a run to a jog. Behind me, Steve's footsteps change audibly—heavier and slower. I turn to look. He's walking, but because his legs are so much longer than mine, it's easy for him to keep up. His stride is long and easy, and he is not breathing especially hard, a fact I find momentarily disheartening—not because I am trying to race him but because if he can walk as quickly as I can jog, I must be moving awfully slowly.

When I turn to look again, he has a pained expression on his face. "My stomach is cramping," he says. "I think I need to find a tree."

Most ultra trail races are staged on remote backcountry trails, with only periodic access to roads or services, so there are few opportunities to use a proper bathroom. Over the years, I've gotten comfortable peeing almost anywhere I can find a bush or a tree or any kind of cover. Leaves or rocks will do for toilet paper, but usually I just pull up my shorts and keep running. Pooping is more complicated; if you can't hold it till the next aid station, you have to go well off the trail and dig a hole.

Steve swerves off the course and disappears behind a clump of shrub oaks, calling over his shoulder, "Keep going! Don't wait for me!"

I'm reluctant to leave him, but I need to keep my momentum up the mountain. I keep jogging, looking over my shoulder now and then, but Steve's nowhere in sight. The solitude is lonely at first, but then I lose myself in the repetitive demands of running: drinking sips from my bottle, forcing myself to eat Gu every thirty minutes. Time means nothing to me; the day is vast and simple. I have only one job to do, and I'm doing it.

The trail to the summit of Pajarito Mountain skirts a small ski resort of the same name. Ski slopes without snow are rarely a pretty sight, and Pajarito's are scarred by raw, treeless cuts and chairlifts tilting emptily, like phantoms from another season. Above me, through the trees, I can just make out the twin tips of the radio towers near the summit and aim for them, my thighs heavy and unresponsive.

When you've been running uphill for more than an hour, you can't help but fantasize about going down. Anything—*anything*—will feel better than this! The sad irony is that while descending a mountain may be a mental reprieve, rarely does it bring much physical relief. Your body is fighting gravity the whole way, your glutes, knees, and quads forced to act like shock absorbers so you don't fall.

The descent from Pajarito shoots down the grassy spine of a double-black ski run so steep that, if my legs buckled, I could rag-doll a thousand feet to the aid station on the deck of the ski lodge. It's all I can do to rein in my wobbly thighs, reminding myself that things could be worse, much worse: I could be the guy I just passed who's crawling *backwards* down the mountain.

Aid stations at ultramarathons are makeshift waypoints with folding tables and shade tents, where you can resupply on food and water. Typically situated about five to seven miles apart, they're stocked with pretzels, squares of peanut-butter-and-jelly sandwiches, orange slices, coolers filled with water and electrolyte drink, bowls brimming with M&Ms and energy gels—all free for the taking.

My plan is to eat my own supply of Gu and to supplement with real food from aid stations if and when I feel like it. Running with most of my own calories means I don't need to linger for long, except to refill my bottles with water and electrolyte tablets, and can be in and out in a minute or less. When I run onto the ski resort deck, at roughly the halfway mark, I'm greeted by a gaggle of volunteers yelling, "You're the first woman! Go, go, go!"

What?!

My race strategy for Jemez had been modest: Finish and don't get hurt. Winning had never factored in, and I'd had no clue I was in front. I don't know how much lead time I have. For all I know, it could be five minutes, a luxurious spread in shorter races but a narrow margin in an ultra, when you can burn through that time stopping to tie your shoes or going to the bathroom. Suddenly I feel like a rabbit being chased.

At mile 25, in my excitement to stay out in front, I stumble on a sharp rock and catapult forward. It takes all my effort to catch myself midfall, a spasmodic jerking that sends the torque of my body weight straight into my right calf. I stop for a moment to catch my breath and assess. My muscle is tightly coiled but seems stable and more or less okay. I have six miles to the finish. It's time to change my strategy. *Don't fall, don't get hurt,* I coach myself. *Don't fuck this up. Do NOT fuck this up!*

For ultrarunners, tripping is an occupational hazard. The trails are strewn with rocks and roots, downed trees and occasionally sand. On technical descents where the footing is tricky, you want to keep your feet light and quick and your stride short, skipping over obstacles. The key to staying upright is to look ahead about ten feet. This enables your mind to register what's coming before you're actually upon it and directs your feet to find the holes between the hazards. As I learned in whitewater kayaking and skiing, it's best to look where you want to go, not where you *don't* want to go—a good strategy for life, too. If you turn your head to appraise a cliff or a tree or a boulder, your body will almost certainly follow.

Whenever I get wobbly on my feet, I know it means my blood sugar has dipped and I need to eat. Not in ten minutes, or two, but right now. I rip open a Gu packet with my teeth and choke down a couple of dollops and keep running. If I stay upright, moving forward and thinking clearly, I can win this.

The next thing I know, I'm on the moon. Almost exactly a year ago, the Las Conchas Fire, the largest wildfire in New Mexico history, raged across these canyons, burning more than 150,000 acres of forest. The scorched, barren mountainside is littered with barbecued trees toppled every which way, like blackened matchsticks. Beneath my feet, the trail is hot and silty with silver ash, and there's not a lick of shade.

There are many excellent diversionary tactics to pass the time and take your mind off the pain and frustration of ultrarunning. Self-loathing is an obvious place to start. I spend a few miles berating myself for the stupidity of trying to run thirty-one miles. Why, when I was perfectly happy running up and down my little mountains, with nothing at stake, did I need to do *this*? I think about Steve and wallow for some time in regret. How selfish I was to leave my husband alone on the trail! I haven't seen him in hours, and it's unlikely he'll catch me now.

Blame works just as well as shame, and soon enough I am silently berating Steve. He shouldn't drink two cups of coffee before running—*what* was he thinking? He should have known not to eat an extra helping of lentils for lunch the day before the race. He should have trained more and run faster, dammit!

Eventually, my petulance begins to bore me, so I try to shut down my mind and look around instead. Someone's hung funny signs on piñon trees every fifteen or twenty feet along the trail. YOU KNOW YOU'RE AN ULTRARUNNER WHEN . . . reads the first one. Each sign continues the theme: YOU NEVER HAVE A COMPLETE SET OF TOE-NAILS. I can feel myself start to run faster, just to get to the next one and the next. YOU DON'T THINK TWICE ABOUT EATING FOOD DROPPED ON THE GROUND . . . YOU MEASURE YOUR TRAINING RUNS IN HOURS NOT MILES . . . YOU LOOK FOR A BUSH WHEN THE LINE FOR THE BATH-ROOM IS TOO LONG.

Then, at last, I'm in the shade of tall ponderosas, descending into Los Alamos Canyon. A couple hundred yards before the final aid station, near mile 30, is another sign hung in jest, this one advertis-ing free tequila and a mirror to fix your hair for the finish-line photos. I don't want either, but I do need salt, and I want to know what the last two miles to the finish line are like.

"It's a climb, right?" I ask a volunteer, thinking back to the spiky, evil contours of the course profile I studied online the week before the race.

"Nope, just rolling!" she replies with false cheer, refilling one of my bottles and pressing three mini pretzels into my palm. "Just rolling!" she says again, as if she can tell I don't believe her. Aid station volunteers are preternaturally kind, upbeat, and results-oriented, and they will lie straight to your face to help you reach the finish line.

The trail isn't "rolling," not even by my warped standards, but whether from the lure of the finish or the salty pretzels, I snap out of my delirium and pull myself together, surging up the last rocky ascent and onto the mesa top. A small crowd of spectators lines the finish chute, clanging cowbells. When they see me, they cheer, "First female!"

I've done it. I'm the first woman across the line, in five hours and fifty minutes, and eighth overall. Dazed, I strip off my damp T-shirt, shoes, and socks and lie back in the grass to wait for Steve. When he finally appears, about an hour after me, he still has an agonized look on his face, but then he sees me and tries to smile. "Well, *that* was a nightmare," he groans. He'd had an upset stomach for miles and spent a long layover in the bathroom at the ski lodge. By the time his stomach cramps abated, his knees had begun to hurt. Still, he'd finished his first 50K in twenty-ninth place, in a highly respectable sub–seven hours.

There's free beer and a barbecue, and, a little while later, an awards ceremony. The organizer calls my name and hands me a small clay pot made by a local Jemez Pueblo artist. "Under six hours—that's one of our fastest women's times!" he exclaims, clapping me on my back. I remember this feeling from my Fodderstack days—of being swift and strong, of proving something specific and measurable to the world. Of winning. How quickly I could get used to it again.

My calf is cramping, my feet are blackened with dirt and soot, and my toes are chafed. I know I ought to savor the moment, but my victory was so unexpected, it almost doesn't seem real. I got separated from Steve, babbled to myself like a maniac, and whipped in and out of aid stations, panicking about who was behind me and how close. Yet even when I was out of my mind, I was *in* my body, flying on fleet feet, skirting the edges of ragged canyons, inhaling the scorched summer smells, riding the waves of my breath up and over ridges and down valleys. I was running from the inside, from the certainty that anything is possible if you just keep going.

The next day I call Mom. "I won!" I cry.

"Oh?" she asks. Incomprehension drips from her voice. She has no idea what I'm talking about.

"The race! My ultra!"

"Oh, that's right. Fantastic," she says unconvincingly. "How many other runners were in it?"

People often ask this question after an ultra, as though there's a chance the answer might be two.

"A couple hundred," I say.

"You're eating enough, aren't you?" This has been her refrain over the past few months whenever I tell her about my running. "You were looking quite gaunt last time we saw you."

I want to tell her she's mistaken, that I wolf down food like a starving polar explorer after I run. But I know she's picturing me at eighteen, the year I went to college and ate Ben & Jerry's ice cream two meals a day and had soft, rounded New York Super Fudge Chunk cheeks—before I moved to the desert and got lizard skin and squint lines. I haven't looked like that in twenty years. There are so many reasons I run, some of which even I don't understand, and staying thin is the least of them.

But I know that it's her job as a mother to worry, because I'm one now, too, and that worrying is another way of loving, so I just nod into the phone.

"Yes, Mom."

A couple of days later, Natalie and I meet for a walk. My legs are still sore, but the euphoria from the race hasn't worn off. We start slowly up our mountain.

"I knew you'd win," she says proudly, "because you didn't care about winning."

19

Practice

Dad outside the M Street Deli, Washington, 1980

In 1980, Dad traveled to France to take pictures of the Seine for *National Geographic*. For weeks, he followed the river from its source in Burgundy, through Paris, to the sea. In one photograph, a young boy on a barge peers through binoculars. He has clipped brown hair in blunt bangs and bare feet. I remember seeing that photograph in the magazine and thinking for a moment that it was me, and, when I realized that it wasn't, feeling jealous of that boy who'd captured my father's attention and held it long enough for him to compose a picture. Dad had made so many photographs of us over the years, but always I wanted more—more time with him, more proof that he loved us. And I remember being ashamed of my envy. I'd grown accustomed to being apart from my father. Shouldn't I be over it by now?

In mid-June, three weeks after the Jemez 50K, I fly alone to a farm in France to write for ten days. Maisy and Pippa are about to turn two and four, and this will be the longest and farthest I've been away since they were born. I cry the whole way to Albuquerque, sad, guilty mama tears—*I love you, I miss you, I hate to leave you, I can't wait to get away. I'm sorry.* I'm not on assignment. I don't have a deadline. I'm going away to work in silence on the novel I've had in my mind for years, even though, in the bedlam of motherhood and anxiety, I can barely remember what it is.

I got the idea on a trip Steve and I took to Florida to visit his parents, before the girls were born. It came at me in a torrent, and I filled a notebook overnight. Then I ran out of steam and put it away, promising myself that someday I'd go back. I hadn't learned to pace myself. Maybe now it will be different. Maybe by training my body to run for hours, I will have conditioned my mind to sit in a chair and write for hours, so that when I'm ninety-five I won't still be talking wistfully about the novel I once wanted to write. I'll have written it.

The night before I left for France, I went looking for Dad's watch. I wanted to bring something of him with me, but I hadn't seen the Timex for months. I'd worn it all through that long first winter after he died, even though it dwarfed my narrow wrist and spun around so that the buckle was where the face should be and the face was where the buckle should be, rubbing on tables, the kitchen sink, the rocky ground when I bent to tie my sneakers. It was getting scratched, and I worried that the leather band—the old arc, the memory of Dad's wrist—would break.

Eventually, I took it off and put it into a drawer. I was grieving

Dad and my own mortality and my babies getting bigger all at the same time, and I didn't need any more reminders that time was passing.

Every so often, I'd retrieve the watch to check that it was still ticking. Sometimes I held it to my wrist, imagining it wound around Dad's, his skin mottled with age spots. As long as the Timex was still ticking, Dad's death was still fresh and my sadness still acceptable, even reasonable. I worried that when it stopped, Dad would be gone all over again, for good this time. Even as I put it to my ear to hear its steady ticking, like a heartbeat, I knew this was arbitrary, the kind of fanciful logic that takes over in the upside-down aftermath of death.

How do we measure grief? In seconds, minutes, hours? Days, months, years? Like love, it can't be quantified. There is no time limit. It's not linear but cyclical. It bears down on me in the darkening days of winter and lifts with the strength of the springtime sun. I'm beginning to predict its comings and goings. It's growing sluggish, as I am becoming quicker and more nimble. Most of the time now, I can stay just out in front, the fear and sorrow trailing behind me with outstretched arms, trying to keep up but falling further and further behind.

It'd been so long since I last looked for Dad's watch that, for a moment, I wasn't sure where I'd left it. But there it was in the top drawer of our bathroom vanity, under an old bottle of hot pink nail polish. It had stopped. I wasn't surprised. Ever since the intern undertaker had handed it to me on a velvet tray at the funeral home, I'd known this day would come. Instead of sadness, though, I felt a faint relief. Dad's watch had finally caught up with him.

I did not press the watch to my ear or bend the band around my wrist or inspect the face for scratches, wondering which ones were mine and which were Dad's. I clasped it only briefly in my hand, and then I put it back into the drawer.

My first day in Paris, I walk for hours through Le Marais, Les Halles, Luxembourg Gardens, the Louvre, the Eiffel Tower, the Seine, back to Saint-Germain. I walk twenty miles or more, thinking of my father, wandering these same streets thirty years ago.

From Paris, I ride the train two hours to a village of two-hundred-year-old stone houses surrounded by green fields. All the houses have cornflower-blue shutters and window boxes spilling over with orange geraniums. Even the cows—the fattest and healthiest I've ever seen, Jerseys, as big as oxen, with cinnamon hides and newborn calves—are exquisite. Poppies grow straight out of cracks in the rock walls. I write at a narrow desk in a second-story farmhouse room with yellow walls. My bedroom window overlooks a church steeple and a small pond with iron-red water, where I swim in the afternoons.

Momentum buzzes through my body, like a motor beginning to hum. I'm hungry all the time, writing like mad, burning with so much energy I can barely sleep. Is it jet lag or insomnia? Separation anxiety? No. It's the silence. No one to talk to, no one crying *Mama, Mama,* no phone calls to make or take. How much energy we expend by talking, by spewing words into the world! The silence is addictive. It's a performance-enhancing drug—free and legal—fueling my body and mind. When I'm not writing, I run or walk alone, before breakfast, after dinner, at sunset, before writing and after writing, in the full sun of high noon. I fold a crinkled map into my shorts pocket and set off in a new direction: long, looping routes past hay meadows, along lanes lined with magenta foxglove and daisies. The roads are pebbly and coarse: predictable, monotonous, delicious asphalt. I don't have to watch my feet. I can look straight ahead and swing my arms by my side. It's just after the summer solstice, and it's light so late that the farmers stay out on their tractors, cutting hay, until 10 p.m.

In the mornings, I wake after four hours of sleep with voices in my head. They are my own words, wanting to write themselves. The church bells chime six. Five clothespins and my bathing suit dangle on a piece of string I tied across the open window; a dove's wings beat the frame. The sky is a bright, shocking cobalt. Every fiber in my body is firing. Maybe this is what running a hundred miles feels like: run, eat a little, run, run, run, walk, sleep a very short time, run some more, walk some more. Writing, like running, is an endurance sport. Keep moving or you'll atrophy.

This is the way time used to feel in the long, empty, drawn-out days before babies. Mornings were the dreamiest. I would sit in the garden and feel the sun on my arms and write a few lines. I didn't know then how much time I had. It was endless, really. I'd had a job, but then I left it and my time was my own and nobody was expecting me, only my words, and I could write them whenever I wanted. I miss this, I want this again—not all the time, not every day, but once a year maybe. This exact room in this exact village: maybe this one time, ever.

For the first time, lying in my narrow bed, I can see how Dad might have left. He didn't leave for yellow walls in France or for wooden shutters that opened to a steeple and a pond shrouded in mist; he left for another woman, but that woman was an excuse. He left for silence and spaciousness, for freedom, and the idea of it, for staying in bed as late as he pleased. Having this now, I can see how easy it would be to want more.

In Eastern religions, practice means something you do regularly, without concern for results or, as the Buddhists say, "a gaining idea." This is the opposite of the usual Western definition, which I grew up with and which implies a persistent striving for improvement, for significance. "Racquet back!" Ron would call to me every single time he thwacked a tennis ball to me at the city courts in Summit; I practiced my ground strokes almost every day the summer I was nine. "I can't go out to play," I'd tell Mom in fourth grade, "until I practice my multiplication."

Sitting meditation, or zazen, is the central practice in Buddhism, but anything you do regularly and attentively, without gaining idea, counts. "It's what you do no matter what," Natalie explained as we hiked down the mountain a few weeks before I left for France. "You don't get tossed away. Continue under all circumstances." This is what her Zen teacher, Dainin Katagiri Roshi, had taught her about zazen, but really it applied to anything. Everything. The first winter we hiked together, Natalie would often email or call first thing in the morning, saying, "It's twenty degrees outside! Should we still go?!"

"I'll pick you up at nine," I always wrote back. Then I'd bundle Maisy in two layers of down bunting and we'd go. Whatever the weather, we met the mountain where it was.

Writing was practice, too—a way to study your mind. "Write like mad," Natalie told me that day on the trail. "Let it rip on the page, puke your guts out on paper. Then sit."

I did it differently. First I ran, and then, when my body was calm and my mind quiet, I wrote. I had a project I hadn't told anyone about except Steve: I was writing a poem every day for a year. By the time I arrived in France, I'd been going for almost six months. Like ultrarunning, it had started as a lark. I wasn't a poet and harbored no illusions of becoming one, but I liked poems. I liked how when I read them I might understand only an iota of what the poet was trying to say. The poem was a mystery I could not fully grasp, but it grasped me.

My own weren't quite so mysterious. I wrote them every night before bed. I didn't belabor them—I could whip out a poem in ten minutes, sometimes less. I did not go back and fix them or even reread them. It didn't matter if they were good or bad—they were for no one but me, the way running had been for me when I was little. The poems were a way of paying attention, looking for lines in my day as though I were fishing and didn't know what I might catch: the hallucinatory scent of saltwater in the desert; a cowboy riding a horse along the Winsor Trail, tipping his hat to me; an old man on the sidewalk stooping over a cane, the man my father might have become. I was all of those people at once and also none of them, and I gathered them in my net as I ran.

Some days I didn't want to write a poem, just like some days I didn't want to run. "Write what's in front of you," Natalie told her students when they got stuck. What was in front of me was a blank screen, my own deafening doubt. *You are the worst poet in the world.* Practice was writing one anyway. It meant showing up for the good days when running felt effortless, zanily optimistic, and the bad days, when it was sticky and hard and I wanted to lie on the ground and cry. Practice was writing at the kitchen table on Saturday mornings while Steve played Old Maid with Pippa in front of the woodstove, and writing by headlamp, with gloves on, in a camp chair in Chaco Canyon in late November, the girls asleep in the tent. It was all my poems, one hundred and counting, most dashed off, some godawful, others secretly sort of sublime.

And now, here in France, it is writing with my notebook propped on my lap in a cobblestone courtyard, for the simple thrill of discovering something unfolding as I put it down. Practice is staying in the muck, the back and forth, the transcendence and the torment.

On my last morning in France, the sky is spitting drizzle, a mist so gentle it's hard to decipher individual drops. I walk past the pretty cows and a red clay tennis court, over narrow bridges. I go slowly, trying to memorize it all. Already I miss my superhuman energy; already I feel it dissipating. Already I feel my feral squirrel girls rising up to meet me, their sweet, soft skin, babies still, but not for long.

The meadows are so green, as green as the fields in upstate New York last spring when we buried Dad. It had been raining for weeks when we arrived, and I could not believe the grass. How thick and tall it was! I had forgotten Dad's slavish devotion to his fields, how they had been his burden and his pride. His grass was like father-hood in the early years, when Meg and I were very small: something he loved and tended but also resented. He hadn't figured out that there was discipline and virtue in staying with the mess. That it was a practice, too. A clean line through the chaos. The grass grows like crazy all week in the rain, shoots up. You mow it. You get on your tractor and you cut it. You ride, you walk—any way you can, you do it.

Dad loved the grass, but it was okay to hate the grass, too, to want to leave. As weird as it sounds, I wish he'd left more. For a weekend, a week. Mowing is not all it's cracked up to be. Everyone needs to go. But you come back; the grass is what you know. There is solace in the grass. History, duty. What do you do out of duty, and what do you do out of love? Where do you draw the line between walking the line and running in the opposite direction?

Time passes so swiftly: a blink and this moment is gone. A dove flaps its wings and flies away, and water drips from the clouds so softly it doesn't make a sound, shooing me home.

There's so much noise in the world, and, back in the happy mayhem of home, it all seems amplified. I'd forgotten how loud small girls can be, piling onto me gleefully as I pull them in. They have freckles and bruised knees and they have lived ten days without me and no one died.

Even silent things make noise: the taunting blue screen of Facebook, the blinking light on my answering machine. I long for the rolling lanes and clear, wide days of France. Attachment—and discontent, too—is its own kind of noise.

One morning, jet-lagged, I wake up before 5 a.m. and tiptoe out for a run. I know where I can find the silence: where it's always been, outside, on the trails. I run hard, and when I get home, my wild, tangled life is all right there waiting for me, pleading for soft-boiled eggs and a bike ride to school. But the silence is also inside me, part of my muscle memory, moving through the trees and into my legs and onto the paper.

20

Spirit Running

Winsor Trail, Santa Fe, 2012

I n July, I sign up for the Mt. Taylor 50K, held in western New Mexico in late September. Like the Jemez 50K, Mount Taylor is a technical course, much of it above ten thousand feet in elevation. I'm forty years old and coming off a surprise win at my first ultra. Maybe I'm good; maybe I could even be *great*. Probably I'm merely above average, but either way, I want to find out. The clock is ticking.

I talk Steve into signing up, too. He's still leery from the Jemez race, but I convince him that he still has the fitness to run another 50K without too much additional training. Selfishly, I want the company, but I'm also hoping he'll fall in love with the sport, as I have.

Stony Lake, where I take the girls for a month each summer, is not the most obvious place to train for a high-altitude mountain race. It's at 600 feet above sea level, and there are few hills. The country roads are narrow, winding between lumpy pastures rife with Queen Anne's lace and limestone boulders. This the scabbiest, lumpiest, least productive farmland on the edge of the Canadian Shield: unforgiving granite all the way to bedrock. The silos are all tilted and falling apart, and I can see sky through the ribs of the barns. There are only a few stop signs, and no traffic lights, so I rarely have to stop, which is good, because you can't slow down for even a second or you will be devoured by mosquitos, especially on roads and trails where the trees are thick—which are almost all the roads and trails—and after a rain, when it is humid. One upside to mosquitoes: they are very good for speed training.

I've known this country my whole life, but running changes it. I notice all the things I previously missed—dry-docked boats for sale and scrap-metal piles and white-brick farmhouses—and I feel proprietary tenderness toward them, not unlike the way I feel about my mountains at home. On the ground beside a mailbox, someone has left a box of toys, free for the taking: Barbies, a small plastic Lion King, rubber balls, mermaids. Each day, there are new ones in the box and I pick one to bring home to Pippa and Maisy.

Near the dock where I park my boat, a network of trails winds for seven miles through the birch and hemlock trees. On hot days, it's shady and cool beneath the canopy; after a rain, the puddles are so big you can't run through them; you have to skirt the sides, slopping in up to your ankles. I've maybe seen one other person on the trails, ever. The paths meander in such an illogical, unmarked fashion that it's easy to get turned around, and when I first discovered them, I would often be several miles in the wrong direction before

I realized I was lost. Now, though, I can run without having to remember where I am or memorize intersections, without having to think. At first my legs are tight, but I also feel fast, as though all the oxygen in the world is available to me, and my lungs stretch wide to breathe it all in—no tension, no hitches, no holding back. If it's hot when I get back to the lake, I run straight onto the dock, pull off my shirt, socks, and sneakers, and jump in.

Some days, the doubt slides in and I wonder how I can possibly train for New Mexico's high, thin air and mountain passes in the flatlands of Ontario, but then I look around, at thick trees and goldenrod meadows and Barbie's blond head shoved into my sports bra, and I know how I'm doing it. By running where I am.

When I get home to Santa Fe, most of my miles are in the bank. All I really need to do is reacclimatize to the altitude and stay healthy. I should be feeling strong, but instead my joints ache and my right Achilles tendon feels tight enough to slingshot a sweet potato. My rational brain tells me that the obvious culprit is too many fast miles. But I can feel my anxiety spiking, taunting me with improbable scenarios. It must be Lyme's disease, from the tick I pulled off my thigh when I was at Huntly last spring. Though I showed no symptoms six months ago, the disease is, right this very minute, worming inside my joints, corroding my heart, zapping me of vitality and stamina.

The blood test I ask Dr. G. to order comes back negative. I ice my ankle twice a day for three days and lay off the hills, and the tenderness in my calf subsides. I'm not sick or injured. I'm just burned out, running for the wrong reasons: not for the pleasure and self-confidence I felt all spring, but because I want to win and am afraid I won't. Because now I have something to prove. That my first ultra wasn't a fluke.

One morning, as I'm running up Atalaya, I think about bailing out of Mount Taylor. It would be so easy to cancel my registration, to let my ultrarunning career fade out after one freak victory. After all, this is what I'd done as a girl, by competing only once a year, at the Fodderstack. Had I given up racing for Meg, or for myself, out of defiance? Or maybe there was another piece: fear. Maybe I hadn't wanted to risk losing face in front of Dad. Now, thirty years later, scuffing my feet up the mountain, my heart a bag of bricks in my chest, I can't fathom why this seemed like a good idea.

When I get to the top, I sit on a rock, looking down on Santa Fe. If I quit now, I would miss so much. I would miss the clarity of purpose I feel when I have a goal and it absorbs me so completely I stop caring about the outcome. And I would miss *this:* the full moon sinking into the Jemez Mountains, and behind me the sun inching up over Thompson Peak, equidistant above the horizon. I stretch out my arms, cupping the moon in one hand and the sun in the other, and they align exactly, as though, in this one moment, the world hangs in perfect balance.

I feel Dad rising around me, through the thick reptilian skin of the ponderosas: *I know it's hard. You are doing a good job. Keep going.*

And so I do, dropping off the north side into the shadows, leaning into the turns. I don't feel strong, but I feel better, less afraid. If I want to stay healthy for Mount Taylor, I will have to let go of my ego's insistent posturing and run instead for the love of moving through mountains, for something bigger than results and beyond myself.

The August days are full of gorgeous, fading beauty. At seven thousand feet, the seasons switch over briskly, without warning. Moths stitch themselves into the tiny checkered squares of the screen doors, manic for the light. We live outside with the girls, hiking beside trickling creeks, collecting pinecones that stick to our hands. We dunk our toes in the Rio Grande and flick watermelon seeds into the current one last time this season. The aspens up high labor from green to pure gold, and all of Santa Fe climbs the mountain to gawk at their brilliance. Days this happy make me a little melancholy. There is not a lot of time left before the snow closes down the high country, but this is the very best time and I don't want to waste it.

On the last day of summer, I run twelve miles to the radio towers, at twelve thousand feet, and back. The season that began with late nights falling over hay pastures in France is ending beneath a million golden aspen leaves in New Mexico. I run as though drawn upward by a kinetic charge that's bigger and stronger than me. All I have to do is let it in and I will never run out. At the top, I sit and eat a peach, the juice running down my chin, the sugar giving me speed. I spread my hands out to the sky and say *"Thank you! Thank you!"* the whole way down.

When race week arrives, I'm frazzled again, as though there's not enough time to get it all done, until I remind myself that I've already done everything. I've trained hard while trying to set aside pride and preoccupation with winning. I don't need to do anything; I only need to do nothing.

A couple of days before the race, Natalie and I are walking around the neighborhood when she says, out of nowhere, "Writing should be for the whole world, for all sentient beings. Maybe your running can be, too." She says this plainly, the way she does everything, nothing to suggest she's transmitting the wisdom of the ages, handed down from teacher to teacher, all the way back to the Buddha.

"You could make an altar for your running, you know, a little table filled with meaningful things to sit in front of and focus on," she continues in her even tone, as if building altars is something I do all the time. As if I have the foggiest idea how. Still, I pocket a couple of pebbles from the trail and pick a sprig of yellow chamisa flowers. They bloom in September along the roadsides and arroyos and smell musky, like wet dog, reminding me of my first fall in Santa Fe.

When I get home, I find a bundle of dried sage I brought home from our last river trip, along with a votive candle and a photograph of Dad. I climb the stairs to my writing loft, a small room under the eaves, and spread them out on a low table. I sit on the rug, looking at the arrangement for a moment, moving things an inch this way, half an inch that way, and light the candle. I'm not sure what to do next. Pray? Cry? Plead to the running gods of Mount Taylor for mercy? Instead I sit in front of my offerings, looking at Dad looking back at me, grinning and quizzical, through his tortoiseshell glasses.

Dad, New Hampshire, 1985

I took this picture, in a diner in New Hampshire, in 1985, the summer I was thirteen. Meg and I went kayaking with him for a week down the Connecticut River. The river was flatwater, with so little gradient we could barely feel the current. At the end of each day, we pulled our kayaks onto the bank and dragged them and all our gear across lawns or down gravel lanes to whatever "riverfront" country inn Dad had booked for the night. Time has distorted the trip so that, when I remember it now, it seemed dominated by an

excessive, even cruel, amount of dragging, when in fact we probably had to do it only once or twice. Memory can be so catastrophic.

The river trip was part of a series of ambitious self-propelled
summer adventures that Dad planned for us. The year before,
we'd gone walking in England. The year after, we bicycled around
Prince Edward Island, where it rained constantly and we were always riding into the wind, no matter which direction we were
going, and somehow we found this funny, even when it wasn't.
Some things are good to learn early in life, and this was one of
them: There is *always* a headwind, just like there is *always* a false
summit—sometimes many.

Meg and me, England, 1984

I study the picture closely. Dad's glasses reflect the light, as they
so often did, so I can't see his eyes, just a blurry, whitish glare, and
for a second I can't remember. They were *green,* weren't they? He
cups his chin with his left hand and leans forward with a thin,
crooked smile, as if to say, *Okay, what's next, Katie? Whaddya have
for me now?*

The house is quiet and empty and I can feel it breathe me in as I
breathe out. Whatever happens on Mount Taylor will be okay. It
will take me someplace new and teach me things I didn't know. I
just need to let go and receive it.

Mount Taylor is an extinct volcano that blew its top two million years ago. On a typical, clear New Mexico day, you can see its hulking profile from nearly a hundred miles away, south and west of Santa Fe. At 11,305 feet, it's the tallest peak in the San Mateo Mountains, but because no other mountain nearby comes within a thousand feet of its summit, it appears to stand alone, wavering in the far distance. For the Navajo, Hopi, Zuni, and Acoma people, Mount Taylor (or Tsoodził, "Turquoise Mountain") is a sacred peak, part of an ancient Native mythology and one of four mountains that define the Navajo people's traditional boundaries.

The day before the race, Steve and I drop Pippa and Maisy at Blair's house for a sleepover with their two daughters. At four, Pippa is old enough to understand that we're going to run a long way, but too young to know what thirty-one miles means. She's more concerned with results.

"Are you going to win again, Mama?" she asks eagerly.

I've been trying not to think about this for weeks.

"Oh, sweetie, I don't know. I'll have to see how I feel."

It's a three-hour drive west to the town of Grants, at the foot of Mount Taylor, and by the time we arrive at the Red Lion Hotel, just off the interstate, the race briefing and pasta dinner have already begun. Volunteers sit behind a registration table in a conference room, doling out goody bags and race bibs, and a hundred athletes wearing fleece jackets and oversize GPS watches hunch purposefully over paper plates sagging under spaghetti and garlic bread.

One of them, tall and lanky, with shoulder-length black hair and angular cheekbones, stands up to address the room. His name is Shaun Martin, and he's an elite Navajo ultrarunner and a high school cross-country coach who lives over the state line in Chinle, Arizona. "It's a sacred honor to be here, running on Mount Taylor," he tells us. "For the Navajo people, the point of running is not to be faster than anyone. We were raised to get up every morning as the sun is rising and run east to meet the birth of a new day. Running is a celebration of life, a way to honor a new day. It's also a prayer. You are out there moving, breathing in all positive things."

A hundred forks hang in the air. Pre-race meetings typically focus on logistics, like carpooling to the start and following course flags so you don't get lost, not personal tributes to the sport's spiritual side.

"Running is a teacher," Shaun continues. "As we run, we experience hardship. In moments of doubt and pain, and we'll all have some of those tomorrow"—at this, the room erupts in nervous laughter—"what you do will define who you are. It's your character shining through at its truest. Running teaches us to balance the negative and positive and to live in beauty and balance.

"Now, if you'll excuse me," Shaun says, eyeing his altimeter watch, "I'm camping on the mountain tonight, so I'd better get up there while there's still light."

It's still dark as night when we pull into the staging area at nine thousand feet on the flanks of Mount Taylor the next morning. An almost full moon hovers above the horizon, and it's cold—barely forty degrees. The course description promised a scenic, challenging circumnavigation of the mountain, which is laced with jeep roads and singletrack trails, including a section of the Continental Divide Trail, a long-distance through trail traversing 3,100 miles, from Canada to Mexico along the backbone of the country.

This time, Steve and I have agreed to run at our own paces, and though we stand together waiting for the start, I quickly lose him in the jostle. Within a hundred yards, the course veers off a jeep road and climbs a steep gully through aspens. Shaun is way out in front. The trees thin, and the road gains an open, grassy slope to a high ridge, the sky getting brighter by the minute, as though someone's turning up the dimmer switch on the sun. As I crest the first high ridge, there it is directly in front of me, beaming above the horizon and straight into my eyes.

Mount Taylor has several false summits, and after the first one, the course drops steadily along a dirt road. In ultra trail marathons, descents are a good chance to make up time lost on the slower, steeper climbs. For the past six weeks, I've been training for the downhills, trying to run fast rather than lean back and coast. Even so, several men whom I'd passed on the climb fly by me with disconcerting speed, and I watch them from behind, trying to mimic the way they lean forward and swing their arms loosely like overcooked noodles. The feeling I have is one of running ahead of myself, restless and striving and a little bit reckless.

Don't look back. Keep running.

At the ten-mile aid station, volunteers huddle in down jackets, warming their hands over a campfire. "First female!" they yell when they see me. Up until now, I hadn't been sure. One runner ahead of me in the twilight had thighs like a woman's but looked to be at least six feet tall; another bounded along, ponytail bouncing, but I was almost positive they were both men.

When I hear this, I know I want to win, but I don't *want* to want to win. I just want to run. *Settle in,* I tell myself. *Settle your body.*

For a long, surreal stretch between miles 10 and 16, I streak beneath blazing aspens on the Continental Divide Trail, not bonking or hallucinating, not thinking about whether I'm in first place or how my legs feel. I'm riding the cusp between pleasure and pain, a simple love of running and the primal drive to win, past and future, start and finish, here and now. All around me I feel spirits— people I've known and loved and have never known and will never know, and those I still know and love. They rise up from the pine-needled earth. They are light as breath, like wind on my lips, floating into the sky.

One day, when I was seven and sat in front of my mirror in my bedroom, I realized I was my own self. I had legs and arms and thoughts, and they belonged to me. But out here on this sacred mountain, the boundaries have blurred. I'm not separate after all. Nothing is. I'd been running for myself, but now I'm running for everyone and everything that's ever lived, that's alive now, and that may someday live. For the stout Douglas firs with strong arms and the ancient sequoias in Yosemite, for my mother and grandmother and Pippa and Maisy and their great-great-granddaughters I can only dream about. For the whole world.

It's the briefest flicker of enlightenment, a slit in the skin of the world big enough to slip through, if only for a little while.

A common misperception about ultrarunning is that races unfold slowly, gradually, over many miles. Running on the thin edge of endurance, your physical and psychological states can shift in an instant. One moment you're in a heightened state of consciousness; the next you're muttering *Motherfucker!* under your breath as a needle-sharp rock bayonets you through your sneaker and your hips feel like they're rolling around, bone-on-bone in their sockets, and you still have the longest climb of the day ahead of you.

"Save your energy for the top," the race director, Ken, warns me when I come into the halfway aid station just before going back up Mount Taylor again. "It's three miles to the summit, but it's gonna feel like more."

Gone is the transcendent bliss. Now I'm just trying to survive. Eating is a job, and I'm all business: every half hour, a Gu goes down the hatch; bananas at the mile 20 aid station, sliced watermelon at mile 25, the long, zigzagging climb through high, grassy meadows more punishing than I feared. I pass a guy but am soon passed by another; I round a bend through a high notch; I alternate between running and walking the steepest parts, hating walking the steepest parts. I wonder where Steve is. I give myself landmarks: run to the next tree, walk to that bush, repeat. I look at my legs, my quadriceps sweat-stained and filthy, flexing and strong. Finally, a small wooden sign announces the summit: MT TAYLOR,

11,300 FEET. Aspens and firs above lumpy brown badlands far, far below.

Four miles to go, then two. Tune it all out: your creaky, rock-pummeled hips and your fiery IT band on the outside of your left thigh; the other runners and hikers with happy cheers; the final, sadistic, boulder-strewn downhill slam to the finish. Focus only on: crossing the line, staying ahead of the women behind you, wherever they are, and setting a personal best in the 50K. Three goals to distract your mind from the torment of your body.

Below, through the aspens, I see the tent and hear the cheers. There is the digital clock and the finish line, and I run hard across it. I've won: five hours and twenty minutes, nearly thirty minutes faster than my Jemez time, half an hour ahead of the second-place woman, and an hour and five minutes behind winner Shaun Martin.

Shaun places a medal around my neck, and I collapse into a folding chair. There were so many highs and lows crammed into thirty-one miles that I couldn't keep track of them all. I wanted to stay on my feet. I wanted to run with the spirits the whole way, forever. I wanted to finish, to stop running. I wanted to be alone. I wanted to see a mountain lion, so that the mountain lion would attack me and put me out of my misery. I wanted to be joyful, strong, egoless. I wanted to win. I wanted to stop wanting. Even at the finish line, when it was over, I wanted something: Steve. Did I ever, for even one moment, want nothing?

On the way home to Santa Fe, Steve drives, and I stick my bare feet out the window. They're calloused and grimy, and the wind feels like water on my inflamed toes. We're listening to a country station out of Gallup and not saying much, and the silence between us feels heavy, like more than just fatigue.

"I don't think I'm cut out for more than eighteen miles," Steve grumbles as we pull off at an exit for chocolate-dipped cones at Dairy Queen. His knees bothered him after twenty miles, but he stuck it out and finished an hour after I did.

"But you hardly even trained! Your knees will get used to it. You could be so good!" There's no question in my mind that this is true, but I can't help but feel guilty and a little sad, as though my running and winning have somehow tipped the equilibrium in our relationship.

Victory is sweet, but also a little lonely. By bowing out, however reluctantly, Steve's giving ultrarunning over to me. It will take me many more long runs and races to learn how to run fast without losing my balance, to run hard for something bigger than winning, and to experience what the Navajo have always understood about long-distance running: It will teach us everything we need to know. Like how to want nothing, even for only one minute.

21

Resistance

After the Fodderstack, 1982

Jumping from fifty kilometers to fifty miles is arguably the toughest transition in ultrarunning. A 50K is thirty-one miles, five miles longer than a marathon. If you've recently run a marathon or even a half marathon and have a solid work ethic and moderate pain tolerance, it's not unreasonable to make the leap to your first ultra in six to nine months.

Fifty miles is a different sort of insanity: nineteen miles longer, nearly two marathons. Twice the commitment, almost double the distance. Un-freaking-fathomable. And yet I know I'm going to try. I want to see if I can run my way back to the oneness I felt at Mount Taylor, that brief but mind-bending sense of being no one, and everyone. I hadn't known that such a thing was possible. I thought that you'd have to sit so still and so diligently, for hours and years, until your face wore an expression of tranquillity and you were free from all suffering. I thought that's what awakening was. I didn't realize it could happen in an instant, a cracking bolt of clarity cutting through the tumult. Here, and then gone.

I'd glimpsed the infinite. It was a kind of ecstasy, really, and I wanted it back.

I sign up for the Jemez 50 Mile, scheduled for May. In January, I begin training in earnest. My first long run is eight miles, low and slow. Starting is always hard.

A woman I know named Margaret has been diagnosed with a brain tumor. Days after I hear the news, I develop a strange pressure in my head while skiing. By nightfall, my ear is ringing like a cricket. By morning, the cricket owns a chain saw and it's clear-cutting my brain. Within days, my mind has reached into its linty pockets and pulled out its old nemesis: anxiety. Within the week, I've convinced myself that I have a brain tumor that's causing not only the ringing in my ear but also my morbid fixations.

"Do you have headaches?" Dr. G. asks when I explain that sometimes the ringing in my ear sounds like belligerent insects and other times the pearly thrum of a seashell.

"Hmm," I say, stalling for time. Do I? Not unless I think about it, in which case yes, like right this very minute there's a chisel in my forehead.

"No, not really," I say finally.

He looks in my ears and eyes and performs a series of simple diagnostic tests, like a policeman making me walk the line during a sobriety check. Can I touch my finger to my nose when my eyes are closed? Yes. Count backwards from twenty? Yes.

"I don't see anything to suggest this is serious," he tells me. "Millions of people get tinnitus, often for no apparent reason." Then he pauses and shakes his head. "I will tell you, though, sometimes it never goes away."

For a few minutes—the length of time it takes me to grab my bag and walk to my car—I am filled with the most delicious relief. My breath swoops all the way down to my feet and back, washing me with beneficence and hope. It's the way I feel after a long run. *I'm strong! I'm still alive!* But by the time I get home, I know with certainty that it won't last. There's no way a doctor's diagnosis will hold up to my anxiety's demented, tyrannical authority. Fear is opportunistic, and it will come roaring back like the ringing in my ear, screeching and unstoppable.

On a snowy Friday in February, I pull up in front of an adobe house. A shepherd mix barks from behind the wall. Inside the sliding glass door, coats are slung over benches, a wooden cane lies at a careless angle, sneakers with the heels pushed down are askew on the floor. The chiropractor shows me in, sticks out his hand. "Call me Dr. Seth," he says. He has bedhead and wears baggy, wide-wale corduroys and sheepskin slippers. On the phone he told me that he's had some luck curing tinnitus with chiropractic adjustments.

"Which ear?" he asks.

"My left one," I say.

There are three massage tables, all in a row. Dr. Seth motions for me to lie facedown on the middle one and looks at my chart. "So you're a Scorpio. Me, too." He takes my neck in both hands and twists, yanks with a terrifying pop.

"Ooh, that was scary!" I squeal, petrified that he'll do it again.

He does. Both hands into the hollow of my high back, pushing.

"Have you ever—" I start. "Never mind." Better not to know.

"What? Broken someone's neck? Not in twenty-one years, not even close."

I can relax now, sort of, except that I want to cry. He's adjusting the part of my spinal column, the C1, that does all the work, that holds up my head.

"It's named for the Greek god Atlas," he tells me.

I think, *Dear Atlas, my spine, what a responsibility you have! You hold up the whole world.* The thought of this is almost more than I can bear. I stifle tears, then giddy, terrified peals of laughter. Seth could hurt me, kill me even, as I lie docilely under his scratchy Guatemalan blanket. And yet I like him, unaccountably.

By the time I leave, I'm so concerned about my neck that I've forgotten all about my ear. "Try not to worry," Seth says as he ushers me out. "Sometimes it takes a few sessions."

When I go back the next week, Dr. Seth greets me at the door. "Still ringing?" he asks.

"Yes, but I'm not noticing it as much."

I get on my table and he cradles my neck in his hands and twists, cracks. The word *Mommy* actually forms on my lips, but I catch myself and giggle instead. The scraping of footsteps, people shuffling in, climbing silently onto their own tables. It sounds like a small army; at most there are two. "Breathe normally, just like your body wants to," Seth instructs them, moving between them like he's the boss of his own private torture chamber, leaving in his wake a nauseating explosion of popping and snapping. I'm wearing a silk eye mask, but what I need is noise-canceling headphones. Next to me, someone coos softly, in pleasure or maybe pain.

Now I feel hysterical laughter welling up, and I reach for it. I could laugh for hours, entire days, staring up at the bumpy stucco ceiling as one by one Seth cracks our joints and puts them back together.

ThereisnothingsofunnyNOTHINGsofunny as the chiropractor's office.

Seth's voice floats down from on high. "Laughter is the best release."

I'm laughing so hard I'm crying, and then I'm just . . . crying. I've put the laughter back inside, stuffed next to the choking sorrow and the fear and anger, deep down where I need a pickax to chip away all the layers and no one can see it.

By mid-February I'm up to fifteen miles. By March, nineteen. Once a week or so, I use an app on my phone to time my runs. I'm curious about my pace. Unlike in road running, per-mile times for ultrarunners are considerably slower and vary greatly based on altitude, distance, and terrain. I won the women's race at Jemez averaging eleven-minute miles on mountainous trails above nine thousand feet. At Mount Taylor, I bettered my pace to 10:30 per mile. This wouldn't win me any awards on the road, but on technical terrain at high altitude, it's solid. At this rate, it will take me ten or eleven hours to run fifty miles.

In mid-April, on what would have been my grandfather Harold's 102nd birthday I run up the Winsor Trail. The pine needles are sugared with snowflakes, dropped overnight in a spring storm, and I chase mice tracks, small, skittering footprints the size of Q-tips in zigzag lines as though they were dragging their tails. The mice carry on for a quarter mile—an ultramarathon for mice—but then I lose their trail in the big, muscular prints of something else. Two coyotes lope out of the bushes ahead of me and turn to stare at me, then trot uphill. I follow them, pouring my love for my grandfather and my sorrow for my friend Margaret, who has died, into my legs. For once I'm not afraid: We move in the animals' shadows. This is their world.

Back at my car, twenty miles later, I feel stronger, more hopeful than I have since I started my training. I pull out my phone to check my stats and do a double take: nine-minute miles.

A weird thing happens. The faster I run, the more I want to slow down. It's a sharp, visceral need, a physical sensation a few degrees shy of panic. Everything is winging by at warp speed: the girls getting older, all of us busier. It's not like I haven't been warned. "Enjoy it—it goes by so fast," everyone tells you when you have kids. This is the single, unifying summation of parenthood. The same exchange is probably happening right this very second in a felt yurt in farthest, deepest Mongolia.

But until recently, I never really believed it. There were those long, foggy days with newborns, days when you held your breath, talking through clenched teeth, admonishing the two-year-old for the third time that day, "DO NOT BITE YOUR SISTER," when they screech like fat, rabid possums because they don't have words for "Please." Wasn't that just yesterday? But there are also the nights camping beside the river, dark and slippery and gurgling below a billion stars, whole other worlds beaming down on you, when you look at the sky and realize that everything you're seeing has already changed forever.

Sometimes the very thought of putting on sneakers and running seems like the most tedious endeavor ever invented. These are the days I have to trick myself. I run the same trails, but in the opposite direction. I leave straight from our house, without a plan, just wandering through the neighborhoods, following my feet. I ride my bike to the mountain and run up it. I tuck a thin yoga mat into my backpack and jog a mile to the top of Sun Mountain, where I take off my sneakers and tip forward into downward dog. Suddenly everything is topsy-turvy: The mountains are inverted, pressing down into the watery sky like the points of a crown. Seeing the world this way, I feel something shift inside of me. I don't have to be a hostage to my own ambitions and habits. I can break my own routines anytime I want, turn them inside out, upside down. Boredom, like anxiety, is just another form of resistance.

One morning along the Winsor Trail, I stop and sit for a long time. There's a log in a meadow where lavender shooting stars grow wild along the creek, drooping their necks as though embarrassed by their inappropriate splendor, blooming fervently in a hundred-year drought. I'm resting here one morning when, twenty feet away from me, a flash of something long and thick catches my eye. It's a gray fox, slinking away under a willow. It turns its coal eyes to me, its tail ballooned up like Peacock on display, and creeps out of sight. I feel as though I've stumbled upon a riddle with no answer: How can I learn to slow down while training to run fast?

In late April, I finally do it. I sign up for a meditation class. It meets once a week after dinner, in a room in a church with stacking metal chairs. Even here, in a space dedicated to silence and stillness, I feel overwhelmed by the crash of time. I raced out of the door after dinner, leaving Steve to put the girls to bed; I'm out of breath and I have black beans smeared on my shirt.

"Meditation is a place of rest," the teacher tells us. His name is John, and he explains that he used to be a hard-charging businessman; now he trains people how to sit. "We are enslaved by our minds, in bondage to our thoughts. Sitting is a way to detach from our thinking mind and to free ourselves from suffering."

I think that if he replaced "sitting" with "running," we would be speaking the same language.

He rings the bell for a ten-minute meditation. I close my eyes, steel myself for the ardor ahead. We sit and sit and sit longer. My legs fall asleep. My eyes droop. I try to count my breaths to ten and then start over at zero, as he suggested. One, two . . . *Is Steve remembering to give the girls a bath?* Three . . . *Is he* watching *them in the bath right now? . . . Five . . . The doctor was wrong; the ringing in my ear must be a sign of . . . Eleven? Oh, right, back to zero.* I'm waiting for my thoughts to drift away like clouds and not come back, but as soon as one passes, another one darkens the horizon.

When John rings the bell to signal the end, I want to tear out of the room, but instead I bow my head gravely and make little prayer hands, like the people around me are doing. I swear he is looking straight at me when he says, "The answer to any problem with meditation is 'More sitting is required.'"

The final four weeks before my first fifty-mile race are the big push, the climax of four months of training. Still in disbelief about the distance my legs will have to travel to get to the finish line, I decide to attempt one last long run of thirty-eight miles—my longest day ever. After that, I'll taper my mileage and rest up for the race.

Coming up with a self-supported thirty-eight-mile route through the backcountry isn't just a matter of choosing one from a list. You have to look at maps, link up trails, cobble together the distance. You have to be resourceful, figuring out how much food to carry and whether you need to cache extra snacks along the way; how much water to bring and where to resupply. For this reason, many people use 50K races as training for fifty-mile races—someone else handles the logistics. But this is what I love about ultrarunning: the adventure of managing food and gear, accounting for weather and altitude, anticipating unknowns. It's my own thin edge, a way to be wild and still be home by dark.

I usually try to start planning my Thursday long run on Tuesday. Preparation is everything: I need to know where I'm going before my alarm goes off, and be able to visualize myself actually doing it. My running vest needs to be packed with Gu and snacks—an hour's more than I think I need, just to be safe—and my electrolyte tablets and reservoir have to be left out on the counter, because no matter how much I love to run, there's almost always the temptation to bail. Long training runs are daunting, and there are so many other things I should be doing instead.

"How do you *do* it all?" my friends ask. Like most people, they assume that you have to be hyper-organized and responsible to juggle ultrarunning, work, and family life. I am proof that this is a fallacy. I don't keep spreadsheets or weekly menu plans or a digital calendar. I write appointments and activities on scraps of paper that invariably end up wadded at the bottom of the ratty nylon backpack I carry everywhere. I forget a lot of stuff. I *always* miss items on the grocery list. I'm a piler, not a filer. Bills stack up beside the telephone and on the stairs to my loft, laundry topples in the laundry room. Multitasking is the biggest scam of motherhood. It doesn't make me more efficient, smarter, or more productive. It just makes me more distracted. I put empty tea boxes back into the cupboard and forget to close the drain when I'm drawing the girls' bath, and Steve scolds me, as if I meant to.

I only have one real system, and it's this: If I can do something only at a certain time or under certain circumstances, I do it then. I can't run trails alone when it's dark outside, but I can write at night, so I write at night and run during the day. I can tidy up when the girls are underfoot, but it's much harder to write coherently when they are, so I pile the plates in the sink until after school and write instead.

I tell myself I'm not taking up family time with my running, but that's not completely true. I'm taking up my time with Steve, just the two of us. Gone are the evenings we lie head to feet on the couch, reading. Lots of nights, after the girls go to bed, we hardly talk at all; Steve's compiling invoices in his office and I'm writing at the kitchen table. In the mornings, we sit across from each other at the same table in the sunshine, hands cupping our coffee mugs while the girls play Going to Texas on an Airplane, packing their imaginary bags. Monumental issues are not discussed.

Some mornings, when I forget to bring the carrot sticks to preschool for class snack, I look enviably at other mothers who have it together. Then I remember that no one has it together, really. We're all just holding on by our fingernails. So I guess this is how you do it all: by being deliberate and disciplined even when you are obsessive, absentminded, and easily distracted, and also by not doing it all, not even close.

On the morning of my big run, I'm at the kitchen sink, filling my pack with water, when Steve walks in.

"God, you're *always* running," he groans, reaching for the coffee maker.

"I know, I know, I'm sorry," I say, mostly meaning it. When the seventy-ounce reservoir is nearly full, I slide the plastic seal across the top to close it and turn it upside down, blowing through the bite valve into the tube so that the remaining space fills with air. Then I suck all the air back out so the water won't slosh like a bathtub on my back when I run.

I turn my back to him to nuke a sweet potato in the microwave. I've gotten so sick of gels that I've started bringing real food on my long runs. I stick the steaming potato into a ziplock, sprinkle liberally with salt and a dash of cinnamon, and shove it into my pack.

When I look up, Steve's frowning.

"How much longer are you going to keep doing this?"

He doesn't mean the sweet potatoes.

"I don't know," I sigh. "I wish I did. But I know it's not just about running."

He huffs a little, spooning oatmeal into bowls. "Well, *I'd* sure love to spend all day on the trails." His bitterness is a hard edge he doesn't try to hide. Steve's right, of course. He has clients with leaky irrigation systems and plant problems, and a dozen employees, and they all need to be able to reach him on the phone. Only seldom does someone need to reach me.

Running may be making me stronger, but it's pushing the thin edge of our marriage. Steve's resentment is growing with my mileage, a rift widening between us. We've always given each other our freedom, but the reality is, I'm so much freer now than he is. His business keeps our family afloat; my freelance income barely covers childcare. I'm neurotic *and* I'm never home. In a perfect world, the latter would cancel out the former, but I know in our case it doesn't. It compounds it.

Now he sighs. "You'd better hurry up and write that bestseller." This is our inside joke, that someday I am going to liberate him from the backbreaking bondage of landscaping, only it doesn't seem so funny anymore. The Florida novel has been dead in my drawer for years.

I laugh unconvincingly. "You could always get up early to run, or go after work," I say. His answer is always the same: His phone starts ringing at 7:30 each morning, and by the end of the day he's worn out from lifting flagstone, planting trees, loading and unloading his truck, and driving for hours all over town.

He just shakes his head and turns away. "You go."

I'm becoming eccentric. The weird mother who drops her kids off at school and drives to the trailhead, runs for six hours, and reappears at pickup with dirty ankles, skin like a salt lick, and hair pulled back into a sweaty ponytail. I stash baby wipes and a clean T-shirt in my car, and a cotton skirt to pull on over my shorts so I can go straight on to the next thing and still look presentable. But the truth is, I don't really give a shit. Appearances no longer bother me. This is good; this is progress. I've never not cared, but I've always wanted not to care. Now I don't.

In writing and Zen, Natalie calls this backbone. Not caving under the withering gaze of your critical eye, or anyone else's. You don't get backbone by being tough. You get tough by having backbone. It takes practice.

In other words, more running is required.

For my thirty-eight-mile loop through the mountains above town, I'll need six hours of food and water—too much to carry all in one go. A couple days earlier, I called my friend Erika and arranged for her to hide a cache of Gatorade and pretzels under a tree at a spot where the trail crosses the road.

The first hour, I'm impatient, pushing hard to know how the day will play out. In the middle miles, between ten and thirty, my mind eases. I pass in and out of all the emotions: boredom, elation, excruciating loneliness, yearning, joy, ambivalence. Just as I feel myself becoming attached to the feeling, it changes. This time, my thoughts *are* like the clouds gathering in the thin wedge of sky visible through the trees. I feel them move through me and I let them go. My legs are the constant, my chugging arms, the rhythmic in-out of my breath. I'm not running fast, but I've found my body's natural state: to be in motion, flowing up hills and down, not always comfortably or easily, but steadily.

After five hours, I'm descending a dusty trail off the ridge to Little Tesuque Creek when my right calf flexes into a sudden, furious knot. I sit down and massage cold creek water into my leg and then take a few tentative steps. My muscle is kinked as tightly as a coil. At the exact moment that I realize I could probably run through the pain, I know that I shouldn't.

For a mile or so, I walk, pleading with my calf to let go. *Light, loose, love,* I say over and over, sending the sensation of the words, with my breath, into my muscle. The world slows with me, and for the first time in months, the race falls away. I pause to admire a tall, lopsided cairn of rocks half-hidden under a ponderosa pine. Someone built it, stacking stone upon stone, and didn't care if it was ever seen.

Mentally, walking is harder than running; it feels like one step closer to quitting. But it's actually the opposite—it's what enables you to run again. Sure enough, twenty minutes later, I ease into a slow jog up the grinding switchbacks to the trailhead. Erika is just getting into her car, about to leave, and I call her name, practically throwing myself into her arms for a hug. My neediness is a little embarrassing, but I'm so starved for company, and for food, that I don't try to hide it. I stuff my face with the yogurt-covered pretzels and an orange she hid in a bag under a bush. The bottle of grape Gatorade I pound in one frenzied swig.

When I straggle home an hour later, my calf is warm to the touch and slightly swollen. I have three weeks until the race. Plenty of time. *Please let it be plenty of time.*

That weekend, Steve and I clean out our gear shed. It's exploding with skis and bikes, tents, drybags, life jackets. From the way back of the top shelf, behind a pile of old backpacks, I pull a large un-marked box, the cardboard soggy from being stored too close to the leaky tin roof. I have no idea what's in it, but whatever it is will almost certainly be ruined.

It's a plastic grocery bag filled with letters.

The handwriting is miraculously un-smudged. The letters are from 1992, my junior year in college, when I spent a semester in Australia. I'd been fascinated with the country ever since I wrote a report on it in second grade. For the cover, I had traced a *National Geographic* map, the continent floating alone in the middle of the loneliest ocean in the world, a far-off land full of marvels. Even its craggy shape, with it bulbous unicorn horn poking from the top, looked animalistic, as though it might get up at any moment and lumber away like the strange creatures that inhabited it.

When the emu stands, it is as tall as a man. It has a dull color. A walkabout is when an Aboriginal family goes to hunt for food and look for a camp. . . . They often build a shelter called a wurley. It is made with twigs, branches and bark. . . . The community is change-ing [sic] but very very slowly.

In the Australia of my imagination, you would eat yams all the time and travel great distances on foot and the sun would always be shining, not so different from ultrarunning.

The real Australia was so far away, it felt like another planet. WELCOME TO THE FAR NORTH! the sign at the Cairns airport announced. I'd never been so far south in my life. Tropical rain pelted the windows. It was 1992, the last season on earth of letter writing, just before the dawn of email. It took my aerograms a week to cross the ocean, and another week for a reply to come winging back. When I called Mom from a phone booth, she sounded tinny and faint, as though she was at the end of a very long tunnel, the telephone line buried beneath the sea for seven thousand miles. She'd made me promise her I wouldn't bungee jump or fall in love with an Australian man and never come home. I was so lonely I cried for days.

Two separate seasons unfold in the letters: It's spring in North America and fall in the Southern Hemisphere. Mom is busy doing her clients' taxes ("The computer makes it *so* much easier. Now a change can be done in TWO minutes!") and hanging laundry on the clothesline; she signs every letter with a flurry of X's and O's. Meg is moving to California with her boyfriend, who will eventually become her husband. Four L.A. police officers are acquitted in the Rodney King trial. My grandfather turns eighty-one and reassures me that it's normal to be homesick. Memories flutter like moths from the pages.

Dad isn't dead yet. He is attending the National Magazine Awards in New York City and winning. He is researching Walt Whitman for a story and mowing the grass, meeting photographers, checking up on me. He writes every Friday from his desk at the Geographic. His letters are the longest and most detailed of all: two or three pages, typed, about kayaking on the Chesapeake Bay and his neighbor who bashed in a rabid fox with a frying pan, about the Australia he remembers from an assignment he took years ago, and about the importance of being brave. Twenty years after he wrote them, his words seem eerily prescient:

Sometimes the things we disliked most or were most uncomfortable with are the things we think back on most fondly, the things we are most grateful to have done. I think we like the things that have tested us, assuming we have passed the test, which is usually the case.

22

Mind Like Sky

New Mexico, 2013

Thinking about racing an ultra and racing an ultra are two very different things. Before the race, it's easy to get caught up in abstract thoughts. *Will I feel strong? Will I get hurt? Will I set a new personal record? Will I win?*

But once the race starts, these become pointless concerns. Anything can and will happen, much of which is impossible to predict. The very scenario you most feared might not come to pass; the thing you least expected might. The best you can do is train well, steady your heart and mind for the long haul, and show up ready for anything.

The week before the Jemez 50 Mile race, I ice my calf three times each day for ten minutes. Before bed each night, I roll my legs with my foam roller. On some days I use a hard wooden rolling pin, kneading out the knots, flattening the lumpy spots, and I feel my muscles clutch the bone like carpet bunching up underfoot. I slather myself in arnica gel, for sore muscles, and swallow handfuls of fish oil and turmeric supplements to reduce inflammation and lie on my friend's floor while she jabs acupuncture needles into my calf until I feel the twangy spasm of release. Recovery takes just as much time as running, if not more.

Each day brings gradual improvement, but I can't shake the worry that I pushed too hard and now I'm paying for it. Am I losing fitness? What if I'm not able to finish the race? Should I even start? It seems I've traded one dark obsession for another, and the very thing that used to soothe my anxiety is feeding it.

For the first time in months, I sit in front of my running altar. The stones and photograph are felted in a fine layer of dust. The bundle of sage is crumbly and dry but still holds its sweet scent of summertime on the river. Dad's bemused expression hasn't changed; he's ready for the next thing, and seeing his face, I know I am, too. It's possible, probable even, that I won't know what this race is teaching me until after I run it. *If* I can run it. And the only way to find out is to try.

I go downstairs and make my lists: what to bring, what to carry— the unpredictability of ultrarunning tempered momentarily by the illusion of control. I remind myself that by Sunday it will all be over: the anticipation, the months of training, the pain, the race.

And I think: *I do not want it to be over.*

I make another list, everything I'm afraid of: Fifty miles. The caldera. Pulling my calf, wrecking it for good. Tearing my Achilles, falling, breaking a tooth. Going out too fast, going too slowly, not being able to finish, getting dehydrated, cramping, throwing up, running into a bear, crying, feeling scared, getting lost, getting beaten. Badly. Losing face, discovering I'm a fraud. Dying.

Seeing my own freak show of fears spelled out in black and white diminishes them somehow. There are so many, and some are so ludicrous and improbable (a *tooth*?!), that statistically they can't *all* happen. So that's a relief, sort of. Maybe just one or two.

Three days before the race, I go walking with Natalie. The mountain pulls me up, the way it sometimes does. I feel as though I'm carrying a plastic jug in each hand. The imaginary pitchers are filled with all my thoughts—to-dos, annoyances, emails to return, mysterious maladies, grocery lists. I'm turning the pitcher over as I walk and pouring them out, not with any rancor or bitterness, but easily, without attachment. I dump one jug and then the other and then it's time to dump the first one again because they're bottomless, really, but I don't care because I'm pouring them out. I don't need them today.

When I get home, I make another list. This one's the psych-up, get-your-heart-in-the-game, mad-mojo list of everything I'm excited about. I want to run my own race, to feel proud, to sing out loud to my favorite songs, to finish strong and see Pippa and Maisy waiting for me at the end. To be transformed and believe in myself.

I have so many resources. I have food and electrolytes. I have music to boost me as I cross the caldera. I have my stamina and will, the fierce force of childbirth, my own labors and my mother's, the determination to be born and to live. I have all the old layers of me: the seven-year-old tomboy who jumped into the creek, the twenty-year-old homesick on the other side of the world, the mother who walked with her newborn into the hills. And I have everyone who showed me I was loved. "We are all with you," Dad wrote to me in Australia. "There aren't any limits, you know."

There are things I know and don't know. I'm in the middle, the deep center of running and life. I want to race from this place, between the lows of anxiety and the highs of elation; from the middlemost point of knowing and not knowing, open to whatever happens.

The caldera *is* the middle. The deep interior of the supervolcano and the halfway point of the race, where you're equidistant between start and finish and the only way out is forward. I've been running all morning, and in the vast, open crater, distances are deceiving. The shag of trees on the far slope looks close, but for a long time it is not getting closer. I'm a dot in the depression, and there are few landmarks to measure my progress: a lone runner up ahead, the white peak of an aid station tent like a distant, happy circus.

It's here, crossing the volcano in the full blast of midday, exposed to shrieking wind and sun, that I go out of my mind and into my body, purely animal. And then even my body I leave behind. I'm running with pebbles and grit rubbing blisters inside my shoes; hours later, I'll take off my socks to find two purplish toenails oozing pus, but for now I'm too entranced to notice.

In his book *Running with the Mind of Meditation*, Sakyong Mipham calls this the third phase of running garuda, named for the Buddhist and Hindu mythological man-bird with wings and arms. "This phase of running is 'outrageous,'" Mipham writes, "because we are ready to challenge ourselves to go beyond our comfort zone." In a state of prolonged effort, garuda runners experience heightened awareness and clarity, a rare presence he calls "mind like sky" that liberates you from the endless striving of ego. "The garuda in particular symbolizes freedom from hope and fear—our hoping that something will happen and being fearful that it will not."

After twelve hypnotic miles in the caldera, something *does* happen. The small orange flags marking the course vanish. I slow to a walk and scour the area for orange course ribbons. They've either fallen over in the wind or been trampled. I'm lost.

Above me on the mountain, the rustling of branches. Something is crashing through the brush. Animal. Mountain lion or bear? I squint through the trees, my scalp tingling. Lanky beige shapes lumber horizontally across the slope. A herd, flashing pale, knobby antlers.

Elk. They shuffle sideways, hooves stamping the soot-black deadfall less than thirty feet away from me. They move by instinct, not fear, and as I watch them pass, their sureness and beauty calms me.

A hundred yards below me, two runners are pacing back and forth. They're lost, too.

"Do you see the trail?" I yell.

One of the runners puts his palms up to the sky. *Beats me.*

I'm not sure what to do. If I wait for them, I'll waste precious time and momentum, but I'll have a better chance of finding the flags. If I don't, I'll be lost *and* alone.

Ultrarunners are predisposed to persevere, no matter how heinous the effort. Within the sport, quitting is called "dropping," and most runners would rather stagger, bloodied and bruised, to the finish than drop. Running for many hours at a time requires a headstrong faith in your own ability, a fatalistic acceptance that discomfort is unavoidable, and a lunatic conviction that it will all be worth it in the end. At its most elemental, ultrarunning is an exercise in extreme, occasionally foolhardy optimism.

There's a tradition among ultrarunners of writing race reports after a particularly long and grueling effort. These are true-life survival stories penned by elite, middle-of-the-pack, and DFL runners ("dead fucking last," not an insult but a point of pride), as though by trying to recount what happened to them on the trail, it will be possible to make sense of the madness. The reports are peppered with moments of dogged determination, sheer misery, and shimmery glimpses of spiritual awakening—all within the span of a few miles. Reading them is like reading about a disaster narrowly averted: improbable tales by otherwise sane people about dislocating their shoulder, face-planting, getting struck by lightning, going blind in both eyes because the wind blew grit into their corneas—and *still* not dropping. Most are average runners you might not pick out on the street.

Despite the physical torment, ultra distances can be surprisingly forgiving. Because you're out for so long, there are plenty of opportunities to get a second, third, even fourth wind. You may bonk and decide to drop, and someone—a volunteer, another runner, maybe your own loopy brain—will talk you out of it. A few miles later, you'll be happier than you've ever been in your whole life.

For as long as I could remember, Dad had abhorred quitting. The summer I was eighteen, I took a job teaching sailing on Deer Isle, Maine. My college friend Susie and I arrived in late May. The ocean was colder and choppier than any water I'd seen, and we slept in a trailer that reeked of sour milk and hamburger meat that had been left to spoil in the mini-fridge all winter. I called home, both my homes, to tell my parents I wanted to leave.

"It's okay, come home," Mom said soothingly.

But Dad was unhappy, urging me in grave tones to "stick with it." I could picture him on the other end of the line, lips pressed severely together, frowning. I could tell he was worried that this might be the decision that revealed my true nature, the one that tipped the balance from she's-going-to-make-something-of-herself to maybe-she'll-spend-her-life-working-in-restaurants. Quitting felt awful, but I knew I was going to do it anyway. I drove south on I-95 and cut west to the Adirondacks, where I moved in with my boyfriend and got a job in a restaurant.

Dad never said another word about Maine. There was no need. Busing dishes all day on tired feet, I knew I'd bungled a good thing and hadn't tried hard enough to make it work. From then on, giving up would be a last resort.

I pace across the hillside, waiting for the two runners to climb up to where I last saw the flags. I don't know where I am in the pack, but I think I'm among the top two or three females. The only other woman I've seen all day was charging up the trail about a quarter mile ahead of me just before dawn. Then she disappeared around a switchback. It had to be Diana Finkel, who's about my age and is one of the best ultrarunners in the country. Finkel set the women's course record at the Jemez 50 Mile and finished second overall at the Hardrock 100 in 2010; she led the whole pack for more than eighty miles, until fatigue and debilitating leg cramps forced her to walk. Two days after the race, she went into kidney failure and had to be airlifted to a Denver hospital. She'd developed rhabdomyolysis, a dangerous buildup of toxins and shredded muscle tissue in her blood. She spent sixteen days in the hospital. A year later, she returned to Hardrock and won the women's race for the second year in a row.

The two guys and I spread out across the hillside, scouring the grass and branches for the course markers. Talking takes too much energy, so we communicate by pantomiming. We're on the west side of Pajarito Mountain Ski Area, and I know the course climbs a couple thousand feet to the radio towers on the summit. But the mountain is wide enough that accidentally straying too far one way or the other will put us out of position once we reach the top. This might add miles to our race or, worse, shorten it, which is grounds for disqualification.

I tell myself there's no reason to panic. We know exactly where we are, but not where we need to go. My brain snaps to attention: *Think, look.* After ten minutes, one of the runners hollers something and we hustle over to see. A single orange ribbon dangles from a branch.

We separate, retreating again into our private worlds, each of us picking a different line up the slope. Just like my acquaintance Jacob had warned me before the race, it's hands-on-knees, clawing-at-tree-branches steep. I bend into the nightmarish pitch, my heart hammering, trying to coax my thighs into as fast a hike as possible. I've lost twenty minutes to being lost. Now there's nothing to do but get out on my own.

Our friends who are taking care of Pippa and Maisy for the day offered to bring them up to watch the end of the race. The plan is to meet at the ski lodge aid station, at about mile 36. Just thinking about seeing their sweet faces makes me want to cry. I've been out here by myself for so long, and I still have so far to go. But this is its own kind of pleasure—the wild emotional swings, so much joy and pain you can't possibly keep it in.

The whole way down the mountain, I'm running back to them, and they're pulling me forward, my desire and theirs two equal forces. I round a switchback and see a posse of kids far below, cheering and waving handmade signs. They are blond and jumping straight up and down, like deranged pogo-stickers. I'd recognize my girls' ferocious energy from a mile away.

Then they're upon me, wriggling bodies and hands reaching up for me and saying "Mama!" over and over. There's a poster with my name on it being waved about in the air, and there are my friends and their kids cheering me, but I have only a few seconds for hugs and kisses, because I still have fourteen miles to go.

"See you at the finish!" I yell over my shoulder, knowing it will be more than two hours before I do.

Steve's waiting for me on the deck of the ski lodge. Instead of racing, he's volunteered to be my crew. A crew's job is to meet you at the aid stations and help you get whatever you need to keep going—food, drink, tough love, forced cheer, and bald-faced lies. You're allowed to bark at them, demanding salt tabs when you are dehydrated. You're allowed to guilt them into bringing you a grande Frappuccino and drink exactly one sip and hand it back because you have to keep running. Your job is not dropping. Their job is indulging your absurd requests to make sure you don't.

I'm glad to see Steve—not because I love him, though of course I do, but because he has things I need. All the way down the mountain, I've been compiling a list in my head, and now I order it all like I'm phoning in takeout from a Chinese restaurant. Salt pill because I'm dehydrated, a few more energy gels to stick in my pocket. Water and electrolyte tablets in my hydration bladder, please. While Steve's restocking my pack, I sprint to the bathroom to pee. Lowering myself onto the toilet is torture on my quads. Urine: murky yellow—dehydrated. Outside, I swallow the salt pill and take two extras and shove them into my pack's tiny magnetic pocket, where before dawn I stashed a handful of dark-chocolate-covered espresso beans. I pop a few, half-melted from my body heat, into my mouth, smearing chocolate on my already filthy fingers.

Steve tells me I'm in second place, behind Diana. Then he buckles his own pack and we take off. I've been in the aid station maybe three minutes.

Steve is running the last fourteen miles with me as my pacer. Pacers aren't registered competitors but crew who run portions of the race with you. "Pacing" is a bit of a misnomer. Often it's not the pacers who are setting the pace, but you, the beleaguered runner. Your pacer's main job is to keep you company, hound you to eat and drink, make sure you don't get lost, and goad, shame, threaten, and cheer you into maintaining forward progress. Late in the race, your pacer might not be running as much as jogging, hiking, or walking quickly beside you. Nothing that pacers do or say should ever suggest that you are running interminably slowly, so slowly, in fact, that the pacer could stroll casually without breaking a sweat and still keep up.

Now Steve tells me that Diana came through the ski lodge aid station at least forty-five minutes ahead of me, maybe more. Barring some serious mishap on her part, there's little chance I will catch her. My legs are heavy but still moving, and I'm just happy to be with Steve. He runs in front and does most of the talking, rattling off his usual barrage of mind-numbing, esoteric horticultural and geological facts that I instantaneously tune out; I can't be bothered to take my earbuds out, and my iPod keeps cycling through the playlist I made for the race: "Girl on Fire," Gary Clark's "The Life," the same songs, the same lines—*this is the life, the life, the life, the life, the life*—over and over until I start to believe them, until I tune them out, too.

At aid stations, Steve raids the buffet for orange slices and peanut butter sandwich squares and hands them to me. (He's not allowed to carry any of my food or gear—that's called "muling," and it's against race rules.) Some I eat, others I squirrel away in my fists or pockets because I can't stomach more calories and I don't want to let Steve down. Suddenly I'm overcome by love. He's so cheerful and kind, my husband! He's doing what he does best, the things for which I have always loved him most: He's talking to me, naming plants, making me laugh.

We pass through the chalky white moonscape left over from the old burn and into the steep canyon, where we begin to catch up to other runners up ahead, the tail end of the 50K pack. While we're still out of earshot, Steve barks in a menacing mobster voice, imitating the woman who screamed at me from the sidewalk during the half marathon years ago. "They're hurting. Take them *DOWN!* Crush them!"

If I had any air left in my lungs, I would have laughed until I peed my shorts, but I don't, and my lips are so gummy with Gu that all I can do is snort, which only makes me laugh-snort harder. This goes on for five or six runners, none of whom I have any desire or need to crush. They're not even in my race. Like me, they're just trying to make it to the finish.

"Great job!" I say each time I pass, raising my hand in greeting. "Way to go!"

"Looking good!" they call. "Awesome!"

We climb out of the last canyon for the final push toward the finish. Pippa and Maisy are there, screaming my name and waving their sign. The digital clock reads 10:14. I'm the second woman, and eleventh overall.

I find Diana in the crowd to congratulate her. She's all smiles and still looks fresh, as if running fifty miles is no big deal when you've almost died doing hundreds. Steve brings me a beer, and one for himself, but my stomach's too bloated to drink anything. I pour a pile of sand and grit from my shoes onto the ground. My big toenail puffs out purple. Tomorrow I will sterilize a needle and lance it along the cuticle to let the pus drain out, but for now I just wiggle my feet in the grass and let it all sink in.

My calf, the thing that had worried me most about this race, hadn't hurt. Not once, ever. At all. I think about the energy I spent inventing stories around that injury, stewing over a scenario that never came to pass. How many different possibilities exist in the world, all at once. How much calmer life would be if I could learn to hold them all, at the same time, without getting attached to any of them.

I hadn't lost my mind in the caldera after all. I'd found it. All the weather in my brain had blown away and I saw everything—my place in the world, the world itself—with a clarity as wide and sharp as the arc of blue above me. I was simply a speck in space, lost and found, adrift in the enormity of earth and sky.

23

Drinking the Wind

South Kaibab Trail, inner gorge of the Grand Canyon, 2013

After a year and a half of racing, I needed a break. Training and trying to win was wearing me out. I wanted to run just to run, but I also wanted to keep pushing myself. I needed a big objective that was mine alone.

It was June, and I had slowly recovered from the fifty-mile race and was wondering what was next. I was feeling strong and fast and didn't want to squander my fitness. Until I figured it out, I would do what I always did: run up Atalaya. Over the course of a few weeks, I kept seeing the same man hiking; he was older, with a peppery mustache and a wide smile, trekking poles, and a couple of dogs, and he always stepped aside to let me pass, cheering me on in his strong European accent. The third or fourth time I passed him, he called out to me, "You're so fast! You should run the Grand Canyon!"

His name was Gerd Nunner, and he was a sixty-one-year-old German expat who lived in Santa Fe. He told me he'd hiked from the South Rim to the North Rim and back sixty-nine times—more than anyone else in the world. (He would go on to do it more than one hundred times.) After that, whenever I saw Gerd hiking, I would slow to a jog or stop and he would tell me about the Grand Canyon. He knew all about the best months to make the double crossing (spring can still be icy on the North Rim, summer is a furnace, and late fall is just right) and the best ways to avoid the mules that leave the South Rim every morning at 5:30 a.m., carrying supplies to Phantom Ranch, at the bottom of the canyon. This was before I had seriously considered running it, when it still seemed like a fanciful pursuit far in the future, but I liked talking to Gerd, and within a month or two my conversations with him had worked their way into some kind of conscious decision to try.

It's forty-two miles to run across the Grand Canyon and back: seven miles from the top of the South Rim down to the Colorado River and then fourteen miles up to the North Rim, and back the way you came, with 10,500 feet of climbing and 10,500 feet of descending. The rim-to-rim-to-rim, or R2R2R for short, isn't an organized race. It's a self-supported trail run that you can do anytime, by yourself or with other people. In recent years, it's become the most popular ultra adventure in the country, famous for its scenery and staggeringly harsh topography.

I liked the idea of traveling across the Grand Canyon in a single day. Even more, though, I loved that it wasn't a competition. I wouldn't have to show up before dawn with a pit in my stomach, wondering how I would fare against other runners. I would just have to show up before dawn with a pit in my stomach from wondering how *I* would fare. And that distinction eliminated the pit in my stomach. I wouldn't have to psych myself up for the competition or hold myself back from the competition. I could just run across the most beautiful canyon in the world any way I felt like running.

All fall I ran my trails in reverse: first I ran down the mountains, and then I ran back up, to mimic the Grand Canyon's topography. Everything about this felt wrong to me. I still clung to the puritanical notion that you have to go uphill first, get the hard part over with, suffer for your rewards, do your homework, and then go out to play.

Steve was going to join me, but at the last minute he couldn't go, so I enlisted two running friends: Meaghen, a twenty-five-year-old editor at *Outside,* and Anna, a disaster relief consultant in her mid-thirties who had a three-year-old daughter. Both were experienced ultrarunners, but neither had been training for the Grand Canyon, so we agreed to start together but then run at our own pace. On the last Friday in October, we left Santa Fe like a bunch of bandits making a getaway, hopped up on lattes and blaring Britney Spears's "Work B**ch," giddy with freedom and the anticipation of trading one kind of hard work for another.

Now we stand on the South Rim, peering into blackness. It's 6 a.m. on October 27, 2013, and only a faint scrim of yellow lines the horizon. Nearly five thousand feet below us, the Colorado River snakes bottle-green and cold between layered rock walls. The temperature is thirty-five degrees, with a light breeze and zero percent chance of rain. Anna and Meaghen and I huddle together, shivering in shorts and thin wind jackets, headlamps bathing our feet in pools of white light. There's no one here but us. Somewhere across the chasm, the North Rim looms indifferently in the dark. It seems inconceivable that before the day is over, I will run all the way there and back.

At 6:05 a.m., we drop into the abyss. Even in my headlamp's beam, the South Kaibab Trail is dark and very narrow and appears deserted, but within minutes we come up hard behind the long, dusty mule train. Our easy lope slows to a brisk, impatient walk. A few hundred feet below us, the wrangler's scratchy voice drifts out of the twilight. "Don't get too close to the last mule," he calls. "We'll let you pass at the bottom."

The last time I saw Gerd, he reassured me, "Don't worry about the mules. They'll only be a problem for a minute or two." Now, though, I can't help but worry. Which bottom is the mule driver talking about, I wonder uneasily, imagining us eating mule dust for seven miles, all the way to the river. The *bottom* bottom? I'd wanted to start conservatively, and to use the darkness to keep my speed in check and save my strength for later in the day, but this is too slow.

After a few switchbacks, though, we come to a widening in the trail and the wrangler *whoas* the mules. "Go ahead!" he calls to us, and we slide by on the inside and leave them behind in the dusk. The trail is hard-packed sand with some rocks, and we settle into an easy pace. The sky is smudged with pink; soon it's light enough to see, and we switch off our headlamps and shove them into our packs, stopping now and then to take a few photographs of the sunrise painting the mesas tangerine. It's hard to overstate the flamboyance of dawn breaking over the Grand Canyon, but I can't gawk too much, because I have to keep my eyes on the ground. Wooden steps have been hammered across the trail every few feet, presumably to keep the sand—the whole trail, really—from sliding four thousand feet straight down to the river. Eventually I find my rhythm, an exaggerated, hopping gait that becomes less awkward with each step.

When you fall off the edge of the world, it helps to give in to gravity.

The Grand Canyon is home to the oldest exposed rock on the planet, dating back two billion years. Layer upon layer of sandstone and shale, quartz and limestone tell the story of perpetual change on an almost imperceptible scale. In its various geologic incarnations, the Grand Canyon has been a mountain range, a vast, shallow sea, an arid desert, and shifting sand dunes. In the uppermost layers, you can find shark teeth and mollusk fossils. As wind and water and sun carved away at the strata, volcanic eruptions laid down new layers of sediment. The Colorado River itself is a relatively recent addition, seventy million years ago, sculpting the canyon's blocky buttes and mesas. Time here is both relentless and outrageously slow; nothing happens in a hurry.

Last night, in our hotel room on the South Rim, Anna and Meaghen and I spread our map out on the bed. The black line squiggling across the river and up the other side looked so straightforward—just run there and back!—but I knew there would be many immeasurable factors to contend with along the way: heat, hydration, the vagaries of our own bodies, which might get battered by the long descents and climbs. We estimated, conservatively, that it might take us eleven hours, maybe even as little as ten, to cover the forty-two miles and 21,000 feet of vertical gain and loss. Many recreational runners take twelve hours or more; Gerd has power-hiked it in as little as sixteen. My plan was to look at my phone occasionally to check our progress, but to otherwise let go of time and external pressures and do my best to run strong, from within myself. The last thing I want to do is rush.

In the last text message I got from Steve just before 6 a.m., he wrote, "Don't worry about your pace. Have fun, and just enjoy where you are."

It gets warm as quickly as it gets light, and by the time I reach the Colorado River, the sun is reflecting off the water and I can feel the heat radiating from the rocks. I stand on the Black Bridge, an iron suspension footbridge, feeling it sway and staring at the river sliding soundlessly beneath my feet. I take out my phone, snap a photo. It's 7:12. A few minutes later, Meaghen arrives, and then Anna.

At various intervals along the main trails, there are pit toilets and emergency phones and spigots with drinking water. Though we'll be able to refill our water at the bottom of the canyon and again on the North Rim, I'm carrying all my own food, my pack crammed with Gu, energy chews with extra potassium and sodium, chocolate-covered espresso beans, a couple of dense protein bars, a peanut-butter-and-jelly sandwich, and a twenty-dollar bill. I don't plan to run out of food, but in case of emergency I can resupply at Phantom Ranch, where the canteen is rumored to serve the best lemonade in the world.

On the north side of the bridge, we pause to take off our jackets, refill our water at Bright Angel Campground, duck into a toilet to pee, and eat a couple of gels. Far above us, the North Rim jabs out above the canyon. The North Kaibab Trail is twice as long as the South Kaibab Trail, gaining 5,700 feet in fourteen miles as it climbs gradually along Bright Angel Creek.

We've entered the inner gorge, where the canyon is at its narrowest, where the river is most constricted. Reddish-gray walls slant down on either side of the trail at jagged angles. Streaked with quartz and burnished black in places, the Vishnu schist layer of metamorphic rock is the oldest in the canyon; geologists call this the basement rock. Sitting directly atop the two-billion-year-old schist is a layer of five-hundred-million-year-old sandstone. The missing layers in between are a mystery, 1.5 billion years of strata, of time, unaccounted for, swallowed by a breach in the earth. This gap in the geologic record is known as the Great Unconformity.

The blackened, ragged schist is older than anything I've ever seen. Compared with the rosier tones of the canyon's upper layers, it appears weary, tormented by time, as though the world has turned itself inside out. I'm turned inside out, too, awed by the canyon and my own body for crossing it, and suffused with a strange joy that feels almost like sadness. Dad has been dead for nearly three years. Where has the time gone? So many bleak months of my own record have gone missing, overlaid by the haste of real life, sliding beneath the surface of motherhood and love. Grief is its own unconformity.

Two months before the R2R2R, Pippa had started kindergarten. On her first day of school, she was up before dawn. "Mama," she asked, holding up her new school-uniform polo shirt for me to see. "Do the buttons go on the front or the back?"

I smiled and pointed to her tummy, my eyes stinging. For days I'd been fighting back tears. Life was about to get busier and faster for my wild baby, time no longer our own.

We biked four blocks to school, and after I left her with her teacher, I hid in the girls' bathroom and cried some more. *She's not really leaving,* I tried to console myself. *This is only the beginning.* But I didn't buy it. What an egregious mistake I'd made! All the precious time I'd wasted trying to carve out space for myself! Gone for good in the blink of a five-year-old's eye.

I was still teary when I met Natalie a couple of hours later for our walk. "I don't want her world to be so structured," I whined on the way down the mountain.

Ahead of me, Natalie bobbed her head. "You're sad Pippa started school," she said simply. "Be in the sadness. Don't make stories around it."

Her words stopped me in mid-stride. I made her say them again. "You're just sad."

For a split second I held everything clearly in my mind, all the jumbled pieces organizing themselves into a neat bundle: The sorrow I'd felt as a girl was so big, it seemed as though it would swallow me if I let it. Instead I'd made up tales and suppositions, trying to crack the case, even when sometimes there were no answers, or the answers I found only led to other questions. "More explanations later," I'd written in my spy book. I was still looking.

Maybe the answer had been in front of me all along. Maybe I'd just been sad. And maybe that's what growing up means: You don't have to believe all your own stories anymore. You get to choose.

The idea, like so much of what came out of Natalie's mouth, was so slight and yet far too big to grasp all at once. It took the top of my head right off. All I could do was keep walking.

That afternoon, Pippa and I rode our bikes home from school. The sun was high, and the late-summer storm clouds had pushed east over the plains. The waxing moon hung sideways above us.

"Mama," Pippa said, pointing to the sky. "How do astronauts land on the moon when it's so skinny?" I could see her five-year-old mind-wheel spinning, and I could see what she saw: bitty, bubble-headed space travelers misjudging their lunar landing and clinging to the narrow arc of the moon, space boots dangling off one side. They plant their flag in the swinging swoop of real estate and hold on for dear life.

The North Kaibab Trail rolls gradually upward through the box canyon from the Colorado River, crossing Bright Angel Creek atop narrow wooden bridges, for seven miles to Cottonwood Campground. Liberated from the awkward cadence of the descent, I lengthen my stride and relax into a steady clip, pulling ahead of Meaghen and Anna. For a few moments I hear their voices behind me, but then all is silent and I'm alone on the trail.

At Cottonwood, I fill up on water from the spigot and dash into the outhouse. From here the trail begins to climb in earnest to the North Rim. I've been in the shade all morning, but above Roaring Springs waterfall, I leave the shadows and cross into the glaring desert sun. I pass cottonwoods blazing gold along the creek and meadows of silver-green agave, some shooting their blooms skyward. I part waist-high swaying grasses, hop lizards, catch up to groups of runners who left the South Rim before us, and try to outrun swarms of flies. A wiry man with grasshopper legs and a tiny pack strides past me and disappears around a bend.

In the last four miles to the North Rim, there are several long sections where the trail is bound on one side by massive cliffs of redwall limestone rising straight up and on the other by thousands of feet of sheer drop-off. There are no guardrails or barriers, just empty air and, far below the cliff's edge, rock and more rock. The trail is maybe three feet wide. I creep slowly along with my hand on the wall, trying not to look down.

Around a bend I see Gerd coming toward me. His plan had been to start from the South Rim at 2 a.m. Now he's on his way back down. I can tell it's him by his black knee braces and his starchy, long-legged gait. We stop to chat for a few moments, and he bends down on one knee along the edge to show me where the trail washed away several years ago in a storm. He was on the North Kaibab that day, in late November; it was icy, and he had to cling to the side and pull himself up, which he reenacts dramatically with a jolly, mustached grin.

"But go, go!" he says, waving me on. "You are rocking it!"

I tuck in for the final push. Though steep, the switchbacks on North Kaibab make the trail fairly runnable. Within an hour, I'm jogging through a tunnel of ponderosas to the top of the North Rim. The North Kaibab trailhead is wedged into a side canyon, so the panorama isn't nearly as spectacular as from the South Rim. The anticlimax is okay, though, because all I really want to do is eat, fish some pebbles out of my right shoe that have been chafing my toes, refill my water, and be on my way.

The problem is, there is no water. According to ranger reports, the tap is supposed to remain turned on until the end of October, when the winter season officially arrives on the North Rim, but it's already shut off. This I learn from Grasshopper Legs, who's sitting on a bench, waiting for his friends. He introduces himself as Chris Vargo, an up-and-coming pro runner from Colorado Springs. In recent years, the R2R2R has become a proving ground for elite trail runners trying to break the fastest known time, or FKT, for the double crossing. The current men's FKT is 6:21:47, set by Rob Krar; the women's record belongs to Bethany Lewis, in 8:15:51. (Both records would stand until in 2017.)

I lean against a signpost and take off my shoes and socks. A backpacker approaches us and nods approvingly. "Halftime!" he calls. Though we've just finished the longest climb of the day, we're only halfway there. Now I have to turn around and run twenty-one miles back the way I came.

Nearby, a runner is sitting on the ground with his head in his hands, moaning.

"Are you okay?" I ask him.

"I'm dehydrated. I thought there would be water here," he says glumly.

My hydration pouch is nearly empty, too, but I hand him a salt tab and Chris pours water into his bottle.

"Good luck, man," Chris says.

I ask Chris to take my picture, wolf down an energy waffle, and check my phone. It's 10:45. Eight minutes after I arrived at the North Rim, I begin the long run back to the river.

In the first mile, I take inventory. My legs still feel solid and not particularly tired, the blistery patch on my foot seems to be gone, my fingers aren't too swollen from dehydration, my stomach is full of Gu, and I still have plenty of battery life left in my iPod. I let my stride lengthen and loosen, and soon I feel like I'm levitating, my feet barely skimming the ground. I pass now familiar landmarks— the crumbling section of trail where a ranger had fixed a rope and the water faucet near Supai Tunnel, where I'd spaced out and lost the trail for a few moments, wandering into a patch of prickers before realizing my mistake. When I stop and refill my water, I see a woman hiker I recognize from earlier. "Are you Katie from Santa Fe?" she asks. I nod and she says, "Your friends told me to tell you that they turned around at Cottonwood." Any hope I had of meeting up with Anna and Meaghen is gone, but there are plenty of other runners—flocks of them now—making the long climb up to the North Rim, some walking, some jogging.

Sometimes I whoop when I run. I do it spontaneously, without thinking. I whoop when I'm short of breath, to regulate my breathing. I whoop when I'm alone and scared, to warn off animals, to blow off nervous energy and to hear the sound of my own voice. But mostly I whoop when I'm so happy I can't keep it in, like now. I hoot as I pass other runners, and they hoot back, pumping their fists in the air.

Below Cottonwood Campground, I round a corner and see Gerd ahead of me, striding back to the river. I've caught up to him sooner than we both expected, and I holler his name. He turns and waves me on, shouting as I go by, "You look like a feather!"

Then I'm back in the basement of the canyon, where the trail narrows and becomes rougher underfoot. Beside Bright Angel Creek, flinging itself toward its confluence with the Colorado River, someone has balanced a few pointy rocks on end. Above me, the Vishnu schist slants into the inner gorge. The rock is so ancient, it has seen everything in the world. It is impartial to happiness and pain, to success or failure. To time itself. I could be anything in this canyon and it wouldn't matter. We are tiny and new, brief flashing dots on the landscape, infinitesimal and infinite. *This* is true freedom. This is why I've come. This is why I run.

Down to the Colorado again, past workers doing laundry at Phantom Ranch, for a quick pit stop at the toilet and faucet. Seven miles and 4,700 feet above me, the South Rim hovers like another planet, so many layers still between me and it. I check my phone. It's 1:10 p.m.

Up on the North Rim, it was a comfortable seventy degrees, but five thousand feet lower, it's closer to eighty-five. I'm flushed and sweaty, and the heat is oppressive. There's no way I'm going to run by the river without getting into it. I detour a couple hundred yards off the main trail to a crescent beach that doubles as a boat launch for whitewater rafts.

I ignore the sign that says NO SWIMMING—DANGEROUS CURRENTS, take off my shoes and pack and shirt, and wade into the eddy past my ankles. The water is invigorating—fifty degrees, straight out of the bottom of Glen Canyon Dam, a hundred miles upstream. I splash it over my face, arms, legs, and bare stomach, cooled by the current that formed the canyon, and keep running, straight into the jaws of the climb. The South Kaibab is relentlessly steep right away, with sandy switchbacks and those dreaded wooden steps. Nothing to do but dig in and run. The Colorado drops away quickly, and soon I can see the river only in pieces, slivers of frothing whitewater on its way to someplace else.

I pass in and out of shadows cast by the steep walls. Ravens circle above me, and a breeze riffles my skin. I've been drinking warm grape-flavored electrolytes all day, but the thought of taking another sip makes me want to barf. All I want right now is plain, ice-cold water. I open my mouth to let the air blow in. I'm so thirsty I could drink the wind. I think I remember seeing a faucet at the Tonto Trail junction, a couple of miles uphill, and I spend many minutes fantasizing about turning it on, lying on the ground, and letting it wash over me. But when I get there, there is no tap, so I take a long swig from my nozzle and jog on.

Above Tonto, the trail climbs maniacally through a dozen switchbacks to gain another steep wall. I alternate between running at a plodding pace and power hiking—a staccato tempo that usually annoys me but now feels like all I can manage. I know I've been running fast and well and toward a good time, and I want to finish strong. For the first time all day, I'm aware of the clock and the familiar pang of time slipping away too quickly.

Through a narrow squeeze in the trail, around a few more hairpin turns, and up the final rise to the South Rim. There's the wooden sign, the South Kaibab Trailhead, the place where we stood this morning, double-knotting our shoelaces. It's disorienting in the daylight, swarming with tourists waiting for the shuttle bus, different somehow. But maybe it's me. *I'm* different. I've climbed out from the bottom of the world. My phone reads 3:20 p.m.: nine hours and fifteen minutes since I last stood on this spot.

Staring out across the rift, I can see the South Kaibab Trail scissoring four thousand feet down its escarpment, past all the sharp drop-offs we navigated in the dark. Below that, the glinting river and the green smudges of trees where Phantom Ranch is tucked into its side canyon. I let my eyes follow the canyon through the jagged, narrow cut in the earth, past Cottonwood to where the trail heaves left and up to the tall ponderosas on the North Rim. I can't believe I crossed such vast time and space and came back again. It's as though I was transported.

I ran forty-two miles today. In three days I will turn forty-two. My legs are scratched from rocks and brambles and red with canyon dust. I'm salty and disheveled, but I've never felt more like myself—who I am in this moment and who I've always been. I didn't try to run fast, but I did, an hour off the record pace. Strength and stamina, will and wonder—and a little bit of luck—aligned. The magic was in *not* trying, in running strong from my heart and bones straight into the heart of the world.

24

Continue Under All Circumstances

Atalaya Mountain, 2013

"You look like you're seven years old," Natalie tells me a few days after I get home from the Grand Canyon.

I think she must be talking about my scabby shins and sunburned nose and chapped lips, my hair pulled back into a messy knot. Possibly this is her way of gently suggesting I ought to clean up and grow up, once and for all.

"I mean that as a compliment," she says, reading my mind. "You seem so young, so full of life."

Seven. The year I ran the Fodderstack and my balloon sailed off and came back and I wore lavender overalls and had Dorothy Hamill hair and rode my bike all over town. Before I cared what anyone thought. Nat's right: I haven't felt so young since I *was* young. I feel as if I'm aging backwards, running stronger and faster than I ever have.

On the surface, my success doesn't make sense. Statistically I'm middle-aged. I don't have a coach or a training plan. Is it just a fluke, or have I stumbled into a magical state that enables me to turn running into flying?

In the early 1990s, the Hungarian psychologist Mihaly Csikszentmihalyi coined the term "flow" to describe an "almost automatic, effortless, yet highly focused state of consciousness." When we're immersed in flow, cognitive thoughts drop away, creativity surges, and time becomes fluid. Hours may pass in what feels like a minute, or a minute might stretch for hours. Circumstances seem to fall into place, aligning at the right time, and coincidences abound, a phenomenon Carl Jung called "synchronicity." In sports, flow is often called "the zone," a state of consciousness where the body and mind move in harmony and we achieve greatness with less perceived effort.

Csikszentmihalyi discovered that people who are in flow become so engrossed in the activity that they don't notice distractions and they forget to feel self-conscious. "We might even feel that we have stepped out of the boundaries of the ego and have become part, at least temporarily, of a larger entity," he writes in *Creativity: Flow and the Psychology of Discovery and Invention*. "At this point the activity becomes autotelic, which is Greek for something that is an end in itself."

Natalie once told me about a sect of Buddhist monks in Japan who run for a thousand days over the course of seven years as part of their journey to spiritual enlightenment. The so-called marathon monks run all night in straw sandals, training their minds and bodies to tolerate pain, boredom, and fear. I liked to imagine their monastery, cantilevered into the side of its mountain, with paths spiraling outward for miles through the thick trees to gain high, open ridges. I felt peaceful picturing the monks spread out on the trails, running alone and in silence, at their deliberate, monkish pace, knowing that the only thing required of them was to get up the next day and do it again. Some days I longed to live that way, too.

By the final year, when the monks run fifty miles a day for a hundred days in a row, they've entered a perpetual flow state. "At the end, the marathon monk has become one with the mountain," writes John Stevens in his book *The Marathon Monks of Mount Hiei*. "He can predict the week's weather by the shape of the clouds, the direction of the wind, and the smell of the air."

Dean Potter's version of flow wasn't all that different. "It's an enhancement of all your senses," he told me in Yosemite in 2007. This was the high he chased until his death in a BASE jumping accident in the park in 2015. "Your vision gets better, you're more sensitive to sounds. The light on the rock is that much more beautiful, the sounds of nature are much sharper. Your mind is firing that much faster and all your thoughts are coming more clearly and precisely. When I'm on the highline, I feel like I'm almost liquid."

You don't have to risk death or run all day to find flow. Dad found his daydreaming. Once, when Steve and I were visiting Huntly shortly after Pippa was born, I found him sprawled out on his back on the shag carpet in the living room. His eyes were closed and his shoes were off, his feet splayed in his ragg socks, his hands clasped across his stomach. He looked so serene, I was sure he was asleep. But then he raised a hand and opened his eyes. He didn't lift his head; he just turned to look up at me, smiling slightly.

"Oh, sorry, Dad," I said. "I didn't mean to disturb you."

"I wasn't asleep," he answered. "I was daydreaming. It's different than napping. It's a chance for my brain's alpha waves to recalibrate. Sometimes I get answers to problems with my pictures I didn't know I had. I always get up feeling refreshed."

This was what happened when I ran. Running was like putting lettuce in a bowl and tossing it with salad dressing, jiggling loose my ideas, so that by the time I finished, everything was coated and interconnected. I saw links I'd missed, and I knew what to do and how to go forward.

Dad motioned for me to come closer. "Want to try?"

"Sure," I said. I took off my shoes and lay down next to him, closing my eyes. The backs of my legs pressed into the carpet, my elbow grazed Dad's. I was aware of each body part as distinct—my fingers raking the pile rug, my feet flopping to the side—but as I lay still, everything began to merge hazily in my mind. I could no longer feel my legs as separate from each other. I could not have lifted a hand if I wanted to. I was uncertain where I stopped and something, or someone, else began. My mind was aware of sensations and sounds, but they receded into the background and I drifted off into dream thoughts and then beyond them.

After a little while, I felt Dad stir beside me. He creaked onto one knee and stood up. I got up, too, blinked my eyes, looked around. Maybe fifteen minutes had passed. He didn't tell me what he'd been daydreaming, and I didn't ask. His eyes were alight, rested but not groggy. Awake.

All my life, without knowing it, I've been chasing flow. I felt it at nine, shooting baskets in the backyard, and years later, writing stories in my head on my way up the mountain and drifting down a desert river with Steve and our girls. And lying beside Dad on the night he died—in a strange way, even then.

For me, flow has never been only about running. It's about paying attention. After Dad died and anxiety reached out its slippery grip and dragged me under, my world shrank. I stopped noticing. But running up Mount Taylor and out of the Valles Caldera and across the Grand Canyon, I found it again. Practice brought me back: skimming through the easy days and putting my head down through the tiresome, fearful ones.

When I began writing my poems, I had the idea of taping them to the walls of my writing loft. I could see it in my mind: the entire room covered in words. Two years later, though, the poems sit in piles on my desk, scattered on various hard drives. It doesn't matter if I hang them; my mind hums with them. Sometimes I skip a day or two or three in a row; someday I'll stop altogether. That's okay. I've learned what the poems wanted to teach me. They live inside of me now.

Little by little, I'm learning the difference between intuition and obsession. Obsession whips and spins and says *should* and *What if?* and worries endlessly and grips hard onto things that are known, visible, and unbearably precious. Intuition is the voice that says *try* and *It's okay to let go.*

In the desert Southwest, erosion creates tall rock hoodoos, boulders balanced upon boulders. These natural towers are both fixed and fragile. You could sit beside them until the end of your life and they would never budge. Yet they exist in a state of constant unrest, as incremental and microscopic as particles of sand. "Geologic time includes now," Steve says when we're deep in the canyons, admiring the cliff bands, rocks the size of small houses arrested mid-crash. What force stopped their forward propulsion, stalled them on their slopes for thousands of years, poised precisely at the angle of repose?

This is what intuition feels like: solid at the core, but agile, too, always shifting. To hear it is to stay open to all possibilities, to accept that the scenarios I'm most worried about won't come to pass and the ones I haven't anticipated might. And either way, if I'm paying attention, I'll learn something.

How long will it last? I want to hold on, but I know I shouldn't. Because that's the conundrum: The more you clutch, the less you flow.

In early December, the top ultrarunners in the country and the world converge in Northern California for the North Face Endurance Challenge, arguably the fastest, most competitive fifty-mile trail race in the country. It's also one of only a handful of ultramarathons to offer a prize purse to the top male and female finishers—$10,000 for first place, $4,000 for second, and $1,000 for third. When I show up at the starting line, in the Marin Headlands, just across the Golden Gate Bridge from San Francisco, I have no illusions about winning money, but I am curious about how I'll fare against a stacked field of female pros.

At 4 a.m., the coastal hills are shrouded in darkness and the grassy field is damp with a heavy dew and trampled by runners milling around, waiting. Steve stayed home in Santa Fe with the girls, so I'm alone. Because of my estimated pace, I've been assigned to the first wave of elite runners, a designation that both secretly thrills me and makes me so nervous I want to puke. I recognize some of the runners around me, pros who've won big races and others who've made the covers of running magazines.

Run your own race, I remind myself sternly. *Don't get caught up.*

Sometimes ultrarunning feels as effortless as floating. Other times, it's as agonizing as giving birth. When you charge off into the chilly twilight, you know you have long hours of hard physical labor ahead of you. Many people will try to help you, but some of them will irk you for no good reason, and you will not be entirely in control of your faculties, and you will most certainly act like a maniac and say things you will later regret. You will vacillate between the black pit of dejection and blinding euphoria, and at some point your only goal will be to make it to the finish line without anyone getting hurt.

And you will promise yourself that you will never, *ever* do that again.

As soon as the gun goes off, I know I'm in trouble, swept up in a tide of runners gunning not only for the finish line but for money. The fire road is smooth and rolling and dangerously fast. For the first five miles, I keep up with a group of three or four elite women who are, by the looks of it, at least ten years younger than me, with burly thighs and the almost certain ability to crush me. They run shoulder to shoulder but are deathly silent. One of them dashes off course to pee standing up and catches back up to us less than thirty seconds later. Ahead of us, a long string of headlamps weaves up a hill. I figure that somewhere in the front pack are the rest of the top females, including Rory Bosio, who shattered the women's course record at the Ultra-Trail du Mont-Blanc, Europe's Super Bowl of ultrarunning.

Run faster, I chide myself. *Keep up.*

The week before I flew to San Francisco, I thought about my race strategy. Plan A, which I didn't dare say aloud, was a top-ten finish, an ambitious though potentially achievable goal. Plan B was to finish in less than nine hours; and plan C, my old standby: finish without doing irreparable harm to my body. I was losing my mind a little in the way I always do before a race, worried that racing was corrupting my running, turning something private and pure into a measure of self-worth, ruining the thing I love most.

For days, Steve watched me yo-yo between excitement and dread, an existential crisis in puny proportions, saying nothing. The night before I left, he took pity on me. We were outside soaking in the hot tub and I had my calves jammed up against one of the jets, trying to maximize the water's therapeutic benefits.

"Okay, so do you want my race advice?" Steve asked. I could tell by his faintly exasperated tone that he'd been holding out on me until he couldn't take it anymore. I switched off the jets so I could hear him better.

"This is what you have to do," he continued. "You have to go a little crazy out there. Leave it all on the trail."

I smiled in the dark. He could really nail it when he needed to.

I realize now, of course, that he was talking about the *end* of the race—the last third, when it's time to put the hammer down and go for it. Not necessarily the first half. And definitely *not* the first ten miles.

I cruise into the mile 8 aid station in just over an hour. My pace is unsustainable for fifty miles. The four pro women I was running with pulled ahead on an eight-hundred-foot climb and are now out of sight. My legs are pudding, whether from the cold air, for which I am shamefully ill-prepared in my thin nylon running skirt, or from dehydration. I gulp down two cups of electrolyte drink, eat a gel, and plod four miles up and over the bluff, high above Pirate's Cove to Muir Beach. Dawn is only just beginning to break, and from these grassy heights it looks like I could dive straight into the Pacific Ocean. If only.

Somewhere above the crashing surf, my wool ankle sock wads up, hot and bothered, under the ball of my left foot. Same old shoes, same old socks (cardinal ultra rule: *Never* try new gear on race day), but if I don't stop to smooth out the lumps, my foot will be mangled before I even make it to Muir Beach. When I pull over onto the side of the trail, a woman passes on my right, and I recognize her face from the cover of *UltraRunning* magazine: Leadville Trail 100 champion Ashley Arnold (no relation). I've been ahead of her for eleven miles? No wonder I feel like I might die.

I'm not a feather today. I'm a fully loaded eighteen-wheeler lumbering up the hills with my hazards on—all weight and no grace, pure mindless momentum, praying I don't jackknife. Someone has taken my legs and replaced them with concrete blocks.

The wind is gusting to twenty miles an hour, and I stupidly left my gloves in my hotel room. Halfway up the long, switchbacking climb to Cardiac Hill (the race's high point, at 1,370 feet), a tall woman with a brown ponytail scampers past me: Rory Bosio. At the aid station on the summit, my hands are so cold they've turned into hooves and I have to ask a volunteer to rip open my energy blocks for me.

It's funny—sad funny, not funny funny—how fast your priorities can change. By mile 15, a top-ten finish is out of the question. On a short three-mile section where the course doubles back on itself, I count the women ahead of me: ten, eleven, twelve. All looking so sprightly. If I hold on, I can still make top twenty. *Keep it together,* I think, steeling myself. *It's still early. Anything can happen. You can turn this around.* I can see now that I grossly overestimated the physiological benefits of training at altitude and grossly underestimated the size of the hills. They're much lower than our mountains in New Mexico, but they're just as steep. There's hardly half a mile of flat ground on the entire course.

Lesley has flown out to stay with Meg at her house in Davis for the weekend, and together they drove down to crew for me. On the descent to the mile 27 aid station, I pass Rory, who's doubled over, running and throwing up at the same time. Meg and Lesley are waiting for me at Stinson Beach, huddled in down jackets, gloves, ear warmers. I'm nearly hypothermic; they're dressed for the Arctic. They hand me a hot Starbucks mocha, of which I take one sip while trying not to look at my hands so I won't see how grotesquely swollen from dehydration they are. My knuckles have disappeared, and I'm having a hard time bending my wrists. I've dug myself into a deep, deep hole and I still have twenty-three miles to go.

On the steep climb up the Dipsea Steps—wooden ladder-like stairs hammered into the ground—a half-remembered line from the Gettysburg Address begins spinning through my brain: "Now we are engaged in a great civil war . . ." I am at war with the trail, and the trail is at war with my body. I think about quitting, but when you're at war, quitting is pretty much the same as dying. I am delirious. I keep going.

Things get murky for a long while after that. My only goal is not to drop. I walk for long stretches. I curse silently and try not to cry. I cry. The scenery is absurdly beautiful—dappled eucalyptus forests and enormous stands of redwoods, dainty coastal inns, high meadows with views to the blue sea—but in my agony the whole world has narrowed down to a pinprick, and I see none of it.

Keep it together, keep it together.

I truck into the mile 44 aid station on cement legs. Meg is going to pace me for the last six miles, and my stepsister, Amy, and her six-year-old daughter, who live nearby, have come to surprise me. I get teary when I see them, but Meg must sense how perilously close to complete emotional meltdown I am, because she grabs my arm and shouts, "Let's go!" I shove a few gels from Amy's outstretched arms into my sticky, bloated elephant paws and we set off on a two-mile climb up a fire road.

After her high school hurdling career, Meg stopped running. She married at twenty-six and had two kids by the time she was in her early thirties. She was either working or taking care of her family, and anything extraneous fell by the wayside. But after Dad died and she got divorced, she started running again. Now she races half marathons.

She jogs beside me, just off my right elbow. Something about this scenario is familiar—prehistorically familiar. I tug at the memory: our first Fodderstack, Meg with the long-legged ease, me scrawny and beaten, eyes glazed with confusion and fatigue, trying to keep up.

In my delirium, I imagine that Dad is here, too, just out in front, running backwards in a low crouch, holding his camera between his knees, pressing the shutter in rapid-fire clicks like a sports photographer. "Okay, okay, one more, just one more!" he's calling.

I know that Meg feels him, too, because she says, "Wouldn't Dad get such a kick out of this?"

And I say yes, I think that he would (while trying to keep the bristle out of my voice; *I* am not getting a kick out of this), because I am definitely, without question, one hundred percent cured of ultrarunning forever. When I say this out loud, Meg nods gravely, as if she's been wondering when I'll snap to my senses.

"I want this to be fucking done," I plead, feeling a pathetic sniffle creep into my voice. "Pleeeeease. Are we at the top, do you think?"

A runner we're overtaking raises his head and hisses evilly, "Don't count on it."

The next moment is one I'll never forget: Meg *growls* at him, the throaty snarl of a wild animal protecting its dead, mangled prey. Then she turns to me and says, in a completely different voice, a bright and hopeful voice that sounds awfully chipper, possibly too chipper, bordering on satanic, "We're getting there!" I recognize this voice, and it almost stops me cold. It's our mother's.

Mom's here, too, because I'm here. *I'm* my mother. Mom may not understand my running, but she made me a runner as much as Dad did. Her unsurpassable stamina, her indomitable optimism, sometimes so cheerful it makes you want to scream. Her sunny-side-up, glass-half-full positivity—she gave this to me, and even in my darkest moments, when I'm tormented by ear crickets or an imminent heart attack or swelling in my calf that Google says has all the signs of deep vein thrombosis, I believe this. We *are* getting there. And we will get there, wherever there is, and it will be okay. It will be better than okay: It will be good, and we will keep going. Of this I've never really had any doubt.

Suddenly I pump my fist in the air and scream diabolically, "I GOT this!"

Meg looks at me like I've gone beserk, but all around us runners shriek and fist-pump in agreement, our hollers rippling in unison down the hillside. Galvanized, I crest the top, swoop down the other side. My legs aren't wobbly anymore, just deeply pained. My fingers have thawed but still look mildly deformed. I see the finish tent and aim straight for it.

"Go, Katie! Go, Katie!" Meg yells behind me.

During a nine-hour run, it's normal to daydream about what you'll eat when it's over: pizza, banana splits, chocolate eclairs, dark-chocolate peanut-butter cups by the handful. The fantasies carry you for miles, but they are just that: fantasies. Because the cruel truth is, when you have run fifty miles, when you have punished your body and pulverized your digestive tract with intense aerobic output and a hideous amount of synthetic, sucrose-infused energy food, the last thing your body will want to do is eat.

After the race, Meg and Lesley and I drive back to Meg's house. I treat us to Thai takeout to thank them for the thankless task of waiting around for me all day in the bitter cold, but I manage only a few bites. Although I've burned through several thousand calories today, I can't stomach a thing.

Later I take an ice bath and lie awake in bed for a long time. My body is too uncomfortable, my muscles too crimped, my adrenaline still revving too high to sleep. Every now and then, my brain tricks me into thinking I'm tripping, my legs spasm, and my heart skids out of my chest. I must doze off eventually, because in the middle of the night I wake up ravenous. I'm in Meg's guest bedroom on the second floor, and there's zero chance I'll be able to make it downstairs to the kitchen. I half roll, half fall out of bed, army-crawl to my suitcase, vandalize the contents until I find half a bag of cashews, and devour them in a ball on the floor.

The next day, I'm crippled. So stiff I have to beg airport security to pull off my boots for me. But once I'm on the plane to Albuquerque, high above the city lights, everything appears small, orderly, in its rightful perspective. The race was just a race: fifty miles. I finished in 8:49, the sixteenth woman; I missed my first goal but hit the other two. I learned that even when the day goes absolutely to shit, when nothing flows, when I'm running from my head, not my heart, I can still hold on by my bitten-down fingernails. In the end, when my legs were wrecked and my spirit crushed, it was my head that talked me through to the finish line. It wasn't the race I wanted, but maybe it was the one I needed.

As the plane descends over Albuquerque, I can make out the long, dark squiggle of the Rio Grande snaking through the city. The sight of water in the desert fills me with hope. It was just an off day; I missed top ten but still got top twenty. And next time, I console myself, I will *definitely* wear tights and gloves.

Next time?

Little more than twenty-four hours have passed since I swore off ultrarunning forever, and already the amnesia has set in.

The day after I get home, I drive north into the Rio Grande Gorge, a deep rift in the desert halfway between Santa Fe and Taos. As soon as I see the river, clear and winter green, my breath deepens, as it always does. Bald eagles roost in the cottonwoods along the bank, and the rock walls shoot up three hundred feet on both sides of the river, so steep they routinely send small boulders tumbling into the two-lane highway. Erosion is unstoppable, the mountains shrinking before our eyes, but life teems on anyway, wild and equally determined.

I was here, at the mouth of the gorge, when Dad called me with the news that he had cancer. Now it's December 9, three years to the night since he died. I pull over and park. The sun has sunk below the rim, and in a small eddy along the bank, the river is skimmed with a brittle film of ice. I pull a votive candle and lighter from the pocket of my down jacket. The wind is gusting, but the flame wavers and holds. Two mallards fly upstream, quacking to the dusk and the gleaming full moon. The eye of Venus beams down like a porthole, a small tear in the black fabric of the sky. To the east rises the sharp point of Quartzite Mountain. Billions of years old, its rock marks another geologic unconformity, a chink in the chronology.

Steve and Maisy, Rio Grande Gorge, 2011

Around me, the layers of time are closed up tight like an onion. Dad on assignment to New Mexico in the late seventies. Georgia O'Keeffe in her studio, her flat-topped peak, Pedernal, shooting up beyond her window, smoke from the kiva fireplace corkscrewing into the winter sky. Me, at twenty-three, climbing my mountain, electric with possibility.

On the surface, nothing has changed. The piñons are still here, weathered trunks with branches outstretched like arms. The rocks lie mostly in the same random jumbles. The dirt is the same, too, clay-brown and damp with patches of snow. Quartzite rears up above the Rio Grande, stones rain down on the road. But what's underneath is invisible. A lump in the kidney the size of a fist, a secret massing hurt, a game-ender. Fear screaming in my ear. But also love. My daughters' hearts hidden beneath downy skin. And courage. Things we see, things we cannot see.

One year, three years, ten. There's no knowing how long grief will last, but tonight it's almost a joy to allow myself the sorrow. The two are so tightly entwined, the flip sides of love, they're almost the same.

Natalie's leading a meditation retreat in Taos, and I've decided that if I'm ever going to get serious about sitting still, there's no better time than now, after a fifty-mile race, when I'm too exhausted to run away. At the old hacienda where arts patron Mabel Dodge Luhan used to host D. H. Lawrence and Georgia O'Keeffe, I sit with the other students in an austere room with wood floors and bare walls. After Natalie demonstrates proper zazen posture, she says, "I want you to sit *completely* still. Keep coming back to the body and the breath. Sit through the pain. Try not to move a muscle."

I cast my eyes desperately around the room at the other students, but no one's showing any signs of distress. They adjust themselves on their mats with stick-straight backs and half smiles, the picture of tranquility.

Pros, I think bitterly, closing my eyes.

"Follow your breath all the way in, and all the way out," Natalie intones.

I screw my mind around a single idea: stillness. A long time passes. So long I stop trying to figure out how much time has passed. So long my butt goes numb and I stop squirming. Each time I'm tempted to shift my hands or jiggle my foot, I breathe instead and stay exactly where I am. My spine is not too crumpled, and I can feel my breath going in and out. I'm alive. That's what this means. Eventually I find that stillness has become a kind of anchor. Every time my mind strays, dozens of times a minute, I reassure myself that my body is motionless. My thoughts are spinning, but my limbs are composed. There is some small comfort in this.

I've resigned myself to sitting here maybe forever when Natalie finally rings the bell. I open my eyes. Her head is bowed, eyes still closed, when she says, "Settle yourself upon yourself." That's exactly how I feel: as though my mind is resting on my body, which is anchored to the earth. Solid.

It's freezing in Taos, the temperature each morning hardly creeping above zero, but gradually my body is coming back to life. In the afternoons, when the sun finally casts a bit of warmth, I walk up a ridge east of town and sit on a rock at the top. Sitting is what I crave most, even more than walking. I'm still restless, but now when Natalie rings the bell, I'm ready to sit through it all—the itchy tremors in my foot and the numbness in my legs and the almost hysterical urge to yell "Sweet Jesus!" and sprint from the room.

Keep it together, I tell myself. *Keep it together*. Meditation, like running, is an endurance sport.

On the last day, Natalie shoos us back into the world. "What I most want for you is for you to become an animal in your life," she tells us. It reminds me of Steve's advice: *You have to go a little crazy out there.* "When you do this," Natalie says, "all beings get behind you and you keep going. When you do something seriously, you pass it on and help others."

25

The Opposite of Emptiness

Lake Katherine from the summit of Santa Fe Baldy, June 2014

After you've been running ultra distances for a while, you will begin to lose perspective. It happens so gradually that you barely notice, until the day when twelve miles seems like a "short" run. When a couple thousand vertical feet of gradual uphill running spread over fifteen miles is "pretty flat."

It's human nature to adapt, to keep moving the mark and pushing your own thin edge. Whatever you do regularly becomes routine, no matter how extreme it may appear. Like Dean Potter, highlining without a safety harness. Like my eighty-four-year-old writer friend who wheels her grocery cart full of food a mile down the beach to her cottage on an island off the coast of Maine because there's no road. If you point out to her that this is remarkable, she flaps her hand dismissively and says, "No, it's what anyone would do. I go at low tide, when the sand is firm."

We are the same, this woman and I.

When the amnesia of your last race has worn off, your thoughts will naturally go to what's next. Your brain will move through a series of reasonings and justifications, some logical, others magical, possibly maniacal. *I've built my base fitness; why back off and lose it now? I've already run thirty-one miles and it didn't hurt* that *much. What's another nineteen?* And so on. As long as you've had success in your last race—and by "success" I mean not dying—chances are good that you will want to keep going. There's always a time to beat. Your own.

I almost don't want to say "one hundred kilometers" out loud. It sounds absurd, obscene even. But I want so badly to find my flow again, and the best way I know how is to push myself beyond my limits, to burn through my pride and obstinate resistance until there's nothing left.

In his memoir *What I Talk About When I Talk About Running,* the Japanese novelist and marathoner Haruki Murakami calls the period after a race the "runner's-blues fog." Whether you win or drop or finish in the middle or DFL, letdown is inevitable. Runner's blues is a lot like postpartum blues—after the euphoria, the entropy. The particulars may change, but the pattern is more or less the same: For a short time, the relief and novelty of doing other things, followed by the lethargy and aimless wondering what's next; then the pathetic, wallowing inertia, the buzzing impatience to resume training. And always the doubt: Will I ever run that way again? Will I ever *feel* that way again?

In the early months of 2014, my sixteenth-place finish at the North Face 50 Mile lingers in my mouth like a bad aftertaste. I don't want to run; I'm dying to run. I need to run, and I hate myself for needing to run. I'm in the eddy again, gyrating in a torment of my own making.

I have my own name for it: runner's block.

"During the outrageous phase we need to be careful about not getting too far out," Sakyong Mipham writes in *Running with the Mind of Meditation*. He's talking about the third evolution of mindfulness, the garuda stage, when it's common to push too hard or become overly identified with our pursuit. During this phase, we risk becoming unsettled, isolated, injured. Going too far, he cautions, often stems from a "subtle level of pride" that "slowly begins to blow us off course."

At the North Face 50 Mile, I was running for the wrong reasons, for some crazy fantasy of midlife heroism. I went too far out. I've turned what for so long had been my secret happiness into a test of my worth. It's time to pull back and remember why I run, to become just a spirit running.

I sign up for the Angel Fire Endurance 100K, in late June in northern New Mexico. It's early February, and I can feel the sun getting stronger, my own self stirring back to life. The fear is there, but bigger than that is the love: I miss moving. I miss the routine of training, the contentment I feel when I come home filthy and exhausted.

I *want* to run.

I start, slow and low like always. Eight miles is my long day. Then ten, then twelve. There's magic to crossing the twenty-mile mark. Under twenty miles, I run from my calculating brain: *How fast can I go? How soon can I be done?* But once I'm on the other side, the distance teaches me patience. It's too far and too long to be in a hurry. There are so many uncertainties, so many hours on my feet, I have no choice but to surrender to the run. Maybe my legs will feel like soggy logs; maybe I will be hungry and homesick. Maybe I will fly.

Once I'm on the other side of twenty, my training usually settles into a more peaceful routine. I worry less. I run a little bit faster and a little bit farther each week. The few extra pounds I always gain over the holidays melt away. The calluses on my feet grow thicker. I know there will be off days, but I'm learning to run with all of it: the insane, nagging fears, the egotistical glory dreams, the dull soreness in my left ankle, the hum in my heart, the old nudge of Dad daring me to do the unexpected.

Even though it's March, the snow is still piling up in the mountains, too deep to run. One day, chasing mile markers south along the Rail Trail, I remember something I heard John, the meditation teacher, say last year. To quiet the mind and become present, he suggested, follow your breath to its furthest point. Picture a door at the end of each inhalation and exhalation. What's on the other side? Sitting upright on my folding metal chair, I closed my eyes and took a deep breath. I could see the door exactly: It was small and black and curved on top, like Jerry's cartoon mouse hole in *Tom and Jerry*. I wanted to get to it and push it open, but just as I reached for it, my breath swept me away and back, only to begin again. It was soothing, like catching a long, gentle wave all the way into shore, then letting it carry me back into the surf, my mind scrubbed clear, in and out, again and again.

Now, as I run along the railroad tracks, my thoughts drop away. The tracks stretch on as far as I can see. The tracks become my breath. At the far end, there is a door. I will get there when I get there, or maybe not. It doesn't matter. I'm here.

Eight miles from my starting point, the suburban adobes with their swing sets give way to ranchettes with Tuff Sheds and horse corrals. The dog walkers and the Kenyan runners usually don't come out this far, and I see few bikers on this section of rutted, washed-out track. Though it's not nearly as wild as my mountains, the flatness of the landscape makes it seem bigger and emptier.

When I get to my turnaround point, eleven miles from my car, I'm baked by the sun, hungry, and completely alone. I unwrap half a sweet potato, still warm and mashed in its bag, and eat it in one bite. I've curved so far around the back side of my mountains that they don't look like my mountains anymore. I'm a boomerang at the far end of my reach, about to make the long arc back, but not before I hang in the air, feeling far away.

After Dad died, I dreamed about him. Unlike when I ran, I could see him, and I held on to the sight of him, almost greedily. In the first dream, he said nothing; he just sat there, one leg crossed over the other, ankle on his knee, his khaki pant leg pulled up slightly to reveal his thick ragg sock. Balanced on that knee was an object, held lightly in his clasped hands. I couldn't see what it was—wine, an egg, or a glass of eggnog, stiff and creamy, like he always drank at Christmastime—but it didn't matter. What I noticed was how he held it: still, with confidence, quietly, as though poised in mid-thought, listening intently to what the rest of us were saying.

In another dream, he was tall and fit, with his flinty hair and strong cheekbones, still healthy but not for long. We were in Africa to see the lions, and I could feel his anxiety rising off him like steam on the lake on a chilly morning. He was waiting for results from his doctor, something about skin. He stood in profile and worried the way he used to, without saying anything, a pinch in his cheeks. I recognized that look; I'd seen it on my own face in the mirror. In the last dream, we rafted down a narrow swooshing river that was also, illogically, a roller coaster. I was in the seat in front, Dad behind, wild and unafraid, brazen even, ways I hadn't known him to be, ever. We made it through without wrecking, and at the bottom

Dad stood beside the tracks, the rushing current, careless and laughing. He had never been worried.

When I woke up from these dreams, he felt close enough to touch, and I walked through the house gingerly, so as not to shake him loose. But he was always gone by breakfast.

I don't remember when Dad stopped coming to me on the trail, but running has become a little lonelier without him, even though I knew his visits were only temporary and had always been only temporary. Does he disapprove? Is he busy being reborn into another life, discovering fingers, growing hair, his ancient soul finding form again? He is fading but for those rare moments when I feel his soul saying *yes, yes,* and mine answering with feet kicking high, and I wonder if his voice wasn't my voice all along.

Dad on his New Hampshire bike trip, 1977

In late April, Anna and I drive west to the edge of a golf development past La Tierra and the city limits, where the last of the fancy houses give way to scrubby grasslands sloping down to the Rio Grande. We run seven miles downhill on washboarded Buckman

Road, with shot-up signs and cattle guards, to the mouth of Diablo Canyon. Blocky five-hundred-foot basalt walls rise on either side. Rock climbers are inching up the dihedrals above us, their voices drifting down on the breeze. For a moment I envy them, moving methodically up the vertical face—the slowed-down, tactile pleasure of all four limbs, ten fingers, ten toes, two feet, two hands on the earth at the same time.

After half a mile, the canyon widens into a broad, sandy wash. In three miles we reach the Rio Grande. The arroyo ends at the river; on the other side are the steep cliffs of White Rock Canyon. I splash cold water on my face and arms and peel an orange, watching the water rush through a small rapid, the same rapid I've rafted on on summer weekends with Steve and the girls. There's no bridge across the river. I've gone as far as I can go.

We run ten miles back the way we came to Anna's car, where we part ways. She'll drive back to town and I will run another twelve miles home on a mix of singletrack trails and pavement. On the final stretch of road, I see a car coming toward me. It's a dark-blue dented Toyota sedan, pulling away from a stop sign. Sticking out of the trunk is a wooden box, long and yellowish, made from unfinished pine. It's unmistakable: a coffin. There's no ceremony in the way it's slung into the dingy car, as though the driver had just come from Home Depot with a sack of nails strewn about the backseat. The trunk hasn't been properly tied shut and bounces open and closed on top of the casket.

On another day, I might have taken the coffin as an omen. I might have wondered who is dying or dead inside, or who might die next, whether it will be me or someone I love. But not today—not after I've plinked stones into the river and run thirty-two miles and followed my own feet, the mountains slowly growing larger above me, pulling me in. I wasn't training; I was traveling. I ran to the river, and now I'm running all the way home.

PHOTO: KATIE ARNOLD

Pippa and Maisy, San Juan River, Utah, 2015

When I run, I long for my children. The yearning comes over me when I am absorbed by the effort, high above the tree line, hours from a trailhead. It comes over me even when I crave solitude and time to think, or not think, after I've rewritten stories in my head and felt the ideas emerge and when I have crossed over into stillness, empty of thoughts. Sometimes it's a lonesome feeling, but it's hardly ever sad: I have daughters at home. Knowing this is what pulls me through the lows at mile 9, 17, or 35. It's what anchors me to the endeavor and helps me go the whole way.

Four weeks before the Angel Fire 100K, I go down in mileage and up in elevation. The high point of the race is eleven thousand feet, but I will have to climb it four times in sixty-two miles. A few times a week, I run thirteen miles to the 12,600-foot summit of Santa Fe Baldy and back. It's early June, and the wildflowers are already blooming—blue sky pilots and yellow cress, impossibly tiny and delicate for such a harsh alpine environment. The damp forest is clear of snow but still smells like fir boughs and frost, the creeks surging high with runoff.

I feel the altitude in the first, steep mile, but then I relax into my legs and my breath, running steadily to the broad saddle at 11,700 feet. Fat marmots wobble their heads out from granite boulders, whistling as I pass. It's just as fast to hike the steep shoulder as it is to run, so I practice jogging all the gentler grades, even if it's just a few strides, and walking the rest. On the summit ridge, the trail is a narrow ribbon of dirt through stubbly amber grass that looks more like Scotland than New Mexico. A cornice of sun-rotted snow, at least five feet deep, curls over the edge, a last holdout of winter. Five hundred feet below, Lake Katherine is frozen and chunked with miniature icebergs. To the north and east are forests, some clipped by recent fire, others chartreuse with baby aspen leaves. And to the west, the terra-cotta desert, rumpled and worn, the lumps and mesas and ridges, the low, brown buildings of home.

The altitude always catches up with me on the way down, and I get klutzier and dumber on the descent. I've been running for three hours above ten thousand feet, the wind whistling in my ears. Depleted of oxygen, my head feels foggy, my reflexes sluggish, as though my body's been burning through brain cells the way it burns calories, and my feet are ten steps in front of my brain, leaving it behind.

Half a mile from my car I stumble over a rock and sail through the air, narrowly missing a tree and landing hard on my left side. Stunned, I sit in the dirt, wiping blood from the large scrapes on my collarbone, thigh, and palm. The race is in two days. Nothing's broken; I'm just bruised and shaken. Eyes closed, I try to breathe the loneliness out of me. It feels like a precipice, this business of breathing. If I allow my mind to stray, I'll slip off the edge. Then I remember: I don't have to be perfect, or even good. I just have to try.

The last time I saw Dad healthy, it was November, a year before he died. He and Lesley and Meg and her family flew to Santa Fe to spend Thanksgiving with us. The grass didn't need mowing, so it was a good time for him to get away. I knew Dad was excited, because a month before he arrived, he emailed me with an idea: Meg and Lesley would invent a fictional premise upon which he and I would make up our own short stories. "Not a plot, just a kernel, a jumping-off place," Dad explained. He loved Updike and Cheever and had always dreamed of writing fiction. "We'll each start there and see where we end up."

By the time they arrived, though, I was three weeks pregnant and Maisy was a pinto bean worming queasily around inside me. I lay on the couch, feeling sleepy and seasick. Dad's idea hovered, unacknowledged, between us. I wanted to try, but I was so tired. And scared. Writing felt too intimate, even more so than talking. What would he reveal about himself? What would I? We played board games and talked about music and books, like we always did, but we did not talk about our stories, nor did we write them. We both thought we'd have other chances.

The day after Thanksgiving, we drove out to the cliff dwellings at Bandelier. Dad wore his blue jeans and red down vest and held Pippa's hand, walking slowly as they searched for broken bits of eight-hundred-year-old pottery. Once you saw one, you saw hundreds. Shards littered the ground, with faded black and ocher designs. We turned them over in our hands and then put them back where we'd found them.

The year after Dad died, I was cleaning out our freezer when I found a container of frozen cranberries left over from that Thanksgiving. As I poured the whole hardened chunk of them into the garbage disposal, it dawned on me that Dad had eaten those very cranberries, with a turkey we'd bought at the farmers' market. I wanted the cranberries back. I felt like I was throwing away Dad's tongue or his taste buds, some part of him that had stayed too long in a freezer-burned Tupperware, ignored. The sadness that came over me as I watched the last reddish bits disappear down the drain was so complete, it seemed to contain everything: love, fear, rage, regret, disappointment, tenderness, shame, surprise, anguish, even awe. For a moment I understood. I *had* felt it after all. Grief is all of these things and more, a big, messy wad of emotion. It is beyond category, as fathomless as desire, as luminous as joy. It will break your heart and fill it up again.

The Angel Fire ultra is a small, local event, with only a hundred people registered in four distances: 50K, fifty miles, 100K, and one hundred miles. Held at the Angel Fire ski resort, east of Taos, it won't be an especially competitive race, and I feel no pressure to perform. I'm not even especially concerned about my time. It's a new distance for me, my longest yet, and I just want to finish.

At 5 a.m. on June 21, the longest day of the year, the night is still black, save for a faint, hopeful brightening behind the ski mountain. But twenty minutes into the race, I've clicked off my headlamp and am jogging through the first light of the first day of summer. Unlike in previous ultras, I feel none of the loneliness that often overtakes me when I realize how far I have to go, all on my own.

For the first time, Pippa and Maisy are here for the whole race. For two years, I've been trying to keep my two lives—running and mothering—separate. I didn't want my running to define our family life. I'd go off alone while the girls were at school, and when we came back together I could give them all of me, because I'd just given everything to the run. Balancing the two balanced me. As much as I loved and craved trail running, coming home was still the best part of every run.

But as I trained for the 100K, my worlds diverged even more. The farther I ran, the more seriously I trained, the more I missed them and the more my running suffered. By separating the two, I'd given myself *too* much time and space to think about running. The more I fretted, the more distracted and impatient I was at home and the more exasperated Steve became.

"Remember, it's just a *race*," he'd say, and I'd nod, chastened, and lace up my sneakers anyway and ease guiltily out the door. Steve never once told me not to go, but I couldn't shake the feeling that I was running through my girls' childhoods, and my marriage, missing out on the best of them.

On the two-hour drive to Angel Fire, Pippa and Maisy sang "This is an annoying song! This is an annoying song!" over and over. It *was* annoying—so annoying that it distracted me from the inconceivable, horrifying prospect of running a hundred kilometers. In the hotel room after dinner, they jumped like maniacs between the beds as I filled my hydration pack and pinned my number to my running skirt. When we turned off the light at 9:30, they lay in their bed chattering while I shoved earplugs into my ears and prayed for them to go to sleep so—*please, God*—I might do the same before my alarm went off at 4 a.m.

The 100K course consists of a sequence of two separate, repeating routes. One is a rolling 10K loop that I will run four times, and the other a nineteen-mile climb up and over the ski mountain that I will complete twice. At the end of every section, I will pass through the base area aid station, where I've stashed a drop bag crammed with gels and bars, a rain jacket in case it storms, salt tabs, and extra socks—most of which I know I won't ever touch. Drop bags are a safety net. You want to cover all possible contingencies— blisters, sour stomach, lightning, and hail—but hope you won't need any of them. It's here that Steve and the girls plan to greet me every few hours.

In the first six miles, I deliberately hold back. I let other runners, and other women, take off in front of me. All four races start together, and it's hard to tell who's racing my distance. The ambiguity works in my favor: I have no urge to push my place in the pack, since it may not be my pack I'm pushing.

This was my plan going in: to be calm off the start, because I hadn't been in California and because sixty-two miles is so far that anything can happen at any point. But mostly because I want to see if it's possible to race simply to run, not to win. And if I run this way, will I win?

All spring, I tried different methods to break my runner's block. I tried to run free of ego and competitive zeal. I tried to run for joy and flow, with humility and confidence. Now, though, I want to empty myself of *all* expectations—good and bad—and run for nothing.

In Buddhism, ridding yourself of preconceived notions and habits is called emptiness. Natalie had explained this to me once, a few years earlier. I pictured a whole universe with nothing in it, an empty home, all the furniture gone. The dog, too. It didn't sound very nice. It sounded lonely.

"Is emptiness a *good* thing?" I asked her.

We'd come to the point on the trail where we always stop talking and start climbing in silence. We had to follow our rules. Nat, slightly out of breath, pulled over to let me pass. The rubber sole of her shoe had come loose and was flapping up and down like a piece of skin. It was making walking difficult, but Natalie didn't stop; she just kept going.

"Oh, absolutely," came her voice. "It is *it*."

A few days before Angel Fire, we went walking along the Santa Fe River. She reminded me of something she often told her students: "Let writing do writing." Now, as the miles tick by slowly and steadily, I tell myself, *Let running do running.* The words, repeated in my head, trigger a visceral sensation in my body, as though my mind is stepping aside on the trail and out of my body's way, to let my legs run free and the race unfold as it will.

The trail to the top of Angel Fire ski resort climbs through a fir-and-aspen forest, switchbacking so often that the pitch is never onerous, almost pleasant. The last half mile, however, is so steep and gravelly that I have to walk. That's when I notice that runners ahead of me are pointing and shouting at something. It's a bear. Black and shaggy and huge. A hundred yards away, maybe less, so busy chomping bushes that it doesn't even raise its head.

The course follows a rough dirt road all the way down the other side of the mountain. The aid station at the turnaround is a beat-up VW bus with its pop top up. An older man with a broad smile hands me a salty boiled potato on a toothpick. I pop it in, swig some Gatorade from a cup, and am gone. My legs are made of wind, and I sail back up the way I came.

This is how it goes all day: up and down and all around. I thought the course might grow tedious with its repetition, but surprisingly, I like covering the same ground over and over; I like knowing what's around the bend, how steep the next hill is, when to conserve energy and when to charge. And most of all, I like knowing that Steve and the girls are nearby. Sometimes they're waiting for me in the base area, cheering me through M&M-smeared mouths. Sometimes they're not, and I worry: *Have they gotten lost? Did they crash their bikes and get hurt?* But I know myself well enough by now that it would be weird if I *didn't* worry. Maybe, finally, I have made friends with my fear.

When I come through the aid station for the last time, Pippa and Maisy are waving signs: GO MOMMY! KATIE, KATIE! and below that my age, with an extra zero: 402. I laugh weakly through my fatigue. Eleven hours into the race, with six miles still to go, I feel that ancient.

I've been maintaining a moderate tempo all day, consciously holding back to make sure I have enough energy for the end. Nothing hurts all that much, but I'm just really, really tired.

"I'm so ready to be done," I whimper to Steve, who's pacing me the last twelve miles while Anna, who drove up from Santa Fe, stays with the girls.

"Do you want to walk?" he asks.

For the first time all day, I start running flat out, my legs turning as though it's mile 1, not 61, racing through the final turns on the dirt road, then onto pavement. The finish line is nearly abandoned. No music pumping through the loudspeaker, no runners eating hamburgers or swilling beer, just a handful of volunteers settling in for the long haul. The 50K and fifty-mile races have been over for hours; the hundred-mile runners still have ten hours or more to go. I'm the first runner across the line in the 100K. I've won it outright, in 12:14.

I'd stepped out of my own way, one foot in front of the other, for many miles and many hours. I didn't have the transcendent highs, but nor did I have the wrecking lows. In this way it wasn't a spectacular race, which made it, in its own way, sort of spectacular.

I'd always hoped that running would make me a better mother, but now I know that being a mother makes me a better runner. I wasn't running from nothingness after all, but fullness, where all possibilities exist equally—winning, losing, hurting, dropping; being strong, being a mother, being alone; being scared—yet I wasn't attached to any one them. So empty of wanting one specific thing, I was full of everything.

26

Belonging

On the CDT, near Leadville, Colorado, August 2014

For the first fifty miles of the Angel Fire 100K, my predominant thought was *Thank God I am not running the hundred-mile race.* I saw the hundred-mile runners, with their blue race bibs, and I saw how much more slowly they were running than even I, who was trying to spread out my energy throughout the whole day, and I saw by the way they bent solemnly into the slopes that they knew what they were up against and that they would be running into the night and possibly all night, and were approaching it with enormous seriousness. The words *Thank God* played through my head, even when I was at my happiest and strongest, hoofing it fast down the back side of the mountain, whooping to other runners, or watching the bear mow the field. Never before had a race delighted me as much as this one had—the knowledge that my daughters were frolicking somewhere nearby; the kind volunteers, sponging my neck with ice water; the emerald valleys far below. I loved this race, and yet I did not want to run *one inch* farther than I had to.

But somewhere during the final ten miles, another thought began to weasel its way into my head. *Okay, thirty-eight miles more. That's not SO much. Yeah . . . a hundred miles . . . I could do that.* I hadn't even crossed the finish line and already I was dreaming of the next big thing.

Six weeks later, in August 2014, I drive north out of Santa Fe, bound for the TransRockies Run, a multiday stage race through the Collegiate Peaks of Colorado. The three-day race that I've signed up for is "only" fifty-eight miles and ten thousand vertical feet over three days. Whenever I do the math, I always come out ahead. It's shorter than Angel Fire, my longest single-day race, and because runners camp en masse near the starting line each day, the race is known for its festive atmosphere, challenging yet fun, competitive without being cutthroat. I tell myself I don't have big ambitions. I just want to run someplace beautiful, reacclimatize to high altitude after a month at Stony Lake, and get ready for what I secretly hope will be an FKT attempt in the Grand Canyon in October.

Road trips always make me wistful. I think of Dad, rambling around in his green VW bus, to the Midwest for college reunions and to see Uncle Phil; to the Great Plains to see no one, to go where he wanted when he wanted and take pictures if he felt like it. He liked seeing where he ended up and what he found when he got there.

After Dad died, I went looking for his bus. I didn't want a bus *like* Dad's; I wanted Dad's bus, *our* bus, with the puckered white vinyl interior and the sliding side door out of which he let us dangle our feet on the way up the driveway at Huntly. I pictured Steve and the girls and me driving it around the West, waking up in ski resort parking lots on powder days, taking it to races. I knew it was a long shot, but I called the public radio station in Washington anyway. The man who answered the phone found the record immediately. "It was sold to or through a company in Brooklyn in November 2010," he told me.

Meg and me in Dad's bus, summer 1978

I scrolled through the picture reel in my mind. That was the month that Maisy learned to roll over. Dad was still alive, shuffling in his plaid bathrobe from bed to bathroom while the bare-boned maples bristled on the far ridge and the stinkbugs crept silently through the house, claiming it as theirs. I thought of Maisy now, learning to ski and ride her bike. Dad would always be dead the same number of years as she's been alive. It had been foolish to think I might get his bus back. Time just kept moving. It made no sense, and it made perfect sense.

"I'm sorry, I don't have any more information," the man said apologetically, and I thanked him and hung up.

Now I fumble for my phone and call Steve. I just want to hear his voice. "Don't worry, everything's fine here," he says, without a trace of bitterness. "You'll do great."

Once, I might have wanted him to say more, to pump up my ego or stay on the phone, reassuring me until I drove out of cell range. I would have wanted him to love and support my running as much as he loves and supports me. But slowly I'm learning these are two different things, as they should be. It's not that we've finally found a magical balance between my running and our life. We're still just making it up as we go. It depends on the weather, the season, our bank account, our moods and the girls'. Some days, my running is fast and free, and our life feels infinite, open-ended. Other days, the two sides stick and catch, like snags on a thread, threatening to pull the fabric apart. It will always be a give-and-take, a thin line between what's good for me and what's good for our family. All we can do is stay on it.

"I love you," I tell Steve before we hang up.

I call Natalie next. "I'm lonely," I tell her. "I want to go home."

"I know," she says. "It's good you're feeling this. Keep going."

Runners come from all over the country to the TransRockies, either solo or as part of a two-person team. It has a jovial feel, like summer camp for adults. Runners are having birthdays, celebrating anniversaries, getting engaged. One morning in the dining tent, I eat scrambled eggs next to a man in his mid-forties named Frank, who tells me that in the nine months since he started running he's lost 150 pounds. His first race was a 50K. This is his second.

(Pause for a moment of awe.)

"I know nothing!" Frank proclaims eagerly. "I'm just here to learn as much as I can. I'm asking so many questions, I think I must be annoying people!"

Though the daily mileages in stage races are shorter than traditional ultramarathons, the wear and tear on your body and psyche is just as intense, if not more so. You have to run smart, but recover even smarter. Unlike in most ultra races, the real work begins *after* you cross the finish line.

Every afternoon, I take an ice bath—in the Arkansas River, murky irrigation ditches, brisk alpine lakes. I stretch and use a foam roller and lather myself in arnica gel. Runners are deeply superstitious: If a strategy worked once, it must be hewed to with ceremonial precision until the end of time. What I do each night in the dining tent feels less like eating and more like force-feeding: second helpings of beets and greens, salad heaped with beans and nuts, brown rice, and any protein I can get my hands on. After the second stage, I eat a whole pizza for an afternoon snack and then conk out in my tent, pitched along with four hundred others in the Leadville high school baseball diamond. Each morning, I wake before sunrise, wiggle my legs in my sleeping bag to see what hurts, and get up and start all over again. The routine burns off my nerves. I'm not just running the race, I'm *living* in it.

I win the first stage, then the second. On the third and last day, the course follows the Continental Divide Trail for twenty miles north from Leadville; it's covered in pine needles, soft and fast. Ten miles in, I round a curve and see a team of two runners ahead of me, weaving through meadows along the base of the big bald peaks. For six miles we run like this, apart but also in unison. They never get any closer or farther away. But I'm not impatient. I'm not trying to catch them. I'm no longer racing against them; I'm running *with* them. The realization makes me so happy that I start whooping—pure, uncontainable joy escaping my body. An hour goes by like this, but I don't care who hears me or how far I have to go or when I'll get there or what will happen when I do. I'm exactly where I want to be.

A few days before I left for Colorado, I went upstairs to my writing loft. I was trying to find the race guide I'd printed out, to study up on the course. My desk and table were stacked with papers: old magazine clippings, bills, and photographs. I justify the disorder by telling myself that things rise to the surface when I need them, but I know this is mostly just an excuse for laziness.

The guide was nowhere in sight, but a manila folder in one of the piles caught my eye. It was one of Dad's; I'd brought it home from my last visit to Huntly and shoved it there without bothering to look through it; sometimes the volume of Dad's stuff still overwhelmed me. The first thing I saw when I opened it now was a piece of flimsy fax paper. I recognized the time stamp—AUGUST 12, 1998 OUTSIDE—and my handwritten signature at the bottom, but nothing else. I had no memory of writing it.

Evidently I was interviewing Dad for an article about becoming a photographer, as told from the perspective of a neophyte whose father was a pro. I'd included twelve questions I hoped he'd answer, generic queries about first jobs and inspirations, tips for beginners, and "biggest challenges." I was still a fact-checker and just starting to write for *Outside,* and it was the sort of earnest letter I sent to other prospective subjects. My questions were always softballs; I didn't want to annoy anyone, least of all my father. "Don't be shy!" I signed off. "It will be worth it, I promise!"

The fax was sent to the Valley View Motel, in Osceola, Wisconsin, where Dad was visiting Uncle Phil. Paper-clipped to the fax was Dad's nine-page email reply, time-stamped 8/21/1998, taking me through the whole trajectory—his early interest in photography, the thrill of the hunt.

> *I wanted to capture "life" happening and have no influence on it. . . .*
> *I loved the life, loved being able to snoop at it, roaming and captur-*
> *ing, loved the fact that the camera kept me separate and apart and*
> *gave me its own needs to answer first.*

He published a photography book, got some attention. The head of the Magnum agency suggested they meet; the great *Life* photographer Alfred Eisenstaedt sent him a congratulatory note.

I never followed up.

This was the one thing about Dad I still didn't understand, the last thing maybe. I knew why he'd let go of us, but why on earth had he let go of photography?

It was "exciting but stressful," he went on. He liked to assemble projects, books and stories, rather than be "on-point" all the time. "I guess those are the reasons. Maybe not all, but I can't figure the rest."

He must have been wondering, too, though, because a few pages later he circles back:

I couldn't fathom how to be a photographer (who I thought was required to "practice" all the time) and be a husband. Mom and I never discussed it but I think there was some feeling on my part that devotion to photography would have meant unfaithfulness of a kind to her. With the editing came a kind of "normalcy." It had a "track" to it; you could go home at night.

Oh, the irony. He *didn't* go home at night, not in the end, when he really *was* unfaithful to Mom.

I looked again at the time stamp. He'd written the letter in 1998, six years before he delivered his big bombshell to me. Either I'd forgotten it completely or he'd never sent it. It no longer mattered. It was here now, like so much of what he'd left behind, popping up like pale mushrooms from damp, dark soil after a rain. A kind of magic.

You can read more when I finish my life-epic (probably five minutes before my last breath!). I still don't know about the wisdom of leav-

ing active shooting. It's easy to think I turned away from it too
quickly. I kind of wish I'd batted at it a little harder. But you make
your choices . . .

Late that afternoon, the last of my TransRockies race, it begins to
drizzle. My time, in just over three hours, is good for first place
overall in the women's solo division. I sit in a muddy pond up to my
waist, shouting myself hoarse for the last racers. The digital clock
shows an elapsed time of 7:26 as a team of two jogs across the line,
soaked but beaming beneath their Gore-Tex hoods. Their finish is
no less impressive than the winners'. In fact, it's *more* impressive.
They've been running through the mountains in the cold rain for
twice as long. Their stamina is humbling.

Ultrarunning isn't a mystery. It's hard work and human nature. I
believe anyone can do it. If it's in you, if you want it, you can do it.
You can run thirty miles, fifty miles, a hundred miles. You don't
have to look like a runner. Anybody can be a runner. You don't
have to be fast. You don't have to know anything. You just have to
start small and break it down. You will be afraid. You will worry
about wild animals and strangers and getting injured and losing
everything. This is natural. This is resistance. You're stronger than
you think you are. Keep going.

As a competitive runner, I'd always toggled between doubting
and striving. Now, though, I've finally stopped worrying that I'm
less and trying to prove I'm more, and I'm no longer thinking I'm
more and trying to prove that, either. For so long, I've tried to be
different, when what I really wanted was to belong.

In his book, the Buddhist running monk Sakyong Mipham explains
that the final phase of mindfulness is "dragon," named for the creature that "is said to live on the ground, but it also flies high among
the clouds." This is when running expands from something we do
for ourselves to something we do for the greater good, for the world.

"Our running and our meditation have undergone a great transformation," he writes. "No longer are these activities solely for our personal benefit."

Dragon seems very far away, like the hopeful mirage of an aid station winking from a great distance. Am I getting any closer? Maybe only by millimeters. Maybe it is around a hundred bends, and then a hundred more. Maybe it will take me this lifetime and the next. I'm not in a hurry.

The next morning, I pack my gear and head south for home through the San Luis Valley. Sunflowers rage along the roadsides, and the Great Sand Dunes pile up against the folds of the Sangre de Cristo range like a tinselly mirage. As always, I'm torn. The runner in me wishes I could stay, but the mother in me wants to go home. I see that this is how it will always be. Some days my running is fast and free, and I move through the mountains writing stories in my head; other days I fold laundry and wonder if I shouldn't run less and act more like a normal person. I'm both at the same time, mother and self. Everything's already here, the joy and madness, beauty, babies, stories, brilliance, luck, and love. All the pieces have carried me here and live alongside the anguish and boredom and uncertainty, the days I can't breathe, the unbearable growing up of my girls. There's room for it all.

When I get home, I meet Natalie for a hike. On the way down our mountain, she says, "You're ready. When you called me and told me you were lonely, I could tell."

"Ready for what?" I ask, but I already know the answer. For this.

27

Lying Down in the Tracks

Old Saybrook, Connecticut, 1964

I t's been nearly four years since Dad's diagnosis. September is losing its gloomy grip on me. I've stopped rehearsing the order of
events in my head as I did in past years, as though by replaying the
dates and details of our phone calls and visits, I might be able to
change the ending.

The Indian summer days are astonishingly beautiful, but I know
they won't last. The season for river trips and mountain running is
winding down. Time to sneak in a few last long runs above twelve

thousand feet. Time to think about what's next: the Grand Canyon, maybe a hundred miles.

One Wednesday in mid-September, I'm on the Rail Trail, day-dreaming that I'm running the JFK 50 Mile, in western Maryland, about an hour north of Huntly Stage. I'm winning the race, tearing up the fast, flat course at sea level. I hear the spectators cheering me on. I can already envision the headlines in the local paper. CHILD FODDERSTACK CHAMPION MAKES GOOD!

I'm in Maryland, making Dad proud again—not in New Mexico, not on the Rail Trail, certainly not in my own body—when I hear a Very Disturbing Noise. It comes from my left knee, like paper tearing. It's so loud, so wrong, I hear it above the din of Rihanna blaring in my earbuds. So loud it sounds like it came from outside of me.

What the *HELL*?

I'm less than a mile from the trailhead. I bend over to look at my knee; it looks normal. I try to run but can't. It's not painful as much as strange, as though something's been yanked out of position. I limp to my car, trying to make sense of what happened. Only moments ago, I was clipping along, doing seven-and-a-half-minute miles. I felt a tug on the outside of my quadriceps and knelt down to stretch. I continued on, passing a Kenyan runner high-stepping in the opposite direction, when my knee made the awful sound. I hadn't fallen or twisted it. It makes no sense.

Within hours of getting home, my knee has swollen with fluid, a massive ugly thing that does not resemble anything that belongs on my body. I can walk and my knee can bear weight, but with each step, the pain is sharp and searing. Even so, I don't cry or panic. Maybe a microscopic part of me is relieved.

We think we know our bodies and our lives. I can run fourteen miles fast today and get up and do it again tomorrow. My knees are strong. They never give me any problem. I can run fifty miles or a hundred kilometers. I can win. The ego required to sustain this illusion of control can be tiresome, depleting, even as the running builds us up, makes us stronger and more confident than we've ever been. Beneath the formidable strength is our weakness: arrogance, the faulty assumption that we are strong and always will be. It takes work to carry this everywhere. Sometimes we want to put it down, rest awhile, remember we are human, and afraid, even though this terrifies us, too.

I can't get in to see the orthopedist for two weeks. Impatient, I call a bodyworker, hoping he might be able to give me a prognosis. He wiggles my engorged knee, tells me to bend and straighten it, which is pretty much impossible.

"Well," he sighs, "I hate to say this, but I'm almost certain you tore your ACL."

No three letters strike more terror in an athlete's heart than these. The anterior cruciate ligament is the connective tissue at the front of your knee that holds the whole joint together. It's most commonly torn during twisting falls, eliciting a sinister, telltale pop. Skiers and soccer players blow their ACLs all the time. Complete or partial tears almost always require surgery, followed by six to nine months of rehabilitation. It can be a year before you get back to sports, and eighteen months before you return to your pre-injury form. *If* you get back.

Now I do cry. The whole way home in the car, sobbing on the phone to Anna. "My running. It's over."

That night, I Google "torn ACL symptoms." I squint at knee anatomy diagrams from all angles. Assess the purple ligaments, the red muscles, the blue tendons. Try to figure out which one is responsible for the dull ache, the stiffness, the ominous buckling sensation, the feeling that someone has taken a hammer to my kneecap. There's no way to tell from the crappy computerized renderings what has actually happened to my knee. The knee that I love and need. That I have lived with all my life. Scarred and strong and mine.

Uncertainty is uncomfortable. It's not a place we like to stay. We fight it, try to outsmart it, convince ourselves we can control where our life will take us. In fact, we live here all the time, in the unknown, in flux. Only seldom are we awake to it. None of us knows anything, really, but this one moment and then the next. How have I forgotten this again?

When I finally get in to see the orthopedist, my knee is almost my knee again. Most of the swelling has subsided, though I'm leery of bending it too far, and I still walk with a halting limp.

The technician x-rays me and shows me into the examining room, where I give the doctor the recap: running, no fall, the cracking sound.

"Hmm, let's take a look," he says, pinning the films to the light board. He takes one look and cries out, "What the . . . ?!"

It's almost always a bad sign when a medical professional is so shocked he can hardly keep from swearing.

"You fractured your patella." And then, because I must have looked confused, he says it loudly, enunciating every syllable for emphasis. "*You broke your knee.* Look," he instructs, pointing to my ghostly kneecap on the computer, a half-moon, pale white and floating on the screen. I have to squint to see the break, straight and faint as a pencil mark. Even cracked, there is something dainty, almost precious, about my patella, this clamshell bone I've never seen before that's done hard work every day on my behalf, the unsung laborer of long-distance running.

"I thought you said you didn't fall?" he asks incredulously.

"I didn't," I say. "I was just running when I heard the tearing sound."

He shakes his head slowly, as if this is the most messed-up thing he's ever heard. My quadriceps, he explains, must have contracted so forcefully that it cracked my knee—a highly uncommon avulsion fracture that occurs without impact. In other words, I was running so hard I broke my own bone.

I've always known I have a high tolerance for pain, but I'm shocked to hear that I've been walking around for two weeks on a fractured knee. This cannot be good.

But when the orthopedist turns back to me, he's smiling. I can tell from his face that it is good news. Fantastic news! Much, much better than a torn ACL or meniscus. He explains that my patella will heal on its own, without surgery, if I'm careful and rest for the next four to six weeks. "Normally I would put a cast on you, but since you've been walking on it for so long already"—here he shoots me a mildly reproving look—"and it hasn't displaced, you should be fine."

I nod earnestly. I've dodged a bullet, and I'm going to be a good patient. A patient patient.

"REST," he repeats slowly, in that talking-to-a-deaf-person way. "Don't even think about running." As if running is even a remote possibility! As if I haven't been limping around on a broken knee-cap for two weeks and can barely bend it.

"Is there anything I *can* do?" I ask, a hint of desperation creeping into my voice. "Can I ride a bike?"

"No, I don't want you torquing it."

"Can I hike?"

"Nope. If you fall, then I *will* be putting screws in it."

"Can I walk downtown?"

"How far is town?" I can see him trying not to laugh.

"Close," I say. "And it's flat."

"Okay, you can walk to town," he concedes. "But whatever you do, don't trip on the sidewalk."

"How about swimming?"

"You can swim if you need a little cardio." He smiles, aware that this is the understatement of the century. "But not breaststroke. And put one of those floaty things between your legs and just pull with your arms. No legs for a while." Then he turns to his nurse tech, rolls his eyes, and says, with an exaggerated sigh, "Runners are the *worst!*"

I'm so overjoyed, I forget to ask him about physical therapy or Advil or icing. He pats me on the back with a grin, and I practically tear out of there, flush with my good fortune.

The relief wears off almost immediately. It's happened: I'm hurt. For real. I knew this day might come, but now that it's here, the realization that I wasted time whining about running or imagining bogus injuries makes me want to beat my fists against the wall.

Without long runs to fill them, my days stretch out blank and empty. It's torture to look at the mountains outside my window, blazing gold with the turning aspens, knowing they're off-limits. I have endless hours to sit and write. Too many. If there's a sitting-down disease, I'm going to get it.

On the good days, I try to be cheerful, grateful. There are much worse things. I know, because I've imagined them all. Real things that real people have had. Tumors, cancer, hantavirus, chronic Lyme disease, mass shootings, Ebola blowing into Texas like the plague. Comparatively, my broken knee is but a blip in the big picture. Anna emails, "It's a great opportunity to s l o w d o w n." I know she's right. I know I should look on the bright side. Now I have time to do all the things I wished I had more time for! Organizing the house, volunteering at school, editing my photos. Now that I'm not running all the time, Steve will not get annoyed at me for running all the time. Maybe this is just what our marriage needs!

Then I see people jogging down the street, and for a split second I despise them. I want to be them and I hate them. I try to be glad for my friends who run up Atalaya before breakfast, but I am small and mean, and I feel only jealousy. Worse, every day that I don't run, I sense the anxiety skulking closer, looking for a foothold. What if the orthopedist was wrong? What if I did tear a ligament after all? What if I have a tumor in my knee that made it snap?

The first year that Maisy was a baby and Dad was dead and my worry was a living, breathing animal scrabbling inside me and I was so worn out I felt like my skin was peeling up around the edges like cracked paint, I often found myself visualizing a set of train tracks. On days when I awoke feeling especially bedraggled, I'd imagine sprawling out in the middle of the tracks and letting the trains run over me, back and forth, again and again and again. In this scenario, I never died, nor was I trying to. Dying was the last thing I wanted. What I wanted was to learn how to stop resisting so much and give myself over to the mayhem, to allow myself to be flattened into submission over and over.

It was a relief to lie there on the tracks in my mind. It demanded total acceptance. Maisy is waking six times a night and Pippa is projectile vomiting? Yup. I'm just lying down in the tracks. It was its own weird kind of meditation: made up and a little loony, but mine. Immobilized, I was pinned to my place in this inexplicable, spinning world, in this one exact moment. Fully conscious and finally present.

Then I would get up from my railroad tracks, feeling better, and go back to changing diapers and putting Pippa back to bed for the twenty-ninth time in fifteen minutes, and the moment would pass and I would be able to breathe again.

This is what being hurt feels like. I'm just lying down in the tracks. For six weeks, then eight. I postpone indefinitely my Grand Canyon speed attempt, accepting the incontrovertible fact of what is: My knee is broken. All I can do is try to burn through some of my excess energy doing leg lifts and crunches, like when I was eleven and scissor-kicked to the Jane Fonda workout video after school. I sit outside and soak up the October sun and let my bones absorb the vitamin D and practice a radical palliative optimism that sometimes feels almost possible. Healing is training, too.

For four years, ultra trail running has been teaching me how to let go: of my grief, my father, my anxiety and anger; of ego and expectation; of my daughters as babies and toddlers. The lessons never end, they just keep shifting. Maybe now ultrarunning, like the wise mentors whose students eventually outgrow them, is trying to teach me how to let go of running, too.

28

The Long Way Home

PHOTO: KATIE ARNOLD

Pippa, Santa Fe, 2015

Running has a way of bringing you full circle. Whether you run a loop, an out-and-back, or a long point-to-point, up mountains or down, you almost always come back to where you started.

By winter my kneecap is healed. Except for some minor stiffness, it's hard to tell it was ever broken. I ski when it snows and hike fast up Sun Mountain with my black Lab puppy, Pete, who, at sixteen months, is finally old enough to start running. The trail cuts up the south face in full sun all day, so it's the first in town to lose its snow.

We hike to the top, run down. The next week, I run halfway up, walk the steepest pitch, and run back down. I'm careful with my goals. I don't want to want too much too soon.

My first day back on Atalaya, I go slowly, remembering something the orthopedist had said. "You might be brewing some arthritis in there," he said, pointing to my knee. That was his story, but it might not be mine. I could choose another story. In that moment I saw my anxiety as a sort of savagery, a way to punish myself for old crimes and shames by beating my body down with fear and imaginary ailments. But my body is not the enemy. It is my truest lifelong ally.

I love you, body, I whispered to myself as I ran. *Thank you.*

There are people who will tell you that running is harmful, that excessive exercise is just another form of abuse. But running teaches me to trust my body. It's one of the best ways I know to love my body, and my world. For now my body is healthy and strong, but someday it might not be, and so it's important to love my body, even when I'm afraid of it. *I love you, body,* I practice saying into the mirror. *I love you, body,* out loud in the mountains. *Thank you.*

Coming back from injury is as mental as it is physical, and there are days when my knee aches and worry creeps back, wobbling in the corners of my consciousness like a loose tooth. But I no longer grip it the way I once did. My ear still rings, but I don't hear it— I've stopped listening. I've begun to think of my anxiety like layers of unstable snow buried within the snowpack. Each layer corresponds to a storm that can be traced back in time. On the surface, the slope may appear pristine and stable, but beneath this veneer of uniformity are hidden layers of rotten snow that make the slope prone to sliding. You can dig a snow pit and scan for anomalies— a prolonged thaw, a wet storm, erratic temperatures—just as you might read rings in a tree stump that reveal severe droughts, evidence of old trauma.

When you ski on fresh snow after a storm, it sometimes makes a soft *whumph*ing sound, a deep, hollow settling. This is the snowpack compacting, holding. But under the wrong conditions, the outward force is great enough to cause the top layer to push down on the weaker layers with a pressure that they are unable to withstand. The whole slope collapses, the avalanche carrying everything in its wake, snow and boulders and trees tumbled over like pick-up sticks.

All my life I've been laying down my base. I'm lucky. It is mostly solid and strong, stable at the core. But I know my weak layers, the jolting, destabilizing shocks: Dad's leaving, the attack on the trail, his letter and death and the anxiety that followed. With every year, the stress of these storms is buried deeper beneath all the very best and happiest layers. Now, when there's a blow, I might wobble, but I will settle. I will hold.

Once I went to see a psychic. In Santa Fe, people recommend psychics the way they might a hairdresser. You can ask a stranger in the grocery store and no one will give you a funny look.

This was in the spring of 2013, when my tinnitus was at its deafening worst, when I was scared all the time. I could hear the South Pacific lapping in my ear and, above that, a swarm of mosquitos operating Weedwackers around the clock, and I was trying to heal it with homemade remedies and leaking so much garlic oil from my ear that I smelled like an Italian grandmother's kitchen. I decided to have my charts read, under one condition: I wanted to know my future only if it didn't involve a brain tumor. I was getting up my courage to tell the psychic this when she said, "I'm not a medium or a prophet." She told me she specialized in "awareness" of past lives.

She closed her eyes and sat quietly for a moment. Then she said, "Yes, yes, yes, yes, yes, yes"—so many times and in such a mesmerizing way that I didn't know who she was talking to or if a response was expected, from me or anyone else.

"This is a story of darkness, of shadow," she announced. "This person was clinging to a tree in a storm on the shore of the ocean.

There was a fierce wind, like a hurricane." Here she paused. "It wasn't the water that killed her"—apparently the person was a woman and I was to extrapolate that she was me, or I was her— "but the wind. She was at home by the water. The sea was her home."

I watched her, and never once did she open her eyes. I marveled at this: how she could sit cross-legged on a sofa and talk for an hour about my calamitous soul without checking at least once to make sure I hadn't fled the room.

"She was trying to save her child, who had gone into the water. The child lived, but she was swept away."

There in the room, I felt tremendous, objective sadness—not for me, but for this person who might have once been a version of me. That she had saved her child but lost her own life. The shock of it seemed to stick to my soul. Maybe it had been there all along.

She said, "One moment, one moment, one moment," and the words hummed off her lips like they were coming from someplace beyond her "It's a feeling I get from your father. You loved him deeply and were very attached. He called you forward from the sea. He was the one who summoned you into being."

The room was cluttered with Buddha statuettes and candles in the shape of Buddha statuettes, but her awareness didn't come from any of them. It had an invisible source. I didn't question or doubt any of this. What was the purpose? It changed nothing. It was just one version of one story. But as terrible as it was, if I contorted my brain and squinted out of one scrunched-up eye, it was also comforting. Had my father moved into another form, and would I someday call him forth, too?

When I got up to go, the day was just as I'd left it, except all the wrinkled parts of the world had shaken out to show their sharp, beautiful edges.

———

In early April, I'm on the phone with Lesley when she casually mentions that she's going to run the Fodderstack 10K in a few weeks.

"The *wha*—?" I ask, stunned.

"I've been training all winter!" she says proudly.

Lesley is seventy, fit and trim, but the last time she went running was a decade ago. The time before that was the first annual Fodderstack, in 1978, when she hyperventilated on the crowded starting line and had to duck into someone's driveway and put her head between her knees so she didn't pass out. "I didn't even make it out of Flint Hill!" she giggles now in her high-pitched, self-deprecating, *tee-hee-hee* British way.

Huntly Stage in springtime comes rushing back to me: the sweet smell of Dad's freshly cut grass, new foals, mountains sloping in the distance, all that green.

"I'll run it with you!" I blurt, without thinking. It will be my first race since I broke my knee. To return to the place where running began for me and to begin again with Lesley is too good to pass up. The race is in two weeks. I'm going.

When I tell Pippa, she says, "I want to run, too!" She's six and she's heard all my stories about the Fodderstack, seen my prize pottery cups. "How far is it?"

"Six miles," I tell her, trying to feign nonchalance. One mile for every year she's been alive. Though the interminable agony of my first race has long since faded, it sounds crazy for a girl in first grade who's never walked alone down a road, let alone run.

She smiles brightly, nods. "Okay, I know. I want to try."

I think, *That's my girl!*

I say neutrally, "It's totally up to you."

I keep it casual, with no expectation or pressure on either of us. I know there's a decent chance Pippa will change her mind; I expect it will depend on the day, the weather, her mood. There's not even one tiny part of me that wants to push her into running, to displace my own complicated ambitions onto her willful little self.

Maybe because my own Fodderstack debut had been such an accident. Dad wasn't trying to foist his aspirations onto me. He just made a chance suggestion and then let me make running my own.

Lesley tells me that her two friends named Jennifer are going to walk with their friend Jeff's ten-year-old daughter, Barney, and that if she'd like, Pippa is welcome to join them. I agree immediately. Now I can strike "Six-Year-Old Kidnapped During 10K Race" from the worry reel in my head.

Before we hang up, Lesley clears her throat, as if she's been saving up something important to say. "The woman who won the seventy-plus age group last year finished in 1:15. I know I can beat that."

The plane makes a long, gradual descent over western Virginia, banking turns above the Blue Ridge Mountains. Beside me is Pippa, the same age I was when we left Washington, almost thirty-seven years ago to the day. Big enough now to understand what has been lost and what it means to return.

Far below, Skyline Drive is a twisting ribbon of asphalt through the mountains, the Shenandoah River curling like a snake through the valley. Forests and farms give way to subdivisions, my father like a ghost shadow of the plane beneath us, crossing office parks, parking lots, power lines, rippling ponds.

Part of me still hopes to find Dad at Huntly Stage. In his basement, in the photographs on his desk, in his dusty camera lenses and the crinkled Post-its dangling from his computer screen, in his barn and in the fields. But he's not there. I sense this before our plane even touches down at Dulles, the ground rising up to meet us. The land, like all land, is impervious and huge, extravagant in its abundance. It has forgotten him, swallowed his memories, freed him. This is okay. This is what the world is supposed to do.

Gone, too, is the anticipation of seeing him in the airport, how this had always been for me a source of a steady gladness, not quite excitement, but a constant happy dependability. Bracing for his silly gags, the hiding behind pillars, the jumping out. The wide-eyed, exaggerated *Boo!*

Huntly is greener than I remember, the mountains gentler, more beautiful, and so full of life. Lesley's three friends, the Jennifers and Jeff, live on neighboring properties and are gregarious and funny and always popping by for a visit. They convene weekly for a formal sit-down dinner that rotates from house to house. It's Lesley's turn to host, and we drink wine in the dining room, and they teach Pippa the polite British way to say she's full: "Thank you very much, I've had an elegant sufficiency." But on her lips it comes out "elephant epiphany." The pall of loss has lifted and I see that Lesley is happy, and this makes me happy.

The next morning, after Lesley finishes her barn chores, we go for a walk. "Did you ever think when you bought this place that you'd still be here thirty years later?" I ask her. It's 8 a.m. and the sun is just cresting the hill to the east, dew heavy on the grass. My running shoes are soggy.

"No," she says, laughing. "We had this plan that Yerdad ended up forgetting all about. We were going to buy the house, fix up the basement, and then sell it. This wasn't the kind of place you'd stay in. It was impractical in every way."

I look around at the trees and grass, the taupe house and the tall barn, the improbable outcome of their life together. I have the oddest feeling that I'm seeing the farm for what it's always been, even when I didn't know it: home. This plot on this hill where Dad rooted in and down, learning, maybe, from this hillside how to give himself all the way, in his own way, to us.

The night before the Fodderstack, I dream that the racecourse is underwater and we have to swim it standing up, in slow motion. The water is so heavy and viscous, I feel like I'm jogging in custard. Partway through the race, another runner swims up to me and hangs on to my arms, like she's trying to drown me. I wake up in a tangle of sheets and sweat and reach for Pippa, who's sound asleep beside me.

In the morning at the starting line, it's damp and chilly, and we're all nervous for different reasons. Lesley because she wants to make it out of Flint Hill without asphyxiating, because she wants to win her age group. Pippa because she has never run so far in her life. And me because I'm scared for my knee, and for Pippa, who, like me thirty-seven years ago, has no idea what lies ahead.

I don't hear the announcer yell *Go!* through the megaphone; I just feel a surge of energy around me and am swept up by the other runners. The first straightaway, up the gradual hill, past the post office. Right on the Fodderstack Road, all the turns familiar. At mile 2, a woman with white hair, holding a stopwatch, calls out, "13:01." Legs on autopilot, mind constantly assessing: the hills, the slope, the legs, and will they hold? Tight hamstring. Lungs. How is my breathing? Never out of breath, but a steady effort. Do I think I might puke? Not yet. Mouth dry and sticky. Where is the woman with the yellow shirt and armbands who looked like a contender? Don't look back, never look back. It takes too much energy. The rubbery slap of soles on pavement growing fainter behind me.

Soon I see houses on the outskirts of Little Washington. A state police officer has paused from his traffic duties to take a picture. Spectators call as I round the first corner into town: "There she is!" and "Bring it home!" Turn right through the last bend, the finish chute comes into view. Now I take a good long look back, a real look. The road behind me is empty. The policeman is in front of me now, stopping traffic so I can cross the intersection. I've run free of it all at last, even the reflexive, split-second urge to scan for Dad.

Two people shout and string a red tape across the line and I break it.

When we get home from the race, I go down to Dad's basement. I'm not looking for anything, really, just trying to feel whatever's left of him. At the foot of the stairs is a pile of things Lesley has set aside for me to take home. On top is the stack of small black notebooks. I sit on the bottom step and pick up the first one, tracing the bumpy red embossing tape with my fingers: LISTENING TO MYSELF. I open at random to a page in the middle.

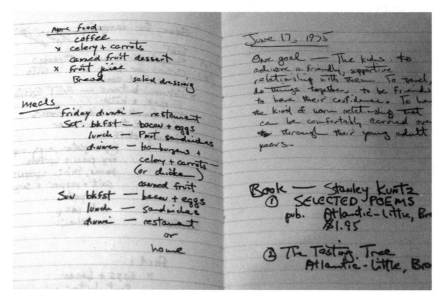

Dad's notebook, 1975

August 1975: "Time in Maine ending. Very successful venture. All of us had a good time—and the kids were introduced to many things: tidal fluctuations, sailing, canoeing, living with 'Daddy' "—the list goes on, thirteen in all. "I feel I have done a good job—no doubts of it."

The entries swing between hope and despondency. I can see that, even in his bleakest moments, he's trying to making a new life for himself—with us, and apart.

To have the girls get this far without knowing the specialness of music is one of my least contributions as a (mostly absent) father. In a way it's almost my most punishable offense.

That was the worst thing? Worse than his leaving?

Once, this would have devastated me. Now I just think, *I got the music, Dad. It just sounds different from yours.* Not a bow on strings but feet on dirt, the cadence of words moving through me as I move.

I was very happy to see the kids Friday evening. We went to the store to buy hot dogs. At times I felt as though I would like to be responsible for them always. I feel that my affection for the kids is one of the more constant things in my life. . . . I think we all have fun together much of the time.

But.

There were moments when I felt tense. I had fixed their breakfast and was trying to eat mine and read the newspaper and they kept interrupting me in spite of an admonishment. And there was a mess of toys, sleeping bags, crayons, and drawings on the living room floor. I remember feeling then that they might really destroy my "world" in my apartment.

I keep reading, flipping forward and back through the pages. I'm no longer afraid, only curious. All his contradictions, his crooked, tangled story, require a detachment I didn't have when he was alive.

What crushes me now is the children. The problems now because I am tired and discouraged seem insurmountable. But perhaps if I love them minute by minute in all our times together it will add up to something.

Dear Meg and Kate, good people, your daddy loves you.

My head spins. He's speaking to me *now,* his grown daughter, forty years later. As though by writing into the future, he would write his way out of his heartbreak, and ours.

Oh, Dad, I think. *You and I. We're so alike. We're so different.*

I wish I could have told him to hang on. That the mess would get better and that he'd get used to it or that he wouldn't and he'd get used to that, too. That he could go away and come home again. Like he'd done on the *Talitiga,* the way Steve and I try to do.

Dad left us because he felt stifled by parenthood, but running is teaching me the opposite: Just because you become a parent doesn't mean you're no longer free. You can keep doing what you love, and encourage your children to live this way, too, outside in the fresh air, without being afraid every single second—or being afraid every single second and doing it anyway. It isn't world politics or human rights. I don't know if Dad would think it is Important. But I can't ask him. I don't need to anymore.

This. *This* is what I've been running from. And running toward.

Running has always held a purity and simplicity for me, existing outside of ego or expectation, at the same time it has always been rooted in ego, a way to seek and find validation, from others and from myself. A way to stand apart and come together. A sign of strength and unending vulnerability. A way of letting go of things lost or no longer useful. A way of being wild on my own terms. A way of leaving. A way to stay.

Both sides now.

Upstairs in the kitchen, Pippa's and Lesley's voices drift through the floorboards, the low thrum of conversation punctuated by laughter and the clatter of dishes. Philip and Merrill, Jeff and Barney and the Jennifers will be over soon for a victory lunch. I'm filled with longing: I want to be upstairs with them, not down here anymore.

All this time I've been looking for one thing. The moment when Dad says, *Wait, I made a mistake. I want to come home.* But I won't find it—I know this now—because he didn't say it. He was too proud, or too conflicted, and Mom was too tired, and their ruined union became a footnote to a bigger story spinning on without them.

You make your choices.

I *had* been mad at him all this time, my anger buried beneath the layers and unconformities, deep in the basement rock. Not because he died. Not because he didn't fight for his life. But because he hadn't fought for us the way I'd wanted him to.

He'd fought for us in *his* way. With adventures and plans, packing lists and wish lists. *Lincoln Logs, punch-out books, barber shears, raincoats + boots. Camping: $3.50. Haunted house! Sheep and ducks, beef, cattle, horses, colts.* He built his life with us the same way he'd built his barn: one piece, one board, one step at a time.

I leave his letters where I found them, in boxes on the shelf. I don't need to read them anymore. The accounting—if such a thing is even possible—will always swing more toward what he gave us than what he took away. But his notebooks, his dreams and schemes—*those* I will keep. I pick up the stack of them and, next to it, a spiral-bound travelogue from one of his cross-country road trips. I turn to the last page; Dad's been driving for weeks and is nearly home.

Tall grass grows to the edge of the road. Now I see a sign for HUNTLY STAGE.

I ease off the gravel road onto a two-track drive, stone walls close on either side. Lights from the house at the top of the hill shine at me. There's evidence of the grass having been recently cut. But not terribly evenly. It can be fixed.

Top of the drive. Engine off, the car falls silent, leaving only the rumble of the road in my ears.

At the door, there's just one more question to ask:

—Anybody home?

I've stopped looking for Dad. He's not lost anymore.

He's here in all of us, in the way we run, separately and together.

At the thirty-seventh annual Fodderstack 10K Classic, Pippa brings her own strategy: Run what you can and walk what you can't. When I double back on the road to find her, she's just cresting the mountain, running straight into my arms, smiling and screaming, "Mama, Mama, did you win?"

She and Barney ran the first two miles, walked the middle two. Together we alternate jogging and walking side by side the last two miles into town, but at the bottom of the final hill into Little Washington she takes off, running as hard as she can, arms pumping, leaving me behind. Around the last corner, down the last straightaway. She is six and I am seven and I know this feeling, only today it's all hers. I'm behind her and she finishes fast and on her own, in 1:38, the youngest runner of the day.

Lesley destroys the seventy-plus age group, in a time of 1:08.

And I win the women's race in a personal best of forty-one minutes.

Afterwards, Lesley, Pippa, and I are presented with an award honoring three generations of Fodderstack runners. Posing together for a photo, I wonder if Dad would ever have imagined this. It had all started as such a fluke. Who could have possibly known where it would lead?

The racecourse was just as I'd remembered it. The winding asphalt and stone walls, brick farmhouses and black barns, farmers sitting in lawn chairs at the ends of their driveways. The rolling hills, nearly constant, one short climb after the next—welcome, really. This is the secret to hills: They make running easier. Run the inclines and then roll through the downhills, building momentum. Keep it flowing and the energy will carry you onward and upward again, flying down the far side. Don't stop. Keep going. Keep rolling through, one after the next. The hills will carry you home.

Ghosts

2015

Meg and me, Washington, 1974

There's one last thing I find.

A box of cassette tapes, pushed into the back of a cupboard in Dad's office, embossed with the same bumpy red letters as his notebooks. I shove them into my duffel and fly home to Santa Fe, where I stash them in my loft and forget all about them.

A few months later, I remember. I'm going on a road trip, five hundred miles from Santa Fe to Wyoming to write and run for two weeks. I don't have a tape deck, but my thirteen-year-old Subaru wagon does.

I drive alone through the Utah desert, doing eighty with all the windows down. It's ninety-five degrees, and the air-conditioning is broken. Just over the Colorado state line, the interstate joins the Colorado River, glittering in its canyon. I want to dunk my feet in the water, but when I pull off the exit and drive past strip malls, I make a U-turn and drive straight back to the highway. If I stop for too long, I'll lose heart.

I'm stuck in between. Here, not here. It's too late to turn back, but it seems an impossible feat to keep driving. Three hundred miles, three states. Harder by far than running.

Now it's night. I've left the interstate for a much smaller highway. I'm tired and my eyes are bleary. Through the windshield, something is wrong with the moon. It's as fat and orange as a tabby cat, but part of it is missing. It's being gnawed away by the night like the flesh of an apple, losing bits of itself by the minute.

I blink, remember. It's a supermoon eclipse, a total eclipse on the moon's closest approach to earth, the rarest of the rare. All along the rural two-lane road, the animals are going crazy, spurred by the strange calamity in the sky. Elk stalk the roadside, rearing up in my high beams. Deer jump out from fences, flick their tails, bob away. The moon is on fire. I squint into the night. One mile at a time. Just like running.

When I lose the country station out of Craig, the car's too quiet, so I fumble for the bag of cassette tapes on the front seat. In the faint green glow of the dashboard, I can just make out one label: MAINE 1976. I push it into the cassette deck, hoping it won't get chewed up and spit out in a tangle. It clicks into position, whirling miraculously to life.

"Once upon a time, there was a ghost in a haunted house . . ."

This is the clear, chirrupy voice of a young girl, vaguely familiar, instantly charming. This is a girl telling a ghost story into the black Panasonic cassette recorder, with its wide buttons and big handle, that Dad slung under one arm wherever we went. The voice is too crisp and mature to be mine. The voice is Meg's, the story is the same one that Pippa told last night, on the river. Goosebumps rise on my arms, and I feel a strange vertigo. I've fallen through a crack in the world, back to Maine the summer after Dad left home.

The burning moon has been replaced by a pale disk drawn with a white crayon, shaded in gray. The constellations seize their moment: Big Dipper, Cassiopeia, and Orion beam out from the blackening sky. My father's voice comes on, young and high-pitched, as though he just sucked helium. He's thirty-nine years old. "This is the evening of August 13, 1976, Friday night," Dad says, "and we are in cabin number four at Bonnie Ridge Cabins." It is September 27, 2015, a Sunday night, Colorado flashing by through the glass. I am singing the ABCs. I am forgetting the order after T. Dad is saying, "Good night, Katie! Good night, Meg!" His voice is deeper now, the gravelly rumble. I would know it anywhere, always. How I miss it.

All our lives, we've been coming together and separating, like mirror images of the same parabola, two lines approaching and then diverging over and over. Even after Dad died, the pattern didn't stop; it just changed, our chance encounters radiating outward on a continuum. *Now you see me, now you don't.* Here again our stories have converged, in a dark car in the middle of the night, Dad somewhere just on the other side of the thin line.

I cross into Wyoming. I am driving backwards and forward in time. I am homesick and full of regret. I steer the car down a long hill into a town with a dingy motel where I will spend the night. Dad's patting his leg: "Sit up on my lap for a minute, Katie." I am singing my ABCs again, the letters running together so that they sound like an imaginary language. *Elem-enoh-pee.* I make it all the way through this time. I am in a cabin by the sea, with lobster boiling on the stove. We are singing "Row, Row, Row Your Boat" in a round. *Merrily, merrily, merrily, merrily, life is but a dreeeammmm.*

Past, present, and future taper to a pinprick on a desolate road veering north beneath a vanishing moon. I have the strangest feeling I've been here before. I'm leaving home and coming home.

I drive all the way through Wyoming, listening to the tapes. In the bleached new light of morning, they're no less haunting, surreal. The darkest, most terrible ones are of my father alone: "Monologues 1974," catastrophe tapes, impossible to bear. The depth of his pain is more awful than I imagined, worse by far than any he inflicted on me. The click of his loafers on the sidewalk as he walked to work down M Street, holding the recorder's microphone close to his mouth so no one would hear. His storms, his secrets, the worst of secrets.

And also anybody's secrets.

The happiest recordings are of us together: Dad and Meg and me. We are at a fair in Maine. We have just picked blackberries and seen Andre the Seal. I remember that seal—the splash of the tank, the hard wooden bleachers, the crowd cheering *Ohhhhhh!* as the seal breaks the surface. At a parade, an old-fashioned car blows its horn at us—*Wubba, wubba*—while we eat rubbery hot dogs on the curb. Nothing has been lost. Not all this time.

PHOTO: DAVID L. ARNOLD

Me on Mount Battie, Maine, 1976

I listen to the tapes, hungrily, one after another, until I get to the last one. I've been saving Dad all this time, uncovering him in pieces, unconsciously but on purpose, to make him last. Now it seems I've come to the end of him. I hesitate, slide the cassette in without looking at the label. One last time, I want to be surprised.

"Okay, let's see if this works," Dad is saying quietly, almost to himself. Then his voice becomes louder, more official: "It's October 29, 1971, in Washington, D.C."

The hairs on the back of my neck stand on end. It's the tape of my birth. A memory beyond memory.

Low murmurings, the clink of instruments on a metal table. My mother huffing and chuffing through each contraction, freakishly metronomic, like a railroad train, never losing her composure. "That one was fifty-five seconds," she chirps gaily, as blasé as someone filing her nails. Her voice is girlish and bright, only half-recognizable, the voice of the first person I ever heard, exactly as I would have first heard it.

The cassette whines and thumps, Dad pressing Stop, then Record again, to make the tape last. "It's one minute after midnight," he says calmly.

The bed is shaking. My mother, who has refused an epidural, can be heard swearing. Once. Nervous sweat beads the back of my neck. In the excitement, Dad's forgotten about the Panasonic spinning on a table in the corner. I know how this ends—and how I begin—yet I can't bear the thought that the tape might run out before I am born, as though that would somehow alter the events that came after.

"Ohhh, it hurts," my mother cries. "Keep pushing," the doctor says in a Cuban accent. My mother lets out a howling screech that trails off abruptly into a whimper. Then a kitten begins to bleat. Somebody has let an animal into the room, and it's wailing. It grows louder, more certain, more rhythmic, ramping up for the bigness required of it. The animal is me. My first wild squawks, summoning everything to come. One breath, the slimmest of margins, holds it all: chance, love, hope, air. Life.

"Well, I'll be damned!" Dad exclaims huskily, relieved.

My mother says, "Oh, look, she's so tiny! Look at her feet!"

She says, "Babykins."

Footsteps: Dad's, crossing the room.

He laughs, giddy almost. "I can't believe the tape didn't run out. Amazing."

Then the car falls silent. Dad's gone again, into the bottomless sky, brutal and beautiful in its brightness, into the sagebrush spreading out in all directions, through the moon and a billion stars and beyond into infinite worlds we can't see but can only feel. A ripple of energy that might someday, still, change the ending.

I've been following the trail, looking for answers. It's the trail that Dad left, but it's also the one I made, dropping clues that form a pattern, words that make an arc. The signs were there all along, cutting a path between truth and illusion, courage and fear, winning and losing. They wobble out of the shadows like images from negatives, comprising light and dark, sun and shadow. It takes time and distance to see the shapes, but even then, they do not reveal everything.

Maybe it's better this way.

"It seemed miraculous, something from nothing, a kind of creation. What had shaped them?" Dad wrote about watching his father develop photographs of his brother, Phil, and him when he was eight. "The first ghosts bloomed and bloomed . . . and there we were, shining and wet. Motionless. Forever."

Years later, Dad would give up his darkroom and then, little by little, his photography. The mystery of his pictures, the purpose they served, was more than he could bear. "What was the use of taking so many pictures when no one would see them?" he wondered in his notebook.

He stopped too soon, before he realized there was joy in making photographs just to make them. They didn't have to mean anything.

But of course they do.

Now the path has led me here, back to Santa Fe and my sunny kitchen on an early fall day. The house is quiet, buzzing with the comfortable hum it has when emptied of little bodies, of their squealing voices, the flinging about of art supplies, dolls; the pleading, the giggling, the whining. I hear the low purr of the refrigerator and, through the open windows, the crickets. In October in the high desert, they go all day—endurance defined. The girls' absence has a presence that reassures me. The house holds their energy, wraps its walls around our clattering joy.

In the near silence, my mind loosens, stretches open. It's the kind of blazingly blue New Mexico morning when anything feels possible. I know this feeling. It's the feeling I get when I run, half-ecstatic, a little bit terrified, but spinning on anyway into the unknown. Through the darkness of early dawn, alone into the wilderness on trails so familiar I've memorized every step, and on others I've traveled only in my mind, with an open heart and fear that falls away with every footstep. I follow the trail as it unfurls, trusting that it will take me where I need to go, where it always takes me: into the story and back home again.

Being alive does not just mean not being dead. For a long time after Dad died, I thought this. But there are so many ways of being alive in this world, of loving the world and seeing the world and feeling it, too. "How many things there were to love; how many things about which to feel sad," Dad wrote on one of his road trips. "I wanted to remember it all."

I thought I was dying, but really I was just beginning. All those hours and days and years on mountains and rivers, across canyons and precipices, alone and with everybody I love most, I'd been writing this book.

ACKNOWLEDGMENTS

Ucross, Wyoming, 2015

PHOTO: KATIE ARNOLD

Many of my earliest recollections exist only as fragments. I'm indebted to my father, David L. Arnold, for caulking over the holes in my girlhood, and to my stepmother, Lesley Arnold, for so graciously allowing me complete access to my father's archives. This book would not exist without your generosity, Lesley. Dad never knew I was writing this book, and for a long while after he died, I didn't, either. For your words, photographs, recordings, and videos, Dad, and for everything else you gave me, I'm forever grateful.

Deepest gratitude to my mother, Betsy, always my sunniest champion and brightest light, who showed me there were no limits, ever. Who bought me all those books at the Lincoln School book fair and let me ride my bike all over town, and who was the first to encourage this project before it had begun to take shape. Thank you for your inexhaustible optimism. And to my stepfather, Ron, you have given so generously and taught me so much about commitment, loyalty, and self-discipline. I love you both.

Enormous thanks to my sister, Meg, for being the other half of my memory, for always having my back, on the steepest hills and fastest flats. And to my siblings Amy and Ron, and their families for their kindness, laughter, and support. I'm also grateful to Philip and Merrill Strange for being such loving friends to Dad, and all of us.

It takes a team to run an ultramarathon, and the same is true of writing a book. So many friends in my Santa Fe family helped me by taking care of my girls while I ran and wrote, keeping me company on the trails, reading early drafts, and supporting me in training and races. Heartfelt thanks to Blair Anderson, Kate Ferlic, Mary Turner, Erika Benson, Erin Doerwald, Carol Norton, and Anna Davis for their encouragement. Much gratitude to Elizabeth Sullivan—some of the earliest parts of this book started with our letters and emails. Natalie Goldberg shared a millennium's worth of wisdom with me, and, though I might never come close to understanding it, I feel it. Thank you.

Special thanks to Sharada Hall, Michael Diaz, Bob Schrei, Meghan Haid Sterling, Kate Reynolds, Bruce Gollub, Ira Berkowitz, Anne Loehr, Wuji Wayfarer, Marise Maxiner, Geoff Kloske, Bill Clegg, Maura O'Connor, Bill Stengel, Alix Kates Shulman, Nallely Chavira, Thais Mather, Rob Wilder, and Lee Lyon; and my fifth-grade language arts teacher, Debbie Kaflowitz, who recognized the writer in me. Thanks to Chris Johns at *National Geographic* and Jenna Pirog for access to and assistance with Dad's photo archives.

I'm appreciative of all my friends at *Outside,* especially the amazing Elizabeth Hightower Allen, champion of writers and words, who read an early draft and saved me with her brilliant, sensitive comments. Thanks also to Larry Burke, Mark Bryant, Chris Keyes, Hal Espen, Stephanie Pearson, Greg Cliburn, Grayson Schaffer, Hampton Sides, Alex Heard, Jonah Ogles, and Hannah McCaughey, who brought her brilliant eye for design to these pages. Much gratitude is owed to Will Palmer, whose thoughtful, exacting attention made this a better book, and whose funny marginalia, as always, made me laugh.

I'm grateful to the Ucross Foundation, in northern Wyoming, where I started writing this book, for giving me a perfect room in an old red train depot, cow paths on which to run through the sagebrush hills, and a neon vest because it was hunting season. The beauty and kindness of Ucross are stitched deep into these pages. And to the MacDowell Colony, in New Hampshire, thank you for so generously providing me the silence and space to finish the manuscript, the freedom to roam in body and mind, and a clunky three-speed bike that healed me.

Big love for my huge-hearted, intuitive, and unshakable editor, Andrea Walker. Your generosity and wisdom can be felt on every page, and the freedom you gave me to find my own way has meant everything to me. Thank you also to Emma Caruso, Andy Ward, Ted Allen, Sharon Propson, Barbara Fillon, Katie Tull, Toby Ernst, and the rest of the team at Random House.

And to my agent, Dorian Karchmar, a steady pulse on the other end of the line, whose immediate and passionate response and invaluable editorial insights helped create the momentum that carried this book forward to the finish. Thank you for pacing me on the long journey. You are truly an animal! Many thanks also to Jamie Carr, Alex Kane, and Laura Bonner at William Morris.

To my daughters, Pippa and Maisy—thank you for your patience and understanding when I needed to run and write, and for always being such game girls. Your curiosity and energy inspire me every day. And of course, forever, to Steve Barrett. Thank you for your never-ending supply of humor exactly when I needed it, your wisecracks and steadiness. Thank you for feeding me, cleaning my smudgy sunglasses, and tolerating my obsessions and dreaminess and all the hours and miles I was gone. Thank you for your faith in me, and for always being here when I get home.

And to the innumerable people who helped me along the way, without acknowledgment, I am grateful. Thank you, world.

KATIE ARNOLD is a contributing editor at *Outside* magazine, where she served as managing editor for twelve years. She is the creator and author of the column Raising Rippers, on *Outside Online,* where she reports on the importance of nature and free play for children. Her writing has appeared in *The New York Times, ESPN: The Magazine, Runner's World, Travel + Leisure, Elle,* and elsewhere. Her long-form narrative nonfiction has been recognized by *Best American Sports Writing,* and her essays have been anthologized in collections, including *Woman's Best Friend* and *Another Mother Runner.* Katie is the 2018 Leadville Trail 100 Run women's champion. She lives in Santa Fe, New Mexico, with her husband and two daughters.

katiearnold.net
Twitter: @raisingrippers
Instagram: @katiearnold

ABOUT THE TYPE

This book was set in Apollo, a typeface designed by Adrian Frutiger in 1962 for the founders Deberny & Peignot. Born in Interlaken, Switzerland, in 1928, Frutiger became one of the most important type designers in the years after World War II. Between 1948 and 1951 he attended the School of Fine Arts in Zurich, where he studied calligraphy. He received the Gutenberg Prize in 1986 for technical and aesthetic achievement in type.